Labyrinths of the Mind

THE SUNY SERIES IN
POSTMODERN CULTURE

Joseph Natoli, *Editor*

Labyrinths of the Mind

THE SELF IN THE POSTMODERN AGE

Daniel R. White
and
Gert Hellerich

STATE UNIVERSITY OF NEW YORK PRESS

Published by
State University of New York Press, Albany

For information, address State University of New York Press,
State University Plaza, Albany, N.Y., 12246

Production by Cathleen Collins
Marketing by Patrick Durocher

Library of Congress Cataloging in Publication Data

White, Daniel R. (Daniel Ray), 1950–
    Labyrinths of the mind : the self in the postmodern age / Daniel
R. White and Gert Hellerich.
        p.   cm. — (SUNY series in postmodern culture)
    Includes bibliographical references and index.
    ISBN 0-7914-3787-6 (hardcover : alk. paper). — ISBN 0-7914-3788-4
(pbk. : alk. paper)
    1. Postmodernism.   2. Self (Philosophy)   I. Hellerich, Gert,
1941–   . II. Title.   III. Series.
B831.2.W43   1998
149'.97—dc21   97-30049
                                                                   CIP

10 9 8 7 6 5 4 3 2 1

Contents

Contents

Acknowledgments

Special thanks to our editors at SUNY Press, James Peltz and Carola Sautter, for their diligent work and support in making this book a reality. Thanks also to our production editor, Cathleen Collins, for her careful preparation of the manuscript. Thanks, finally, to the Division of Sponsored Research at the University of Central Florida for providing grant money to support this research.

Revised forms of the following articles have been reprinted, with permission, as part of this book. We would like to thank the editors for their support. Chapter 1: "Nietzsche at the Mall: Deconstructing the Consumer." *Ctheory: The Canadian Journal of Political and Social Theory* (Spring 1994): Electronic text: *http://www.ctheory.com*. Chapter 2: "Psychiatry in the Labyrinth: Deconstructing Deviancy." *The Humanistic Psychologist* 21.1 (Spring 1993): 65–80. "A Postmodern View of Modern Psychiatry: *The Diagnostic and Statistical Manual of Mental Disorders* (DSM III-R)." *The Humanistic Psychologist* 20.1 (Spring 1992): 75–91. Chapter 4: "Nietzsche at the Altar: Situating the Devotee." *Postmodern Culture* (September 1995): Electronic text. *http://muse.jhu.edu/journals/postmodern_culture/index.html*. Chapter 5: Nietzsche on the Table? Critical Narratives of a Postmodern Impatient. *Nietzsche Studien: Internationales Jahrbuch für die Nietzsche-Forschung*. Berlin: DeGruyter, Bd. 27 (January 1988). "The Ecological Self: Humanity and Nature in Nietzsche and Goethe." *The European Legacy*, MIT Press and Haifa University, Israel, 3:3 (1998/99).

Introduction

Into the Labyrinth: The Self enters the Postmodern Condition

Why write a book on the self in the postmodern age? It seems that individuals nowadays are beset with a crisis that rocks the very foundations of their personalities. The self, a traditional and commonsensical basis for human experience, is being fragmented by a variety of forces: from the breakup of the nuclear family, itself a fragment of the previous extended family, to the diverse demands of the economy, to technological change that creates new jobs and makes old ones obsolete overnight, to political upheaval which, as in Germany or the former Soviet Union, realigns whole societies and makes their members rethink and reconstitute their lives on a new basis, to the constant inundations of information from the mass media and the expanding realm of information processing, to the fashioning and refashioning of the self in the marketplace, where new selves are fabricated weekly by Madison Avenue and projected in magazines, conjured in TV advertising, and glamorized in MTV videos. This fragmentation has momentous consequences not only for society at large but also for the individual subject, who seems to experience the pain of dissolution in isolation. But even though people may seem to be isolated, to experience fragmentation alone, nevertheless the process that has brought subjectivity to this crisis is characteristic of the larger modes of communication that constitute the self

1

as a cultural agent. Language, including the entire realm of semiotic practices—from words to gestures to video images and music—is, as Lacan has argued, the domain in which the self is constructed. For subjectivity is created by self-reference, in Lacan's view, by the identification of self with an external, mirror image and the introjection of that image as the personality.

Amidst this fray increasingly people are turning to various forms of therapy to help them adjust or cope or maintain their sanity. This in itself suggests that the roots of "mental instability" are social, even if therapists argue that the problems should be approached on an individual basis. In effect, when a person enters the therapeutic process she or he enters an artificial world constructed to simulate problems and to organize solutions for the "client." In this respect therapy is akin to a variety of social practices—from counseling, to social work, to public or private education—intended to lead unconventional selves toward a more conventional reality. This broad spectrum of therapeutic processes shares a common set of assumptions organizing the discourses of various social scientific disciplines. The assumptions are often unstated and implicit in the discourse of psychology, say, or education, but nevertheless serve as codes that constrain and shape communication.

A seemingly innocent institution, the school, as Ivan Illich has argued, is not only a place to foster learning but also one where students are inundated with an authoritative and highly conservative bureaucracy: the rules of schooling, not discussed as part of the content of the curriculum, function as implicit messages about learning and hence about self-formation. On the level of what Gregory Bateson calls *deutero* learning, or learning how to learn, the codes of schooling are set and not open to discussion or renegotiation by the students. Therefore, regardless of the content of education, the school repeatedly teaches the same message about learning: do it as teacher, as principal, as textbook, says, preferably in rows. But if higher learning, of the *deutero* variety or beyond, involves the realignment of learning's assumptions, then very little of it is likely to take place at school so long as the assumptions go unchallenged. Postmodern theorist Jean-François Lyotard thus argues that education is most always "in the center," by which he means that from the administration to the faculty to the design of the curriculum, the school is a set structure just like those of private and public administration. So in the everyday lives of students, they find themselves shaped in ways that are beyond their control into persons who, in the current scene, are beset with crisis. Expectably, since the assumptions of their education and personal formation remain hidden, the roots of the crisis remain invisible. So of course they go for more "therapy," which leads them farther down the same path, for its assumptions are the same as those of the school.

As Michel Foucault has argued, one of the key assumptions that underlies modern institutions is the idea of the self as an autonomous entity, not subject to continuous change or reformation, but a stable and rational being: *res cogitans*, in Cartesian terms. This is opposed to the Heideggerian notion of being, including personal existence, as "rising into presence," as openness instead of closedness. Likewise, it is in contrast to the Derridean notion of *différance*, which, as Caputo has argued, is the linguistic equivalent of Heidegger's rising into presence: a continuous play of language in what Foucault would see as the archaeological conversation producing selves and cultures. If the conversation stops, the society dies. Thus the idea of the self as a mental substance, *res cogitans*, created by the Enlightenment is only a limited one, which can be expanded, or radicalized, into an open-ended identity. Expectably the attempt to impose a rigid framework on a living process will result in fragmentation; the glass cage of selfhood, the hypostatized mirror image of self, will shatter when living, evolving, and learning; thus it will open up to new experience that can no longer be readily controlled. Thus the postmodern critique of modern institutions would probe the assumptions underlying the mirror of selfhood, to open the conversation of self-formation once again.

The contours of the postmodern labyrinth of self are diverse but may be traced from the rebellions against and increasing breakdown of the modernist order of things. The forms of rebellion are clear in the dissatisfaction of individuals with the institutions in which they work and live—the school, university, church, family, state, corporation. Modern politics and democratic institutions are perceived as no longer serving their original stated intent: to involve the greatest number of people in the shaping of their own destinies. The modern framework of institutions, evident in the marble facades of neoclassical architecture in Washington or Paris, now functions as an image of democracy. It is wielded by governments which—as Bill Moyers has shown in his television series *The Public Mind* and Noam Chomsky has demonstrated at length in various works whose perspective on American politics is perhaps best summed up in his recent title, *Deterring Democracy*—work by principles that are far from democratic. Although the postmodern cultural logic of images without clear foundations is already evident in this political setting, the difficulty is not so much that the play of information is somehow wrong or false in itself but rather that it is used for modernist motives of prediction and control applied undemocratically to whole populations. As Charles Jencks has argued in *What Is Post-Modernism?* postmodernists by no means reject the democratizing tendency of the Enlightenment but rather *radicalize* it by their commitment to, say, an architecture designed to *communicate* to a diverse public. The difficulty is in part that power is communicated from the top down even in allegedly democratic institutions. Consequently the attempt of *people* to make decisions about their lives from the bottom up is viewed, in Chomsky's analysis, as the crisis of democracy, read, "the unmanageability of populations" in the wake of the broad-based skepticism about government following the Vietnam War. This attempt at management has its spectrum from the right Republicans to the left Democrats in the United States, but the assumptions about control are not seriously challenged by any who would please the monetary powers that be. For these are necessary to get elected by the current system of image management and voter conditioning.

This political system of control, which uses Enlightenment democratic images for rather unenlightened goals, has its analog in the human sciences. Here the ideal of disinterested knowledge for the benefit of humanity is still maintained when in fact social scientific theory and practice are utilized in the service of "management" on a broad scale: from the managing of the mentally disorderly in the psychiatric and other therapeutic communities, to the direction of students and employees in school and business by counselors, social workers, and industrial psychologists, to the consulting work for governments, business, and media provided by "professional" sociologists and political scientists. The universalization of the ideals of knowledge and humanity is similarly utilized in this system for goals that are not congruent with the diverse needs and interests of actual people, so that the everyday lifeworlds of human beings are edited out of the statistical accounts of their participation or lack of it in modern institutions. Local political and social movements are subordinated to the interests of larger conglomerates like the corporation or the state and recalcitrant populations are alternatively ignored or slated for "welfare" to keep them appeased. Thus cultural diversity is reduced in favor of monoculture or the *simulation* of diversity in a sterilized form, as at Epcot Center. Thus the world is increasingly cast in a form appropriate for "tourists," who as Thomas Pynchon dramatized in his novel *V*, are the alienated personae of modernity, the mechanical ghosts of human beings, consuming images of the world through their travels just as surely as developers consume the bio- and cultural diversity of rainforests.

The irony is that the institutions and ideals of enlightened modernity have failed in their original explicit goals of freeing people from oppression and want, and have come to serve interests of economic, social, and cultural élites. Thus in our view the postmodern movement is not so much an anti-Enlightenment one, but as we have argued above, a *radically* enlightened diversity of movements. Thus it is not tolerant of everything; it does not argue that everything goes. Rather, as Marcuse and others argued in *The Critique of Pure Tolerance*, certain forms of oppression and limitation of freedom—economic exploitation, suppression of people's perceived rights to political, social, and cultural expression, wanton violence—are intolerable. This does *not* commit the postmodern movements to specification of universal standards to which people must conform; rather it insists only on some universal proscriptions of oppression. Thus limitations on freedom are the only ones acceptable and freedom does not include the freedom to exploit. The key to this—politically, socially, and economically—is a postmodern *decentralization* of power so that local coalitions of people become empowered to organize and communicate their interests: to develop local economies, local police, local schools, local health centers, local arts, a culture decentered from the modern axes of power but nevertheless having access through global satellite and computer networks to whatever information is desired and to communicate whatever is desirable.

This process of decentralization will surely have consequences for the postmodern self, which will no doubt become diversified, "schizophrenic," multiform, and more difficult to define and control. The difficulty for individuals enculturated into the social identity of the Enlightenment will be to adapt to a new array of self-images, a different sense of personality that is not understood as substantial but rather as a collection of convenient masks, as the Latin for self, *persona*, indicates, for a variety of characters one might play in a new social drama.[1]

A Sketch of the Labyrinth

The modern age has been constituted by a dichotomy between the objective world of nature subject to the normalization and technological control implicit in universal laws, on the one hand, and the transcendent, autonomous self striving for freedom from natural necessity, on the other.

The Cartesian *cogito* and the Kantian transcendental ego and moral subject in the First and Second Critiques are prime examples of the modern self, as is the supposedly free citizen of bourgeois democracy and ethics in Locke and Jefferson, as well as in Mill and Bentham. In economics, the free entrepreneur idealized by Adam Smith and Ricardo is a parallel example, as is the "genius" of science and technology like Newton or Darwin or Freud or Edison supposedly responsible for creating the "new." In the same vein, the self—as worker or entrepreneur—is defined in terms of productivity, so that lack of productivity is blamed on the lazy or impoverished individual and not in terms of the structure creating the inactivity or poverty, as Marx saw. The result of these oppositions is an ambivalent self presented with alternatives, which are in fact not alternatives at all but the polar oppositions of a new form of control.

In the first chapter of *One-Dimensional Man*, Herbert Marcuse writes about "New Forms of Control" that characterize the emerging late capitalist society evident in the early 1960s. These included the productions of the consumer society with all its pleasant commodities—Pleasure Island. Marcuse referred to social control through a culture of commodities as "repressive desublimation." It is the more advanced form of this commodity culture, ramified by what Marshall McLuhan called the electronic media of communication and Mark Poster has called the mode of information, superseding the Marxian mode of production, which Frederic Jameson has called "The Cultural Logic of Late Capitalism." Whether postmodernism is tantamount to this cultural logic remains an open question, but clearly the forms of control in the postmodern age are related to those in the modern one, and we might expect that the forms of liberation will be related as well. Yet important differences exist between control and liberation in both stages.

Modernist control has been delineated clearly by Foucault, on the one hand, and Mumford, on the other: the constitution of the rational self and the megamachine in which the self functions, respectively. Normality, as a principal mode of control, applies to nature in the form of natural laws, and to the society and the self in terms of norms. The culture industry, as criticized by the Frankfurt School, imposes by its marketing strategies and products a certain subjectivity on the consumer, whose choices are imposed by the cultural logic of advertising epitomized by the iconographic landscape of the mall. Thus, in "Nietzsche at the Mall: Deconstructing the Consumer," we show that, contrary to the imposed subjectivity of consumerism, Nietzsche offers a self-chosen individuality, a form of *Kulturmachen* or culture making instead of culture consuming, which leads to self-transformation through a creative will to play.

We will thus consider how the self has been constituted within the modernist framework, stemming initially from the Renaissance and subsequently in the nineteenth and twentieth centuries. In spite of the norms that have been imposed in the rise of modern industrial and bureaucratic postindustrial society, nevertheless individuals have "deviated" considerably from the standard cultural types and constituted themselves as unique. Thus, as Foucault has shown, there has been significant recalcitrance against the seeming monolith of modern industry and the state, even if this does not always appear in the history books. Furthermore, this "will to differ" that is evident in people who have resisted normalization can be thought of as the social base for the postmodern movement, which, for example, surfaced in the 1960s as the counterculture, in the so-called First World, and as national liberation struggles in the Third World. Thus the institutions of the Enlightenment have provided a context designed to edit the text of the self, keeping its narratives within certain limits established by reason. But the postmodern self is emerging as *intertextual* and, in Derrida's terms, "on the margins" of the Enlightenment page, providing tangential commentary and fiction that deterritorialize modern discourse.

The dichotomy between subject and object is a key to the modern self: inner versus outer world; rational versus irrational psyche; mind versus body; what Morris Berman calls the "spectral" or what Lacan calls the "mirror" self versus the kinesthetic/somatic experience of the body unmediated by the social looking glass; or by the hierarchy of subject over object in the logic of domination, especially pointed out by Laing/Bateson/Wilden. The postmodern self is a mode of being/awareness not bifurcated into subject and object but participating in/interactive with the emerging spiral of differences that make up phenomenal experience: the wave-form of Derrida's *différend*. Traditionally the self is thought to be the center of experience, but, as in some forms of meditation or yoga, the postmodern self is relocalized, decentered, merged with various aspects of the body or the natural world—out of the head or the heart and into the spine or the toe or, as in Hesse's *Siddhartha*, into a passing flock of birds, into trees, water, the life cycle, or the electronic circularities of what de Chardin called the Noosphere. "What thinks," as Bateson says, "is man plus computer plus environment."

In "Psychiatry in the Labyrinth: Deconstructing Deviancy," we examine a central concept of psychiatric theory and practice: "deviancy," or, in German, Abweichung. This is a key concept in psychiatry and other therapeutic disciplines because it dramatizes the way in which they depend on the establishment of norms in order to justify their theory and practice. The deconstructive writings of Derrida, however, as well as Goethe's analysis of Abweichung, provide a different view of both the concept and the psychiatric framework it reflects. For they show that "deviation" from a "norm" can be viewed as fundamentally important to the well-being of the norm in question, just as genetic variation can be seen as fundamental to the life of a species. Thus deviancy can be viewed in a much more positive light, not as something to be corrected but as a creative possibility to be encouraged and shaped in productive ways. As a case of deviancy a fortiori we have selected the writings of what editor Gregory Bateson calls the "great schizophrenic" John Perceval, whose Narrative provides a deconstructive critique of the mental health establishment of his day, particularly the asylum, and offers a creative alternative to prevailing nineteenth-century views of lunacy. Finally, his "schizophrenic" commentary on his "psychosis" and its treatment we see as analogous to the deconstructive, "schizophrenic" discourse of postmodernity, which is similarly critical of the reigning, modernist psychiatric order.

We next offer a critique of the DSM-IV as sign, symptom, and practice of modernity. We argue that the DSM-IV manual embodies the premises of modern science as well as its methodologies, both of which include the categorization and systematization of phenomena, whether they be in the natural or human sciences, in order to "discover," or as we see it technologically impose, order on the alleged chaos of nature and society. Thus the chapter not only puts the manual in its historical context by examining its roots in the tradition of science, but it also shows how the manual defines and suggests therapies for what it takes to be various species of mental disorder. The manual thus, we argue, implies an ultimately fixed idea of mental order, in terms of which it defines disorder and suggests strategies for transforming the latter into the former. It thus attempts to overcome what its authors take to be a threatening mental chaos—threatening to "what" we also consider—and so limits what, from a postmodern perspective, is the creative potential of human beings, in favor of a narrowly utopian penchant for a predictable and orderly world. The section finally suggests some possibilities for creative human endeavor implicit in the so-called forms of mental disorder which the manual would extinguish. Thus, once again, the will to differ and the variegated lifeworld that it opens up are seen as a genuine human alternative to the rationalized and standardized ideal of modernism. It is not our intent to provide a guidebook to alternative forms of therapy. Rather, we attempt to situate psychology and psychiatry within a broader realm of social and cultural practices that provide critical and creative strategies for the development of the postmodern self. Hence the idea of therapy is transformed into a heterogeneous variety of life-affirming communicative activities.

We go on to consider Kafka's *Verwandlung/The Metamorphosis* as a paradigm for the broad cultural shift of the self from the modern to the postmodern eras: from the normal, unitary, rational, productive ego to the abnormal or paranormal, diverse to the point of schizophrenic, postrational, communicative, androgenous, ecological personae of postmodernity. We thus present a genealogy of the postmodern metamorphosis by viewing Kafka's literary transformation, and transformation of literature, as analogous to the philosophical transformation into postmodern philosophy, especially in the work of Jacques Derrida, to the 1960s political and cultural transformation whose tremors ran from Ed Sullivan to the Pentagon, to feminism as gender transformation overturning dominant patriarchal icons, to ecology as scientific/technological transformation, to TV/video as artistic/ communicational transformation. Finally, we suggest an end to interpretation and the transformation of the modern rational self into the narrative self of postmodernity; we thus point to Kafka, despite his reputation as a literary modernist, as one of the first postmodern storytellers, in a tradition that spans from Homer to Douglas Coupland.

Increasingly now we turn to Nietzsche's genealogical critique of Western culture and consciousness; we go on to uncover the relationships between Nietzsche's thought and the philosophies of postmodernity. We focus particularly on two aspects of Nietzsche's work that are also fundamental aspects of postmodern thinking: the critique of "normal" language and that of the normal self. Nietzsche's radical genealogy of the discourse of modern science and culture, with its etymological dimension, sets the precedent for the profound rethinking of language in Heidegger, the archaeology of Western culture provided by Foucault, the deconstruction of metaphysical language in Derrida, the critique of master narrative in Lyotard, and the psychoanalytical-linguistic critique of phallocentric discourse developed by Cixous. We consider, finally, whether the postmodern self cannot become an open and creative process, an ongoing work of art, rather than a closed, given, static subject as in modernism. Here, in "Nietzsche at the Altar: Deconstructing the Devotee," we consider the way in which modern "conservative" Christianity, particularly in the United

States, has functioned in tandem with capitalism and militarism to provide sanctimonious forms of control enforcing the interests of multinational corporations and of the last great nation-state. We also deconstruct, via Nietzsche's writings, the moralizing aspects of religion, offering a vision of cultural practice "beyond good and evil."

Parallel to Perceval's rebellion against the normalizing power of psychiatry (Chapter 2), or to Gregor's "monstrous" satire of bourgeois institutions in Kafka's *Metamorphosis* (Chapter 3), is Nietzsche's dissent against medicine. This is the principal focus at the outset of Chapter 5. Specifically, we are concerned with Nietzsche's critique of the cultural assumptions underlying medical discourse. Drawing on various sources in his widely published works, as well as his "Unpublished Manuscripts" (*Nachgelassene Fragmente*), we show how Nietzsche writes narratives depicting the relationship between "doctor" and "patient" in the foreground but representing the edifice of European civilization as a backdrop. Like a more radical version of Hans Castorp in Thomas Mann's *The Magic Mountain*, Nietzsche confronts the institutional illness of Western culture and envisions a "great health" that takes on evolutionary dimensions.

The idea of nature, particularly with respect to ecology, is perhaps the most vitally contested ground in contemporary intellectual history. Is the natural world to be utilized as a cache of resources for human consumption? Is it the aesthetic repository of the Romantic imagination, and hence the final solace of the alienated individual of industrial civilization? Is it the domain of a Gaian intelligence, *including* human consciousness? We argue that Nietzsche's view of nature, significantly influenced by Goethe's, provides a postmodern alternative to modern industrial exploitation as to its Romantic antithesis. Indeed, it projects a new idea of the human psyche in relation to the natural world which is communicative and interactive, suggesting a new ecological ethic.

We inquire whether new light may be shed on Nietzsche's environmental philosophy by considering his view of Goethe and by taking a careful look at some of the latter's scientific writings (which we have translated from the German). Moreover, we criticize the understanding of Nietzsche's *Übermensch* "heroically transhuman individual" questing for what we characterize as power over other human beings and the natural world: the industrial ethic personified. We further show that Nietzsche, like Goethe, develops a significant alternative to Romanticism by suggesting a new, "joyous" science which, we argue, envisions a new "ecological" identity. Thus, we seek to develop an alternative reading of the *Übermensch* as expressing an "overfullness of life," in Nietzsche's terms, and hence as a viable ecological persona—a communicative identity—encompassing the self and "other" of man and nature.

Finally, we explore the ecological and ethical dimensions of a post-modern self, arguing that the transformed self is opened to a new world of alternatives unforeseen by its predecessor. Thus the new persona seeks the freedom to reject the simplistic and controlling dichotomies of the modern era, along with their normalizing, controlling effects. Its ethical alternatives are not typically limited to either-or, as Kierkegaard saw the polarities of modern decision making, but rather to combinations of what diverse modern thought considered to be incompatible positions. Thus the postmodern individual is both a single persona and a multiple of selves functioning in various social and cultural capacities. Thus we explore, in "The Ecological Self: Humanity and Nature in Nietzsche and Goethe," the possibilities of human identity understood by analogy with ecosystemic forms, including biodiversity, providing a dynamic and open-ended—morphogenic and creative—idea of personality. We interweave Nietzsche's writings with those of his respected predecessor, Goethe, and with those of ecological theorist Gregory Bateson, so as to offer a new aesthetic ecology of human identity. We furthermore explore, via Nietzsche, Foucault, Cixous, and others, in "The Ethical Self," the connections between the creative persona that emerges from the foregoing discussion and the ethical concerns of the postmodern age.

Critics of postmodernism have pointed out that it offers an untenable pluralism. As Peter Münz articulates it, "Foucault described the postmodern world, or rather, the world as seen by a postmodern person, as a hetero-topia, a world in which disconnected positions, forms, stances, and beliefs rub shoulders and jostle side by side. . . . Heterotopia consists in the preservation of these disconnected fragments and the complete acceptance of pluralism" (348). But, he argues, "we all live in one and the same world; and its separate parts must be consistent with one another and cannot be irreducibly disjointed. . . . Heterotopia, in other words, cannot possibly be the final word." For (Münz cites Habermas) "a species which depends for survival on cooperative action and linguistic communication, must of necessity rely, in the last resort, on some kind of reason" (349). On the contrary, we argue that heterological coding is possible, that there is a heteromorphous "pattern which connects" the various aspects of the postmodern world together, that the concept of a species cooperating in terms of reason is a monological concept of the Enlightenment that imposes overly limiting concepts of nature, self, rationality, culture, and communication, as if human beings and evolution could not have gotten along in the millions of years of history predating the rise of reason in the West. Furthermore Münz's criticism, characteristic of many attacks on postmodern alternatives, implicitly employs a binary opposition between order and chaos that ignores even the latest developments of science, especially chaos theory, which sees order and disorder as correlative and supplementary rather than as alternatives between which we, or nature, must choose. This fusion of chaos and order in a heteromorphous pattern is emblematized by the generative image of the labyrinth: the unfolding pattern of the postmodern mind.

The Metaphysical Triad of Modernity

In German, there is a triad of concepts that are often used to characterize the Nietzschean-postmodern critiques of modernity's three V's: *Vereinzelung* ("isolation"), *Vergegensätzlichung* ("dichotomization"), and *Verewigung* ("perpetuation"). *Vereinzelung* refers to the critique of the decontextualized individual—the utterly alone modern persona, autonomous, not interdependent with the patterns of "otherness" surrounding him or her. Hence the "consumer" criticized in Chapter 1, the "patient" or "doctor" of Chapter 5, the "psychiatrist" or "patient" of Chapter 2, the bourgeois functionary, the "salesman," satirized and transmuted by Kafka into the strange new persona of Chapter 3, the "devotee" of Chapter 4, and the unecological self decontextualized from the patterns of adaptation in evolution of Chapter 5. *Vergegensätzlichung* refers to the hypostatization of opposites into metaphysical realities characteristic of both ancient and modern metaphysics. So consumption and production, passivity and creativity, self and other, freedom and control, pleasure and work, capital and labor are discussed in Chapter 1, doctor and patient in Chapter 5, therapist and patient or client in Chapter 2, boss and employee, overlord and underdog in Chapter 3, devotee and sinner, sacred and profane in Chapter 4, man and nature, culture and nature in Chapter 5. *Verewigung* refers to the positing of eternal entities in metaphysics, including the metaphysics of everyday life: the soul of the eternal consumer in Chapter 1, medical authority and knowledge in Chapter 5, the universalization and hypostatization of medicalized categories like mental illness or deviancy as well as "schizophrenic" and Cartesian "doctor" in Chapter 2, the invariant human persona and the eternal functionary of bureaucracy in Chapter 3, the sacred and the saved in Chapter 4, and the medical ideal of the "healthy individual" as well as the industrial ideal of "technological man" transcending natural history in Chapter 5. Thus, overall, the decontextualized individual becomes contextualized, the hypostatized opposites become dynamically interrelated, and the eternal verities become animated by historical time.

The consequences of the modern triad of *Vereinzelung*, *Vergegensätzlichung*, and *Verewigung* have also been our concern throughout. So the plight of Perceval (Chapter II) is only revealed in his narrative and in fact concealed by the discourse and practices of the psychiatric institution that isolates him from meaningful dialogue with others. Just as he is decontextualized from the processes of communication that would validate his experience, so also his commentary is delegitimated by the authority of medicine as symptomatic of a mental patient. Similarly, Gregor's anguish (Chapter 3) is that of the deviant from the normalizing institutions of bourgeois society: the business and the family. For as he undergoes his metamorphosis, his story becomes a critical commentary on those very institutions while, at the same time, being viewed as "monstrous." As Haraway (1991) points out, the etymology of that term in itself indicates "demonstration" and "pointing out" directed precisely at the routinizing powers of normalcy from which the "monster" is designated. This form of demonstration further suggests the role of Nietzsche's madman, who by his stark opposition to the strictures of herd consciousness in Christendom— the apparent light of day or of salvation—becomes, too, a rebel whose very madness is a description of the limits of the world he confronts. The madman is, furthermore, an analog for the "ill" Nietzsche surrounded by his doctors, railing at their diagnoses as themselves symptoms of a sick culture. The ecological self (Chapter 5) embodied by Nietzsche's environmental philosophy, furthermore, is one not alone at all but rather a challenger to the framework of modern aloneness who posits an identity that is always in interplay with its environment, always balancing on the abyss of the "other" surrounding it.

The consequences of *Vergegensätzlichung* include the oppositions not only between the normal and the deviant so evident in the aforementioned figures, but on a broader scale the historical development of the what Mumford (1970) called the megamachine of modern industrial technology, bureaucracy, and economy. The human consequence of this is what Marcuse called "one-dimensional man" (Chapter 1), the mere "consumer" of prefabricated culture in the commercial environment of the mall.

The edifice of the megamachine is built in turn on oppositions between primary and secondary qualities (Chapter 2) as between health and illness, medical professionals and laity (Chapter 5). Here we have suggested that the Nietzschean way out of the opposition between consumer and producer, controller and controlled, and their constitutive polarities is to understand power in the sense not of "power over" but of "power to create" and the "will to differ." So our reading of *über* as a form of "supplementarity," which like a stream overflows and breaks through the boundaries demarcating the self in its various prefabricated oppositions with the "other": mad and sane, monstrous and routine, profane and sacred, evil and good, nature and man, and so on. The deconstructive will to differ thus becomes at once critical and creative, not only breaking down metaphysical oppositions but also inscribing new possible lines of activity amidst the fractures. This we see as the very strategy of ecological adaptation for a new, diversified, self (Chapter 5).

The consequences of *Verewigung* are nowhere more clear than in the virtual heaven that is the endpoint of so much tourism in America, Disney World, as it is in the contrived serenity of the mall, built by analogy with the cathedrals of old and serving a similar function for the devotees of consumerism (Chapters 1 and 4). It also functions in the same vein to provide theistic justification for various ideologies and attendant practices of modernity, particularly the use of high-tech warfare to implement neoimperial designs (Chapter 4V). It furthermore hypostatizes and anchors the metaphysical ideas underlying modernization—the self, nature, things, knowledge, truth, gender, ethos—so as to give them seemingly unassailable authority. The power of Nietzsche's critique in this regard is to reveal the historicity and genealogy of the supposedly transcendent verities, showing them to be part of the strategies of what Foucault called power-knowledge (Chapters 2, 5). Overall it is the vision of "eternal" salvation waiting at the end of the road to progress that ties the entire system of modernity together in what Nietzsche thought was at best a lopsided dream.

CHAPTER 1

Nietzsche at the Mall

Deconstructing the Consumer

hodos anō katō mia kai hōtē.
The way up and the way down are one and the same.
—Heraclitus

The Church of the Consumer

The concept of self, especially the Cartesian *cogito*, has received a great deal of critical attention from postmodern and neostructuralist theorists. The rational ego is posited as the subject of knowledge in modern science and technology, animating the utopian projects of industrial civilization and culminating in great urban conglomerates, in theme parks like Epcot Center, and in the sealed universe of commodities that constitutes the omnipresent mall. The selves that in the modernist tradition have become the subjects of knowledge and scientific power were, in the Christian tradition supplanted by modernism, the eternal souls that provided an invariant substratum for the fluctuating experience of human emotion and sense perception, providing spiritual continuity in the quest for salvation: the stable vehicle bound for the static endpoint (*eschaton*) of history. That *eschaton* provided the template on which the modern idea of technological utopia has been modeled, from Bacon through Disney. The Magic Kingdom is, after all, a rarefied and idyllic image of suburbia with synthetic manifestations of American fantasy, from fake presidents to the eternally childlike persona of Peter Pan, both thinly disguised forms of the national self-image of incorruptible innocence. It is as if America wanted to go to heaven so badly that it created its own version of it, with prices accessible to almost everyone, improving on Christianity by insuring salvation to anyone for a nominal fee.

The mall, a pervasive expression of the same sensibility, provides an environment where the self, transformed from pilgrim or scientist to consumer, can achieve happiness, the realization of dreams, by the purchase of commodities. Thus the original quest for salvation has been transformed into one for consumption without end through the mechanisms of the science, technology, and capitalist economy created by the modern *cogito*: "I consume, therefore I am." But has the freedom that was originally to be achieved through salvation from sin, and later to be won by the twin revolutions of modernity—the industrial and the political—really been provided by the culture industry of consumer choice? The notion of freedom is based on the concept of the will: it is a characteristic of the will, which is supposedly capable of uncoerced volition. If a consumer chooses to buy a product, is she or he then expressing free will? The advertisers would have us believe it, and many of us have been convinced, at least implicitly accepting the idea that shopping is the good life and inscribing the desiring subject of consumerism into ourselves by our daily practice of mall strolling.

Decentering the Consumer Subject

But if, in our quest for happiness through shopping, we should happen upon one of Nietzsche's works in the bookstore—they are curiously available, even in mass market shops—and begin to peruse, would we be able to consume it, like any other product, and still retain our sense of security as free subjects empowered by the ubiquitous mechanism of the marketplace? For instance, what if we flip to section 488 of *The Will to Power*, where we read, of "'the subject': interpreted from within ourselves, so that the ego counts as a substance, as the cause of all deeds, as a doer." This is clearly the Christian/Cartesian persona, the medieval and modern forms of the classical Platonic *nous*, the internal mirror of the noetic intellect into which shines the sun and the paradoxically immaterial specters of the Forms. But in section 490 of Nietzsche's tome we discover his considered view of the specter:

> The assumption of one single subject is perhaps unnecessary;
> perhaps it is just as permissible to assume a multiplicity of subjects,

whose interaction and struggle is the basis of our thought and our consciousness in general. . . . My *hypothesis*: The subject is a multiplicity.

Would these descriptions, spoken by the ghostly voice of the philosopher rising out of a consumer product in the mall, jibe with the act of consumption that awakened it? Which "voice from the commodity" is more compatible with the machinery of late capitalist modernity? Is the unitary modern subject still viable, can it still speak, within the enveloping semeiotics of advertising, or is the postmodern multiplicity of selves more at home in the mall? Or, denying the binary terrors of this consumer dialectic, is there an alternative?

The neostructuralist deconstruction of self provides one resounding answer to this question: the modern subject is defunct. This concept of self will not withstand the criticism that it exists within a language game requiring its opposition to, differentiation from, the "other." The self-other opposition is a difference which itself must be accounted for: the binary opposition, "self–other," is, in Derridean terms, a structure that provides for the stability of its constituent opposites but cannot account for its own structurality, its own center. If Derrida is right, this structurality is not a static, metaphysical reality but a relationship created by the play of *différance*. So the elementary deconstruction of the idea of self—that it is in necessary opposition to the other and that both opposites fit within a structure whose structurality is generated by a process of playful differentiation—provides a neostructuralist view of self as a form of inscription in a dynamic language game that can only come to rest through the failure to think, or the agreement to stop thinking, that is metaphysics (see Kamuf 1991, 64ff.). This is the insight that prompted Heidegger to write "The End of Philosophy and the Task of Thinking." But what about Nietzsche's other alternative? What view of self is implicit in the critique evident in the second quotation from *The Will to Power*? Is it not the deconstructed, heterogeneous "schizophrenic" persona of postmodernity? Is deconstruction, then, a form of empowerment? Does it animate the self it recontextualizes as inscribed within the play of *différance*, or does it simply make it into a passive design in an unfolding pattern?

As Foucault argues,

In fact, among all the mutations that have affected the knowledge of things and their order, the knowledge of identities, differences, characters, equivalences, words—in short, in the

midst of all the episodes of that profound history of the *Same*—
only one, that which began a century and a half ago and is now
perhaps drawing to a close, has made it possible for the figure of
man to appear. (*The Order of Things*, 386)

If "man" is the product of this evanescent historical structure, of its
"arrangements," then Foucault's as well as various neostructural and
postmodern views are no doubt correct so that, as Foucault concludes, "if
those arrangements were to disappear as they appeared, if some event of
which we can at the moment do no more than sense the possibility—
without knowing either what its form will be or what it promises—were to
cause them to crumble . . . then one can certainly wager that man would be
erased, like a face drawn at the edge of the sea" (387).

The crumbling of the structures that generated the Occidental self is
broadly evident amidst the mode of information that Mark Poster says makes
up late capitalist society, and particularly so in the widely documented loss of
identity and "neurosis" that people increasingly experience in advanced
industrial civilization. Should postmodern and neostructuralist theory leave
its adherents adrift in the Sea of Consumer Products (as the Beatles called it
in "Yellow Submarine"), to be swept away and collected as so much
psychological landfill, or should it provide a form of empowerment, of
creativity, not the loss of self but its reinvention: the persona as self-writing,
constructed identity, or more broadly, as culture making: *Kulturmachen?*

Nietzsche's work seems ambivalent in this respect. On the one hand,
it seems to deconstruct and dissolve the self. Thus Michel Haar argues
regarding Nietzsche's genealogy of logic:

> The destruction of logic by means of its genealogy brings with it
> as well the ruin of the psychological categories founded upon this
> logic. All psychological categories (the ego, the individual, the
> person) derive from the illusion of a substantial identity. . . .
> Moreover the "self," once brought into relation with the Will to
> Power, proves to be a simple illusion of perspective insofar as it is
> posited as an underlying unity, permanent center, source of
> decision. (1992, 17–18)

On the other hand, it seems to reconstruct and empower it. So Kathleen
Higgins counters the postmodern reading of Nietzsche:

> Although both Nietzsche and the postmodernists advocate a
> fragmented, perspectivist orientation toward our experience,

Nietzsche's purpose distinguishes him from his alleged intellectual heirs. Nietzsche's primary concern is the possibility of rich and meaningful subjective experience. (1990, 191)

We suggest that the combination of these two tendencies—in Heraclitean terms, the way down and the way up—can be made part of one and the same critique and recreation.

The way down is aptly illustrated when Nietzsche says, in *Twilight of the Idols*,

> The conception of a consciousness ("spirit") as a cause, and later also that of the ego as cause (the "subject"), are only afterbirths: first the causality of the will was firmly accepted as given, as *empirical*.
>
> Meanwhile we have thought better of it. Today we no longer believe a word of all this. The "inner world" is full of phantoms and will-o'-the-wisps: the will is one of them. The will no longer moves anything, hence does not explain anything either; it can also be absent. . . . And as for the *ego*! That has become a fable, a fiction, a play on words: it has altogether ceased to think, feel, or will! (Kaufmann 1976, 494–495)

Likewise, in *The Will to Power*, he proclaims: "There exists neither 'spirit,' nor reason, nor thinking, nor consciousness, nor soul, nor will, nor truth: all are fictions that are of no use" (sec. 480).

This skepticism about the self, taking it on the way down into dissolution, is, however, contrasted by Nietzsche's confidence in personal power, the way up, as he indicates in *Thus Spoke Zarathustra*:

> A new pride my ego taught me, and this I teach men: no longer to bury one's head in the sand of heavenly things, but to bear it freely, an earthly head, which creates a meaning for the earth.
>
> A new will I teach men: to *will* this way which man has walked blindly, and to affirm it, and no longer to sneak away from it like the sick and decaying. (Kaufmann 1976, 144)

Similarly, in *Beyond Good and Evil*, he says that the will has a countertendency to diversity and dissolution:

> Perhaps what I have said here of a "fundamental will of the spirit" may not be immediately comprehensible: allow me to explain.—That commanding something which the people call

"spirit" wants to be master within itself and around itself and to
feel itself master: out of multiplicity it has the will to simplicity, a
will which binds together and tames, which is imperious and
domineering. In this its needs and capacities are the same as
those which physiologists posit for everything that lives, grows
and multiplies. (sec. 230)

How are we to reconcile these two roads in Nietzsche, to offer both
multiplicity and unity, critique and creativity—*Kulturmachen*—while
perhaps, at the same time, escaping from and imagining an alternative to
that abode of the consumer self: the mall?

From a neostructuralist perspective, Nietzsche may be seen as
providing a deconstructive semeiotics of Christian culture, a revelation of
the systems of language and signs that make up the dominant tradition of
Europe. His attack on Christianity amounts, furthermore, to a protest
against the literalization of metaphor and to the closed system, the closed-
mindedness, that results from the privileging of the Christian "story" over
all other possible stories, and the creation of a Western master narrative.
The master narrative closes the open play of discourse by denying the
radical tentativeness of culture as play; hence Nietzsche's laughter at the
unconscious ludicrousness of Christian civilization. As he says about the
Christians,

> By letting God judge, they themselves judge; by glorifying God,
> they glorify themselves; by *demanding* the virtues of which they
> happen to be capable—even more, which they require in order
> to stay on top at all—they give themselves the magnificent
> appearance of a struggle for virtue, of a fight for the domination
> of virtue. . . . One should read the Gospels as books of seduction
> by means of morality: these petty people reserve morality for
> themselves—they know all about morality! With morality it is
> easiest to lead mankind *by the nose!* (*The Antichrist*, Kaufmann
> 1976, 621)

The point here is that the pious have hypostatized their idea of the good
into a reality—God—into whom they project their own judgments and by
whose "authority" they absolutize their ideas of virtue in order to impose
them on themselves and others. The texts of Christianity are rhetorical,
forms of seduction in Baudrillard's sense, which entice folks into the fold by
the idea of morality, the self-image of righteousness. But Christian goodness

is spurious, in Nietzsche's view, one more power play, and a particularly dangerous one because it is constituted by a metaphor turned into an idol: it is not, Nietzsche might say, following Feuerbach's *Essence of Christianity*, that man is an image of God, but rather that God is an image, a metaphor, for man who has been, in turn, fabricated as absolute reality and moral authority: a master author for a master narrative for a master civilization bent on colonizing the world for Christ. Significantly anticipating Derrida, Nietzsche neatly, in effect, deconstructs the artificial oppositions, or more precisely the lopsided oppositions, on which this master narrative is based:

> What really happens here is that the most conscious *conceit of being chosen* plays modesty: once and for all one has placed oneself, the "community," the "good and just," on one side, on the side of "truth"—and the rest, "the world," on the other. This was the most disastrous kind of megalomania that has yet existed on earth. (Kaufmann 1976, 622)

God is a magnification of the Christian ego into the absolute, with all the attributes of morality—"community," "good and just"— foisted upon Him, creating an irreconcilable opposition to "the world" (read other peoples and cultures, nature, woman, the devil, evil, the Iraqis) which are, therefore, the proper objects of "salvation" (read conquest and exploitation). But the oppositions are artificial in the first place, and the Christian privileging of one half—the "good" half—is wholly chimerical. This would not be so bad if the Christians, and Eurocentrists generally, understood that the creation and selective privileging of oppositions are no more than a peculiar kind of play, invented by *Homo sapiens*; this realization, however, creates not the Apollonian wise man but the Dionysian reveler, *Homo ludens*. Of course, as Nietzsche's *Philosophy in the Tragic Age of the Greeks* clearly indicates, the Apollonian and Dionysian are themselves correlatives in the game of Western culture, separated at our peril.

The Christian ego is not only posited as God, in Nietzsche's view, but also as the soul, insuring not only that the world is "meant" for Christian colonization, but also that the converted are insured eternal life, independent of the play of time and change. According to Nietzsche, the absolutization of God is *internalized* by the Christians in a kind of meta-idolatry: first a superentity is fabricated and set up as the ontological foundation of all existence; then the Father in heaven is introjected as the soul in the body, or the ghost in the machine, in moral terms as the superego or conscience. Thus man comes to live under the shadow of God and so accept the limits that this imposes on him: God hands down the law. As Nietzsche argues in *On the Genealogy of Morals*,

> All instincts that do not discharge themselves outwardly *turn inward*—this is what I call the *internalization* [*Verinnerlichung*] of man: thus it was that man first developed what was later called his "soul." The entire inner world, originally as thin as if it were stretched between two membranes, expanded and extended itself, acquired depth, breadth, and height, in the same measure as outward discharge was *inhibited*. (II, sec. 16)

Thus the self or soul is created through constraint on "instincts," which would otherwise be turned outward. Here we can see Nietzsche's downward and upward paths juxtaposed, for as he takes apart the inner life of the soul via genealogy, he suggests the expansion of "instinct" outward. This latter idea needs clarification, for it can be misinterpreted as an excuse for imperialism, but it can also be seen as the play of creativity unconstrained by the idols of metaphysics and the seductions of empire.

Learning and the Self-Transformation of the Consumer

This creative version of Nietzsche's upward path is evident in his view of learning, which dovetails with Gregory Bateson's theory of Learning III. Consider Nietzsche's view:

> Learning transforms us, it does that which all nourishment does which does not merely "preserve"—as the physiologist knows. But at the bottom of us, "right down deep," there is, to be sure, something unteachable, a granity stratum of spiritual fate, of predetermined decision and answer to predetermined selected questions. In the case of every cardinal problem there speaks an unchangeable "this is I"; about man and woman, for example, a thinker cannot relearn but only learn fully—only discover all that is "firm and settled" within him on this subject. One sometimes comes upon certain solutions to problems which inspire strong belief in *us*; perhaps one thenceforth calls them one's "convictions." Later—one sees them only as footsteps to self-knowledge, signposts to the problem which we *are*—more correctly, to the great stupidity which we are, to our spiritual fate, to the *unteachable* "right down deep." (*Beyond Good and Evil*, sec. 231)

The idea of learning here is, first and foremost, one of radical self-transformation, where human identity is not static, knowledge not sure, but both subject to continuous reevaluation and change. This tentativeness of identity and knowledge that Nietzsche's idea implies echoes his aforementioned idea of culture as play, in Derridean terms, as the play of *différance*. But the unfolding of identity is limited by the constraint of self, by the "granity stratum of spiritual fate," by the "predetermined" answers to questions, by the "unchangeable" "this is I," as by its "convictions," all amounting to the "unteachable 'right deep down.'" This analysis is similar to Bateson's theory of Learning I, II, and III. Learning I includes simple habit formation as well as Pavlovian and Skinnerian conditioning: a programming of response by repeated pairing of stimuli. Learning II involves a systematic change in Learning I, as when a dog becomes *better* at Learning I, say, at learning to associate meat powder and bell as in the classic Pavlovian experiment, or as when a human subject gets better at memorizing nonsense syllables, after repeated trials. Learning II is "learning how to learn."

Bateson argues, interestingly, that the premises of self are encoded at the level of Learning II: the self is a complex of codes or, in Nietzsche's terms, "predetermined decisions way deep down," which punctuate the stream of experience: codes which, themselves learned and relatively "hard programmed," come to determine the future learning patterns of an individual. In most of us these codes become, as Nietzsche says, "unteachable," so that character and personality solidify; "we know who we are" and act "characteristically," determined by the programs of Learning II or by the constraints of self. But Bateson, like Nietzsche, does not leave the matter here. For both, the self is constructed, fabricated, a learned structure that functions to limit further learning. Both are therefore critical of this limitation and provide a theory of escape. For Bateson, this is Learning III: a change in the premises of Learning II, in Derrida's terms a deconstruction of its codes and constraints, and hence, in Nietzschean terms, a transformation of the person and a new freedom. As Bateson says in "The Logical Categories of Learning and Communication,"

> Certainly [Learning III] must lead to a greater flexibility in the premises acquired by the process of Learning II—a *freedom* from their bondage. . . .
>
> I once heard a Zen master state categorically: "To become accustomed to anything is a terrible thing."

But any freedom from the bondage of habit must also denote a profound redefinition of the self. If I stop at the level of Learning II, "I" am the aggregate of those characteristics which I call my "character." "I" am my habits of acting in context and shaping and perceiving the contexts in which I act. Selfhood is a product or aggregate of Learning II. To the degree that a man achieves Learning III, and learns to perceive and act in terms of the contexts of contexts, his "self" will take on a sort of irrelevance. The concept of "self" will no longer function as a nodal argument in the punctuation of experience. (*Steps*, 304)

Thus Learning III, in Bateson's terms, is analogous to learning as self-transformation in Nietzsche's, and both imply that the construction of cultural codes, of which the ciphers of self, like the idea of deity, are a prime example, are constraints on the open play of creativity, in Derridean terms of *différance*. Thus culture making becomes a creative, upward path, only tentatively constrained by the strictures of self, of metaphysics, of morals, and of various other kinds of civilized "order." The tentativeness of self-making becomes part of the play of culture making, the primary Nietzschean "rule" of which is, "Don't forget that this is a game," "Don't start worshiping the king," just move your chess piece or carve a new one or make up a new form of play.

The upward path in Nietzsche, like Bateson's road to higher learning, involves a generative idea of identity. Identity is to be shaped in terms of values that in turn must be shaped by the creative will to power. This active dimension of the self, counter to the passive acquiescence of the slave, is the command of the master. This latter idea might cause, and has caused, postmodern and feminist theorists to wince because of its frank assertion of power and dominance as opposed to passivity and submission. But it is possible to interpret what Nietzsche says in this regard so as not to uphold the patriarchic dominance of master narratives and phallocentric discourse but rather to open the way to polymorphous self-making. It is also possible to develop the Nietzschean idea of mastery without invoking the master–slave dialectic, delineated by Hegel and Marx as well as by Sartre.

The idea of commanding and mastery in Nietzsche may be understood by analogy with that of Zen discipline and mastery, itself compared to Learning III by Bateson above. As Shunryu Suzuki says, "the purpose of studying Buddhism is to study ourselves and to forget ourselves. When we forget ourselves, we actually are the true activity of the big existence, or reality itself" (1985, 79). Here "reality" must be understood antimeta-physically as "true activity." In this regard, to "command" and to "master" are not to impose rules from above or to assert power over, but rather to break free from rules and ascend to a perspective where structures, including the self, are fabricated. Thus, in spite of Nietzsche's railing against the asceticism and herd mentality of Buddhism that supposedly imperils Europe by, as he says in his preface to *On the Genealogy of Morals*, "the will turning *against* life, the tender and ultimate signs of the ultimate illness" (sec. 5; cf. *Beyond Good and Evil*, sec. 202), to the creative Nietzschean as to the Zen Buddhist, mastery consists not in asserting domination over the slave but in transcending the double-bind of the master–slave dialectic. This is the will to mastery that Nietzsche contrasts to the preference of the spirit for the dissembling, trivializing power obtained from the masks of everyday identity, the "will to appearance":

> in this the spirit enjoys the multiplicity and cunning of its masks, it enjoys too the sense of being safe that this brings—for it is precisely through its protean arts that it is best concealed and protected!

The will to mastery is quite different, however, counteracting the will to appearance. As Nietzsche continues,

> *This* will to appearance, to simplification, to the mask, to the cloak, in short to the superficial—for every surface is a cloak—is *counteracted* by that sublime inclination in the man of knowledge which takes a profound many-sided and thorough view of things and *will* take such a view: as a kind of cruelty of the intellectual conscience and taste which every brave thinker will recognize in himself, provided he has hardened and sharpened for long enough his own view of himself, as he should have, and is accustomed to stern discipline and stern language. (*Beyond Good and Evil*, sec. 230)

This path to a profound mastery appreciative of multiplicity and achieved through stern discipline and language not only connotes Zen practice but also suggests that, like Learning III, the identity to be created by the Nietzschean master is not a superficial phenomenon, not the mask of prefabricated identity readily available in the myriad consumer images on display in the mall, but rather the power of image making, of self-formation. This identity requires not the acquiescence of the consumer slave but rather the intellectual conscience, bravery, and even cruelty of self-scrutiny and reevaluation characteristic of the creative master. It also leads, because of the tentativeness and multiplicity of the roles it invokes, to the metalogic of play.

The Will to Power and the Will to Play

Nietzschean, like Derridean, play invokes the unfolding power of *différance*, of what Bateson calls the "difference which makes a difference" (381), the generative identity of the rule-maker unconstrained by any strictures except those created by herself or himself, including of course the gender codes of selfhood implicit in the aforementioned pronouns, for the game. As Nietzsche says, in his typically contemptuous way,

> Wisdom: that seems to the rabble to be a kind of flight, an artifice and means for getting oneself out of a dangerous game; but the genuine philosopher—as he seems to *us*, my friends?—lives "unphilosophically" and "unwisely," above all *imprudently*, and bears the burden and duty of a hundred attempts and temptations of life—he risks *himself* constantly, he plays *the* dangerous game. (*Beyond Good and Evil*, sec. 205)

What is the "dangerous game"? If our reading is correct, it is the play of *différance*, which emerges at the level of Learning III and makes irrelevant the premises of the spectral self created by the will to appearance or by Madison Avenue, creating the extraordinary risk and responsibility of self-making, the impetus of the will to power. To give up prefabricated identity is to play the dangerous game of having to make one's own, of going "mad." As we have argued elsewhere (White and Hellerich 1992, 1993), the therapeutic disciplines of the social sciences, like psychology and education, are in the business of regulating and enforcing norms of identity consistent with the bureaucratic structure of modern states and corporations. To challenge those identities and what Nietzsche calls the "slave sciences" that help maintain them, is to set out on a hard climb, the upward path, which as Nietzsche says requires discipline. This is where Nietzschean postmodernity differs from that of Fredric Jameson, at least if we understand his "cultural logic of late capitalism" pessimistically as defining the limits of postmodern coding. For the pastiche of codes that make up postmodern artifacts and representations, including the schizo-phrenic post-self, are on this reading the result of the commercialization of culture by what the Frankfurt School called the culture industry, and the pervasive dominance of advertising, even identification of advertising, as the logic of culture. But that makes those in the postmodern condition no more than schizophrenic consumer slaves, in Nietzsche's terms, hardly an ideal hoarde of twenty-first-century culture heroes, or even anti-heroes.

New Forms of Empowerment

If postmodern consumers are slaves, then those who make the rules for consumption, the capitalists, are the masters; together they produce the master–slave dialectic of late capitalism. Consuming more will not make the slaves masters, and becoming capitalists will not free them from the dialectic, for their power is constrained by the need for slaves to feed profits. In late capitalism, as Marx foresaw, both capitalist and consumer, like capitalist and worker in earlier phases, are prisoners of the logic of capital in its game of masters and slaves: the game of power as *power over* the other. The Nietzschean and, we think, the postmodern game is to get out of the dialectic altogether: power as *power to create* (*Kulturmachen*). As Nietzsche says, contrasting his ideal with thinkers in the tradition of Kant and Hegel,

> *Genuine philosophers, however, are commanders and legislators.* . . . With a creative hand they reach for the future, and all that is and has been becomes a means for them, an instrument, a hammer. Their "knowing" is creating, their creating is legisla-tion, their will to truth is—*will to power*. (*Beyond Good and Evil*, Kaufmann trans., sec. 211)

The social philosophy of Nietzschean postmodernity is emerging as a Neo-Marxism embracing both a critique of capitalism and an incredulity at the master narrative of collective liberation through state socialism. Pluralism, decentralization, feminism, environmentalism, local empower-ment, in the Nietzschean sense, of diverse peoples and cultures are the semeiotic formations of the new movement. As Grossberg and Nelson argue in *Marxism and the Interpretation of Culture*, a volume embodying the new diversity of discourses in this domain,

> As *Marxism* has been challenged and rewritten, both by its dialogue with other bodies of theory and by its effort to acknowledge the diverse political realities of the postwar world;

as Marxism has attempted to find more sophisticated models of
the relations between culture and power, more reflective understanding of its own position within these relations, and more
politically insightful and relevant tools for the analysis of contemporary structures of power—so has it become a much more
varied discourse. (11)

In this context, the ideas of self and self-formation are crucial to the understanding of what empowerment might mean and what it might achieve.
Empowerment of the creative self requires a critique of the dialectic, which
makes a master or a slave out of the spectral self: the consuming logic of
images in the mall. The logic is so pervasive and so dominant that it is not
unlike that of the stained glass in the medieval church, except consumer
icons have replaced religious ones.

Herbert Marcuse's critique of late capitalism provides a useful beginning point from which a deconstructive critique may proceed. Marcuse
utilized Freudian theory to highlight the subtle forms of repression emerging in the advanced industrial West during the 1950s and 1960s, when
consumerism was burgeoning into what Jameson, Lyotard, Baudrillard, and
others would recognize as the postmodern cultural formation. In *One-
Dimensional Man*, Marcuse develops his most telling analysis of the way in
which the capitalist economy was reducing the complexity and autonomy
of collective and individual power by the mechanisms of the market,
transforming workers and citizens, both potential revolutionaries, into
consumers. A key to his analysis is the concept of "repressive desublimation," which inverts the traditional Freudian analysis, where civilization is
said to be formed by the sublimation of desires and the structuring, in
capitalism the exploitative repression, of *eros* into alienated labor for
someone else's profit. This dimension of Marcuse's work was an expansion
of his earlier *Eros and Civilization*, in which he supplemented the traditional
Marxian interpretation of capitalism in terms of economic exploitation
with the Freudian one in terms of psychological forms of control. What was
new in late capitalism, particularly consumerism, Marcuse argued, was that
the work ethic analyzed so well by Weber in *The Protestant Ethic and the
Spirit of Capitalism*, which required that the desire for pleasure be sublimated
in order for worker or capitalist to succeed, was now being overturned.

The logic of consumerism was precisely the repressive structuring of
pleasure for the purpose of control. Consumers were encouraged to desub-
limate and indulge their desires for a myriad of products, which were made

all the more alluring by the glossy images of advertising. Thus where capital-ism once required hard work and sacrifice, it now requires leisure and self-indulgence. The flagrant contradiction between these two tendencies is no doubt at the basis of the contradictions and irony pervasive in developed consumer economies, especially in the United States, where people are simultaneously told to work hard and to enjoy themselves, to diet and to eat, to save and to spend, until they are understandably confused and lined up for therapy. This contradictory rubric is at the basis of Jameson's pastiched "cultural logic" of late capitalism, mentioned above, or what Jameson, Baudrillard, and others have referred to as postmodern "schizophrenia," and what Charles Jencks, speaking of architecture and the arts, calls postmodern "double coding."

As these theorists, especially Jencks, suggest, this logic, while it has a great many destructive features—consider the mass control of the con-sumer population by the "soft" methods of the market that have invaded every sphere, from health care to politics—also opens some creative possibilities. For the masters of the consumer kingdom, the patron saints of the consumer church (Lee Iacoca, Jim and Tammy Baker, Donald Trump, Bill Gates) are not necessarily in control of the Pandora's box of pleasures they have opened. What may be taking place—what we hope is taking place—is a splintering of the very mechanisms of control that gave us the structures of consumerism in the first place—and the opening up of a creative option for politics and culture. We may still accept the sacraments of the consumer church, but we may no longer believe in the religion. This disbelief is part of what Lyotard has called the postmodern incredulity about master narratives—progress, enlightenment, salvation, and, we would add, consumption. With economy and ecology crumbling, increas-ingly we are willing to admit that there is trouble in consumer paradise.

Interlude: Nietzsche Goes to Hell (and so do we)

In the textual world of the *Comedia: Inferno*, Virgil leads Dante through the hordes of the damned, all engaged in activities that epitomize their forms of entrapment and self-torture, revealing the semeiotics of sin to the pilgrim and his guide. So let Nietzsche be our guide as we purchase his commod-itized tomes and enter the stream of consumers in the mall. "Buying and selling have become common, like the art of reading and writing," our guide proclaims with mild disdain. "Everybody has practiced it even if he is no tradesman, and gets more practice every day—just as formerly, when men were more savage, everybody was a hunter and practiced that art day after day" (*Gay Science*, 31). "So we go foraging for products as a way of life," we wonder, "even as your metaphor indicates, writing by our consuming practices the language constituting our lives?" "One can imagine social conditions in which there is no buying and selling and in which this art gradually ceases to be necessary," our guide says (31), intimating, we assume, the Other Place, which we've heard of but never seen. For now we're in the realm of the carnal, and indeed we observe a neon sign blinking in time with neo-disco pop rhythms, just ahead, reading, in Nietzsche's translation, "Prostitution of the Spirit" (31).

"*Ecce!*" Nietzsche remarks with a glare. "After all this do I still need to say that they too will be free, *very* free spirits, these philosophers of the future?" (*Beyond Good and Evil*, 44), by invidious comparison with whom we get the uneasy feeling that he is referring to *us* in *our* rubric of consumption. "In all the countries of Europe and likewise in America there exists at present something that misuses this name, a very narrow, enclosed, chained up species of spirits who desire practically the opposite of that which informs our aims and instincts. . . . They belong, in short and regrettably, among the *levellers*, these falsely named 'free spirits'—eloquent and tirelessly scribbling slaves of the democratic taste and its 'modern ideas,' men without solitude one and all . . . unfree and ludicrously superficial" (44). After this, we are a little ashamed to try something on, despite the friendly pose of the salesperson beckoning us, like a siren, to simulate the perfect electric images of the body-apparelled emanating from the video monitors above. We are so taken with the images of delight dancing with digital ecstasy on the screens, like writhing forms in pain on Prozac, that we are nearly overcome with awe, and so apparently is another salesperson with our guide's mustache, which he describes as "awesome."

Escaping from that gap in the mall's glittering, woeful stream, we reenter the consumer traffic, the souls rushing as in a stampede toward what at first seems to be an apparition; but, our guide explains, "What with all their might they would like to strive after is the universal green pasture happiness of the herd, with security, safety, comfort and an easier life for all" (54). We are taken by our host's prophetic powers, too, when his very words are soon echoed by another person selling, this time, the images of suburbia from a real-estate booth, high above us up a glittering escalator, emblazoned by the skylight. As we ascend amidst the herd our guide bids us to listen, and explains that the celestial music we hear is actually the sound of Musak augmented by the strains of an electric fountain with plaster boulders and "real" plants. He also explains that suburbia is where the souls go who, having escaped the tortuous delights of the mall, seek a place of rest and so are given the simulations of "home" that best fit their (our?) televised imaginations and budgets. So Nietzsche asks, "Is it any wonder we 'free spirits' are not precisely the most communicative [televised?] of spirits? that we do not want to betray in every respect *from what* a spirit can free itself and *to what* [and in what model auto] it is then perhaps driven?" (44). But we are not yet to receive our estate, and our guide motions us again downward, toward further wonders of the consumer cavern.

As we descend into the lower level, we notice that the souls move in an aura of purely artificial light, the blaze of the sun absent here, and that the mall stretches out before us as an avenue of glittering surfaces, the ice of electronic Cocytus, under the gloss of which entities swim in every conceivable form of simulated self-betterment, mannequins like pieces of straw bent this way and that behind the glass. Our host explains that this is the realm of Love Gone Awry, where the nobler inclinations of the spirit entombed are subjected to the frigorific contortions of style. Refracting language through a prism of applications like his Florentine counterpart, Nietzsche says, "Avarice and love: what different feelings these two terms evoke! Nevertheless it could be the same instinct that has two names" (*Gay Science*, 14). The *Amor* of Dante's *Paradiso* is also the Love entrapped in his *Inferno*, we assume he means to suggest, so that love and avarice have a common thread. Thus Nietzsche says, "A full and powerful soul not only copes with painful, even terrible losses, deprivations, robberies, insults; it emerges from such hells with greater fullness and powerfulness; and, most essential of all, with a new increase in the blissfulness of love. I believe that he who has divined something of the most basic conditions for this growth in love will understand what Dante meant when he wrote over the gate of his *Inferno*: 'I, too, was created by eternal love'" (*The Will to Power*, 1030). We are on the verge of forgetting that our journey is one of exploration, a kind of archaeological expedition to the mall, and approach the encased images, ready to consume with plastic drawn, when Nietzsche warns us: "Our pleasure in ourselves tries to maintain itself by again and again changing something new *into ourselves*; that is what possession means" (*Gay Science*, 14).

We ponder the result of becoming those mannequins under glass, and are about to sheathe our credit cards when there appears on our right, in an aura of incandescence and perfume, a pane that offers plastic women dressed in as little silk as possible—the perfect consumable items! The idea seems to be that the lingerie has some Secret power to transform real women into icons, thus making them much more amenable to male taste. But once again our guide warns, much to our disappointment,

> Sexual love betrays itself most clearly as a lust for possession: the lover desires unconditional and sole possession of the person for whom he longs; he desires equally unconditional power over the soul and over the body of the beloved; he alone wants to be loved and desires to live and rule in the other soul as supreme and supremely desirable. If one considers that this means nothing less than *excluding* the whole world from a precious good, from happiness and enjoyment; if one considers that the lover aims at the impoverishment and deprivation of all competitors and would like to become the dragon guarding his golden hoard as the most inconsiderate and selfish of all "conquerors" and exploiters; if one considers, finally, that to the lover himself the whole rest of the world appears indifferent, pale, and worthless, and he is prepared to make any sacrifice to disturb any order, to subordinate all other interests—then one comes to feel genuine amazement that this wild avarice and injustice of sexual love has been glorified and deified so much in all ages—indeed, that this love has furnished the concept of love as the opposite of egoism while it actually may be the most ingenuous expression of egoism. (14)

As our benevolent shepherd prods us past the store, he points to a sign with stark white letters on a black background, oddly enough standing out amidst the glittering icons all around, saying "Limited": "At this point linguistic usage has evidently been formed by those who did not possess but desired. Probably, there have always been too many of these," our guide explains (14), apparently meaning that the name indicates the underlying dynamic of consumerism: desire unlimited in a semeiotic formation that paradoxically spells out "Exclusive" in pastiche with images of unlimited conformity through consumption: "*From Paradise*: 'Good and evil are the prejudices of God'—said the snake" (*Gay Science*, 259). We are, at this point, feeling uneasily like Nietzsche's "free spirits," and are ready to escape to the suburbs.

Beyond Good and Evil: *fröhliches Kulturmachen*

"We Gotta Get Out of This Place"
—The Animals

The church of consumers may be deconstructed by the Nietzschean critique—the restrictive premises of late capitalism, of bureaucratization, of channeled and conditioned desire revealed—and in their place the possibility of a new game opened. The deconstruction is achieved by Nietzsche's simultaneous criticism, on our reading, of the oppositions of the master–slave dialectic and his provision of an upward path that transcends it. This is a transcendence not of "the world" but rather of the polarities of a game, the restrictive logic of dominator and dominated, and hence into the freedom to be a true player—a maker of games, instead of a piece (whether king or pawn)—in a prefabricated game. It is the opening up of the domain of play as the metalogic of Learning III, of the possibility of identity unconstrained by the spectral self, which Nietzsche offers as a "philosophical" alternative for the individual psyche. Beyond the entrapment of the child in the introjected imagery of the culture in the mirror phase, as Lacan theorizes it, Nietzsche offers the image of the child as the open possibility of creativity, through the looking glass into the realm of play:

> The child is innocence and forgetting, a new beginning, a game, a self-propelled wheel, a first movement, a sacred "Yes." For the game of creation, my brothers, a sacred "Yes" is needed: the spirit now wills his own will, and he who had been lost to the world now conquers his own world. (*Thus Spoke Zarathustra*, Kaufmann trans., 139)

We should understand this affirmative spirit that wills itself not as the traditional ego of the West, of which Nietzsche was so critical, but rather as the play of *différance* in the psyche, creating the personae of selfhood via the multilevel paradoxes of play. The latter, and the host of creative options they open by making communication ever incomplete, are generated by the peculiar self-referentiality of the message, "This is play," which Bateson translates as "These actions in which we now engage do not denote what those actions *for which they stand* would denote," so that, for example, the playful nip denotes but does not mean the same thing as the bite ("A Theory of Play and Fantasy," *Steps*, 180). It this opening up of communication via paradox to the expanding indeterminacy of play that,

Bateson suggests modestly, "may have been an important step in the evolution of communication" (181). The opening up of communication to indeterminacy is also an opening up to creativity, as Nietzsche and affirmative postmodernists suggest. It is a way out of the stylized rules of the static game of control, imposed by the powers that be, and a way into culture making by powers that become. For as Bateson concludes, more profoundly, regarding play,

> we believe that the paradoxes of abstraction must make their appearance in all communication more complex than that of mood signals, and that without these paradoxes the evolution of communication would be at an end. Life would then be an endless interchange of stylized messages, a game with rigid rules, unrelieved by change or humor. (193)

So perhaps we can put down our copy of Nietzsche that we have been contemplating to see that the mall, no matter how powerful and encompassing, may itself be transformed, its consumer gods dethroned, by the deconstructive power of laughter.

CHAPTER 2

They Might be Giants

Mental Patients in Rebellion

Psychiatry in the Labyrinth: Deconstructing Deviancy

Deconstruction is a term that has received considerable attention and currency in a variety of disciplines, perhaps most prominently among literary critics in the United States, but also in philosophy and the social sciences. It is perhaps necessary, given the polemics that the idea has generated, to specify as clearly as possible what *we* mean by it, before discussing its applications to psychiatry in general and the idea of deviancy (*Abweichung*) in particular.

Derrida is clearer, it seems, when he is explaining what deconstruction is not. As he says when considering the difficulties in translating it in "Letter to a Japanese Friend,"

> deconstruction is neither an *analysis* nor a *critique* and its translation would have to take that into consideration. It is not an analysis in particular because the dismantling of a structure is not a regression toward a *simple element*, toward an *indissoluble origin*. These values, like that of analysis, are themselves philosophemes subject to deconstruction. No more is it a critique, in a general sense or in a Kantian sense. The instance of *krinein* or *krisis* (decision, choice, judgment, discernment) is itself, as is all the apparatus of transcendental critique, one of the essential

35

"themes" or "objects" of deconstruction." (Kamuf 1991, 273; cf.
Derrida, 1973, 129ff.; 1982, 3ff.)

But if the term denotes neither an analysis nor a critique, then what *does* it
mean? Derrida suggests this later in the same essay: "Deconstruction takes
place, it is an event that does not await the deliberation, consciousness, or
organization of a subject, or even of modernity" (274). Here we are to
understand that deconstruction is an *activity*, but it would perhaps be easier
to specify what kind of activity, insofar as we can do so with a term that
defies classification into kinds, by using Heidegger's term *Ereignis*, "a
coming into presence," which is also suggested, in his view, by the Greek
term *physis*, often translated statically as "nature." Derrida goes on to
explain that

> the word "deconstruction," like all other words, acquires its value
> only from its inscription in a chain of possible substitutions, in
> what is too blithely called a "context." For me, for what I have
> tried and still try to write, the word has interest only within a
> certain context, where it replaces and lets itself be determined by
> such other words as "écriture," "trace," différance.". . . By
> definition, the list can never be closed. . . . In fact, I should have
> cited the sentences and the interlinking of sentences which in
> their turn determine these names in some of my texts. (Kamuf
> 1991, 275; cf. Derrida 1982, 3ff.; 1973, 129ff.)

So deconstruction is neither analysis nor critique but an activity that is
determined by the context in which it occurs, just as the meaning of a word
may be specified by the context of the sentence or paragraph or essay in
which it occurs.

    With respect to activities other than writing, which are of interest
because structuralism, like neostructuralism, is in part based on the general-
ization of linguistic processes to ones that were formerly thought to be
nonlinguistic, Derrida's most fruitful definition of deconstruction is in terms
of play. So in "Structure, Sign and Play in the Discourse of the Human
Sciences," as he considers the tendency to "totalization" evident in the
social sciences in general and Lévi-Strauss in particular, Derrida says, again
attempting to define a concept by what it is not:

> But nontotalization can also be determined in another way: no
> longer from the standpoint of a concept of finitude as relegation
> to the empirical, but from the standpoint of the concept of *play*.

If totalization no longer has any meaning, it is not because the infiniteness of a field cannot be covered by a finite glance or a finite discourse, but because the nature of the field—that is, language and a finite language—excludes totalization. This field is in effect that of *play*, that is to say, a field of infinite substitutions only because it is finite, that is to say, because instead of being an inexhaustible field . . . instead of being too large, there is something missing from it: a center which arrests and grounds the play substitutions. (Derrida 1978, 289)

The word "play," therefore could be another substitution instance of the word "deconstruction," as both exist within a field of infinite substitutions and are determined by the constantly shifting configuration of that field. The result is that the concept of deconstruction, of play, connotes what Derrida calls *différance*, listed by him as a substitute for deconstruction above, and hence as he explains in his essay *"Différance,"*

every concept is necessarily and essentially inscribed in a chain or a system, within which it refers to another and to other concepts, by the systematic play of differences. Such a play, then— *différance*—is no longer simply a concept, but the possibility of conceptuality, of the conceptual system and process in general. For the same reason, *différance*, which is not a concept, is not a mere word; that is, it is not what we represent to ourselves as the calm and present self-referential unity of concept and sound. (Derrida 1973, 140)

Interestingly, this association of the ideas of play and *différance*, suggests that what Derrida is talking about is not only the freedom connoted by the idea of play applied to the sober disciplines of the "human sciences," but also about the idea of innovation and creativity—unruly concepts at best. However, we shall argue that this understanding of deconstruction, applied to the psychiatric concept and practice of deviation and its correction, reveals the limits and the possible violence of that and related sciences— psychology, counseling, therapy—to various strains of creative discourse, from poetry to politics.

It is appropriate to consider the concept of deviancy as it is employed in some texts of the human sciences. *The Encyclopedia of Psychology* (1984), for example, defines deviancy in terms of two principal viewpoints:

The first has viewed deviance as an exceptional but consistent variation from statistical norms. . . . The second prominent position has seen deviance as defined by occurrence of single critical events. . . . From this point of view, deviance is defined by the single occurrence of an unusual high-intensity behavior, cognition, or emotion. (367)

Another shade of the concept's meaning is evident in the definition offered by *The Social Science Encyclopedia*:

Although the word *deviance* has been employed for over three hundred years, its sociological meanings are rather recent and distinct. In the main, sociologists and criminologists have taken deviance to refer to behavior that is banned, censured, stigmatized or penalized. (199)

Although various schools of thought, ranging from phenomenologists to Marxists, have developed variations that alter the meaning of the term somewhat, as the aforementioned texts point out, nevertheless its essential meanings are rather constant: deviancy is some "exceptional" variation from a statistical norm, or a single "unusual" act or thought or emotion, or a piece of behavior that is somehow censured. Foucault perhaps could not have found better examples to illustrate his idea that the individual is constituted by a process of "normalization" in which the personality, even if subjectively experienced as unique, is in fact standardized to meet the needs of social institutions and systems of communication (see Foucault 1977). As Freud saw, we learn a good deal about how norms are constructed by considering abnormalities, and so we can learn a good deal about how the mental health establishment enforces dominant types by its conception of and practices to "correct" deviancy (see Freud 1989). Indeed, the above definitions of deviancy may be seen as establishing boundaries, fixed outlines, for thought, emotion, and behavior outside of which its "clients" fall into the "deviancy" category and so become the subjects of "treatment." Furthermore, a binary opposition between "normal" and "deviant" is assumed in the definitions, so that a phenomenon falls into one or the other—it is either statistically normal, say, or it is not; the line must be drawn somewhere, even if gray areas are admitted.

Indeed, as behavior approaches the borderline, enters a gray area, it becomes increasingly suspect, indicating that principally mainstream statistical types are privileged in this system. As Luhmann argues in

Soziologie des Risikos, the sciences depend on the concept of normality in order to establish their basic concepts of measurement, classification and evaluation: norms provide the standards or reference points to which scientists must refer. This in turn suggests not only that the binary opposition between normal and deviant is at the foundation of the human sciences, but also that the opposition between normal and abnormal—read order and chaos—is at the foundation of science as such. Thus psychiatry, as Thomas Kuhn would say, depends on a paradigm that defines certain classes of behavior as "normal" or "deviant." But since psychiatry is a *social* science, its practitioners are themselves subject to the reference of psychiatric classification, so that the doctors are presumably "normal" and their patients "deviant" (see Kuhn 1962). This sort of definition, however, is likely to be self-serving, as we point out below.

A case study from the history of psychiatry may be illustrative of how the norms and classification systems of early-nineteenth-century society constructed a standard individual who, if he deviated from the norm, was diagnosed as "mentally ill" but whose very alleged mental illness provides a commentary that deconstructs the doctors, the mental health institutions (especially the asylum), and the psychological and social norms they represent. In fact, we shall argue that the commentary of what psychiatry defined as a "schizophrenic" amounts to a deconstruction in terms tantamount to those of contemporary "schizophrenic" postmodern discourse, of the very idea of sanity or mental health. We are not arguing that a case of "schizophrenia" is reducible to one of "deviance"; rather we are saying that the behavior defined as schizophrenic is not only deviant but also, due to its peculiar form, a deconstructive commentary as suggested above. We also do not want to imply that the particular case and context in question are generalizable to all cases and contexts; however, they may well apply to a variety of circumstances where the etiology of deviancy is social. The document is *Perceval's Narrative: A Patient's Account of his Psychosis 1830–1832*, edited by the originator of the double-bind theory of schizophrenia and longtime critic of the psychiatric establishment, Gregory Bateson.

John Perceval, as Bateson explains in his introduction, was one of twelve children of the British prime minister, Spencer Perceval, who was assassinated in 1812. John entered the army and served as an officer, but throughout his military career he was beset by religious conflicts, especially as he came under the influence of evangelical doctrines. At one time, after relations with a prostitute, he believed that he had contracted syphilis, and, as Bateson comments, "he narrates with retrospective humor the characteristically schizophrenic dilemma in which he then found himself—whether to trust in God for the completion of his cure or to take the medicine which his doctor had ordered: he took half the prescribed dose" (vii). Soon his behavior became disorderly, and he was put under restraint in the inn where he was lodging on 16 December 1830. In January 1831, his eldest brother, Spencer, placed him in an asylum operated by Drs. Fox at Brisslington in the vicinity of Bristol. He remained there until May 1832, when he was relocated to another asylum until the outset of 1834, when he married Anna Gardner, with whom he had four daughters. He published his account of his psychosis in two books, the first appearing in 1838, the second in 1840, both of which are contained in Bateson's volume. Little is known about the remainder of his life, except that he gave testimony to the Select Committee for Lunacy at the behest of a group called the Alleged Lunatics Friends Society. He also wrote various letters to *The Times* concerning the lunacy laws on behalf of the "insane."

First, it is important to discuss the construction of Perceval as a mental health patient in the context of the established norms of his day. It is clear that in Perceval's society a person holding ideas that were extraordinary, especially if they resulted in speech or behavior that did not fit established norms, was considered a threat and was subject to chastisement. As Perceval describes it, "Then when I became insane, the knowledge of that fact appears to have given to every one who had to deal with me carte blanche to act towards me, as far as seemed good unto himself, in defiance of nature, of common sense, and of humanity" (69). It is interesting to see how Spencer Perceval, John's brother, reacts to his behavior:

> When my brother [Spencer] first appeared by my bedside, "I have hopes now," said I, "I shall be understood and respected"; . . . When, however, I first told him, "I am desired to say so and so," "I am desired to do this, or that"—he replied to me, in an ill-judged tone of levity, and as if speaking to a child; ridiculing the idea. (52)

Clearly the brother is already beginning to function in loco doctoris, and if we consider the internal double-bind imposed by the logic of Perceval's "schizophrenic family," *in loco parentis*, enforcing the categorization of John as deviant and so as mentally ill. The family is thus, already early on in John's break from normality, functioning as an institution of control, suppressing the deviancy of the sibling, making his voice inefficacious, and finally silencing him. As John goes on to explain, "My hopes of being comprehended were blighted, and my heart turned from him. I reflected; my brother knew my powers of mind, he ought to consider that it can be no light matter that can so change me. I then resumed my silence" (52). This silencing is significant, especially in terms of double-bind theory, for, as Bateson argues, it is precisely the silencing of the schizophrenic's commentary on his situation, particularly his description of the role that "normal" family members play in generating the symptomatology of the "abnormal" one, which precipitates the more outstanding "symptoms"— read signs or commentaries—of schizophrenia (*Steps*, 206–207).

The doctors, as indicated above, step up the surveillance and control of John's behavior once he has been committed to the asylum. They impose various kinds of restraints on Perceval, some of which are no longer employed today, but the logic of which is still very much operative in modern, more humane forms of treatment. As Perceval comments on the chemical restraints, "My mind was not destroyed, without the ruin of my body. My delusions, though they often made me ridiculous, did not derange my understanding unaided by the poisonous medicines and unnatural treatment of my physicians" (69). Physical restraints play a similar role:

> Since boyhood, I had never been confined to my bed for more than two or three days, nor to my room, for so much as a week together; and on an average had never had less daily, than three hours' active exercise. Now, after a fortnight's confinement to my room, I was fastened on my bed, with the liberty of my arms and legs denied to me. (39)

The chemical and physical restraints applied to Perceval are expressions of a psychiatric discourse that was purportedly for the health and security of the patients. But, as Perceval explains, "this restraint was kept on a great while longer then was necessary. A lunatic doctor, in one sense, is pretty sure to be on the right side; he will run no risk that will do his reputation for security, an injury" (91). Security entails control, so that the patient may be returned to normality, and the medical establishment has an implicit self-interest in doing this successfully. Nowadays the forms of restraint are far more sophisticated and overtly far less damaging, but even the "soft" techniques of engendering normalcy are forms of control that serve the implicit interests of social/medical institutions while purporting explicitly to serve the interests of their clients.

In contrast to modern forms of control, schizophrenic discourses from Perceval to the postmodernists provide an opening in which a new language of social critique and human creativity may be written. In this light, an alternative term and an alternative definition for "deviancy" might be considered, for it provides for the possibility of a genuine dialogue between schizophrenic, or more broadly deviant, and the normalizing power of mental health workers. The German word *Abweichung* is now used by psychologists, social workers, and others in Germany to mean roughly what is meant by "deviancy" in the United States. However, if we consider the history of the term's usage, a different view of deviancy emerges, one that is less prone to the seductions of power and control. In the literary and scientific texts of Goethe, for example, the related verb *abweichen* emphasizes "the process of moving away from something or somebody, from an accepted or established line, and taking a new direction" (*Goethe Wörterbuch*, 218). It also means, consequentially, *differieren*, *verschieden sein* ("to differ, be different"), and hence "divergence of opinions, viewpoints, attitudes, methods" (*Meinungen, Ansichten, Gesinnungen, Methoden*) (218). Similarly, it means "to differ in form and appearance, to form nuances, to vary a basic form" ("in Form und Erscheinung sich unterscheiden, nuancieren; eine Grundform variieren").

Obviously Goethe's language, itself diverging from that of the human sciences, approaches the deconstructive language of Derrida: *differieren* clearly resonates with *différer* and *différance*. Goethe's language thus provides a genealogy of "deviancy" that suggests an alternative to classifying it in pejorative terms and subjecting it to "correction" as psychiatric discourse now does. "Deviancy," understood as *Abweichung* in the sense of *differieren* and ultimately *différance*, suggests a new meaning of the term that entails creativity, play, innovation, and critical engagement.

Our positive assessment of the creative possibilities of deviancy raises the question, Isn't it necessary for psychiatric institutions to constrain mental patients so that they do not harm themselves or others? In a small percentage of cases this is doubtless true, and in Perceval's case it sometimes seemed called for. But it is important to understand the motivation for and the context of Perceval's "abnormal" behavior. Consider the following account Perceval gives of his conduct:

> A few nights after my arrival, I threw myself off the bed, in my waistcoat on the floor, in obedience to my monitors [his inner voices]; the command was usually given about the time the keeper came into the room either to look after me, or to sleep; fortunately I did not injure my limbs. In consequence of this trick, my arms were tied down to each side of the bed, by bands

of ticking. Still I contrived to excite alarm, and subsequently my feet were fastened to the bottom of the bed, in leather anklets I had on in the day time. (90)

Perceval's acts are, as he says, "contrived to excite alarm" and are prompted by the arrival of his keeper. Regardless of whether his "monitors" or inner voices suggest the conduct to "him," the schizophrenic complex of John and his monitors acts in a manner intended to be *critical* of his keepers: the institution provides a context, like the schizophrenic family in Bateson's analysis, in terms of which Perceval's behavior makes sense and to which it is a defiant response.

Even though the doctors are attempting to treat Perceval humanely by restraining him from behavior they think might harm him and others, from Perceval's point of view—that of the supposed beneficiary of this treatment—the therapy seems anything but helpful. This is evident in Perceval's insistence on silence in the face of his doctors, silence that is a response to, and commentary on, the fact that he is not being addressed as an intelligent human subject:

> I was not, however, once addressed by argument, expostulation, or persuasion. The persons round me consulted, directed, chose, ordered, and force was the *unica* and *ultima ratio* applied to me. If I were insane, in my resolution to be silent, because I was sure that neither of the doctors, or of my friends, would understand my motives, or give credit to facts they had not themselves experienced; they were surely no less insane, who because of my silence, forgot the use of their own tongues,—who, because of my neglect of the duties I owed them, expunged from their consciences all deference to me; all hope of sifting the cause of my delusions; all hope of addressing my reason with success; all hope of winning me to speak. (121)

Here Perceval's will to differ is not only a direct response to his caretakers' indifference to his opinion; it is also a commentary on their methods of control, their treatment of a sentient being in terms of force, shunning all deference to his viewpoint, to his authorial voice. His silence is, therefore, in deconstructionist terms, both a narrative that is tangential to the voices of the supposedly sane institution and precisely the space displaced by the discourse of the doctors but nevertheless commenting on and negating it. As Foucault argues in *Madness and Civilization*, confinement, prisons, dungeons, even tortures, engaged in a mute dialogue between reason and unreason—the dialogue of struggle. This dialogue itself was now [in the neoclassical age] disengaged; silence was absolute; there was no longer any common language between madness and reason. (262)

Perceval's "diary" voice, the one published in his *Narrative*, furthermore, critically inquires into the assumptions of his benefactors:

If the insulting and degrading treatment I have described, was indeed designed to mortify and probe the feelings, it was pre-posterous, without explanation, expostulation, or remonstrance; and impolitic, without a thorough knowledge of the temper and humor of the individual to whom it was applied. Why was I confined? because I was a lunatic. And what is a lunatic, but one whose reasoning cannot be depended upon; one of imperfect and deranged understanding, and of a diseased imagination? (100)

On the one hand, Perceval notices that he is being mistreated because he falls under the category "lunatic," which is defined as one whose reason "cannot be depended upon," which is to say, an individual who does not satisfy the Enlightenment concept of the rational individual and who does not present that consistency of mind and behavior necessary for rational institutions, from state to business to medical establishment. Furthermore, the "temper and humor" of the individual is beneath consideration if it does not conform to the Enlightened criteria. It is as if Perceval were presented with an ultimatum: "think and act as a rational and dependable individual, or you will be defined as a lunatic and treated accordingly." "Either you have a voice that is reasonable, or you have none at all." As Foucault also argues, the psychiatric institution as a mirror of the bourgeois world is threatened by the discourse of the mad, which speaks of an "other" world:

It was in this *other world*, encircled by the sacred powers of labor, that madness would assume the status we now attribute to it. If there is, in classical madness, something which refers elsewhere, and to *other things*, it is no longer because the madman comes from the world of the irrational and bears its stigmata; rather, it is because he crosses the frontiers of bourgeois order of his own accord, and alienates himself outside the sacred limits of its ethic. (1973, 58)

Thus not merely the Enlightenment preference for a rational ego as human persona but, more significantly, the power of social and economic interests underlies the doctors' treatments.

Like the schizophrenic family which, according to Bateson, imposes the double-bind, so the psychiatric institution provides the crucial link in the definition and perpetuation of "madness" by suppressing "lunatic" discourse as the discourse of the "other," deviating unacceptably from politically expedient or, from a more limited perspective, "normal" communication. From one alternative perspective, the aforementioned one offered by Bateson, the communication of the so-called schizophrenic is established within the context of the schizophrenic family, which serves as a kind of niche to which the schizophrenic's behavior is adapted and in terms of which it makes sense. Indeed, the question underlying Bateson's theory is similar to those asked by Perceval: not "What can we do to cure this madman?" but "What is a madman?" and "Under what conditions does his form of communication make sense?" From this point of view he argued that the schizophrenic is typically presented with a double-bind: paradoxical messages of different logical types being imposed on a subject and the subject's being prevented from commenting on the paradox.

This double-bind is typified by an example Bateson gives of a mother who says to her child, "I love you," while simultaneously reacting kinesically (cringing from the child's touch) "I hate you," but implicitly requiring the child's silent complicity in his entrapment by the assumption, "How could you point out that I say I love you when I react as if I hate you? I wouldn't do that because I'm your mother!" (*Steps*, 201ff., 271ff.). Similarly, the doctors give Perceval the message, "We love you," in their alleged attempts to "help" him, but in fact their abusive behavior signals to him, "We hate you," and, of course, they silence his commentary on the situation by their assumption that *they*, after all, are the "doctors" and so the embodiments of reason. Thus the critique of the psychiatric institution and its discourse in particular, and the bourgeois order in general, apparent in *Perceval's Narrative*, is not allowed to surface within the confines of the insane asylum.

No doubt Perceval's "lunacy" is a commentary on his own family life, before it becomes a commentary on the institutions in which he is placed, as is clear from the aforementioned treatment he receives at the hands of his brother, who clearly acts *in loco doctoris*, ignoring John's attempts to communicate. To what degree the family itself is the bearer of this kind of tyranny has been discussed by R. D. Laing in *The Politics of the Family* and other works. In more traditional terms, Freud's analysis of the primal, Oedipal scene seems translatable into Bateson's terms; indeed, Lacan's linguistic reading of Freud may well form the necessary bridge. For Laing, the very ghosts of generations past, like that of Hamlet Senior, haunt the current generation of the family, who are condemned to reenact the political struggles—for dominance, for love—of their forebears. Similarly Freud's Oedipus is condemned, by the logic of the parent–child dialectic, to displace his father and marry his mother. And in Bateson as in Lacan, the process of communication, or the signifying practice, of familial discourse inscribes identities—of self versus other, of child versus parent—on family members; when these practices "deviate" too much from normal patterns of communication, the phenomenon of schizophrenia may be diagnosed. But, from the critical perspective of deconstruction, clearly anticipated by Freud, the "abnormalities" of schizophrenic communication provide a critique of the family, its signifying practices, and the larger "normal" social order of which it is a part (see Laing 1972; Freud 1949; Lacan 1982; Bateson 1972).

The point, and the shame, is, as the *Narrative* clearly suggests, that a dialogue with an extraordinary mind of perhaps unlimited creative potential is often lost through the operations of "therapy," no matter how well-intentioned. "His [Perceval's] theoretical position is perhaps midway between that of Freud and of William Blake," Bateson argues. "What Blake called the Creative Imagination Perceval assigns to some inner action of the Almighty. His language is often that of theology, where his thoughts are those of a scientist" (*Perceval's Narrative*, vi). "I conceive . . . that the mind acts by beautiful and delicate machinery," Perceval says. "That we have no idea of the beauty of diction and of conversation—of the grace and majesty of action—of the perfection of the mental faculties which might be attained to, if more liberty were given in early life to the fancy" (291). Similar critiques of therapy are provided by Masson in *Against Therapy*, as by Deleuze and Guattari in *Anti-Oedipus: Capitalism and Schizophrenia*. The opening of human discourse to the commentary provided by the rich language of "lunacy" or "schizophrenia" or, for that matter, "postmodernity," no matter how seemingly irrational and hence valueless the doctors of established discourse may find it, provides a view into the aforementioned realm of what Bateson called Learning III: learning how to learn how to learn—a level at which the personality itself, not simply the subroutines created by the stable character of an established human subject, can be constituted. If Learning I is habit formation, any freedom from the bondage of habit must also denote a profound redefinition of the self. If I stop at the Level of Learning II [the learning of the contexts in which Learning I takes place, e.g., learning repeatedly in Pavlovian or Skinnerian sequences leads the learner to punctuate the stream of experience in Pavlovian or Skinnerian terms, the former tending passively to await stimulation, the latter actively seeking it], "I" am the aggregate of those characteristics which I call my "character." "I" am my habits of acting in context and shaping and perceiving the contexts in which I act. Selfhood is a product or aggregate of Learning II. To the degree that a man achieves Learning III, and learns to perceive and act in terms of the contexts of contexts, his "self" will take on a sort of irrelevance. The concept of "self" will no longer function as a nodal argument in the punctuation of experience. (304)

This is precisely the locale at which we would place Derrida's *différance* or Foucault's discourse of the mad other or Perceval's lunatic narrative: it is a form of "schizophrenia" set free from the debilitating binds of family or factory or madhouse or benevolent therapy or even of school, and allowed to trace the differential course of *Abweichung*, like Odysseus or Parmenides Kouros wandering (*planein*) through all the cities of humankind, but not to get back to Ithaca, necessarily, or even back to Parmenidean being (*to eon*) but, "for others, more creative, the resolution of contraries [of Learning I and II] reveals a world in which personal identity merges into all the processes of relationship in some vast ecology or aesthetics of cosmic interaction" (*Steps*, 306). But what might this emergence of what Bateson would call a "mental ecology" out of the traditional strictures of the rational ego mean in the context of a postpsychiatric era?

In evolutionary terms, an ecological instead of an egotistical form of consciousness, where "human" identity is not separate from and in competition with the social or natural "environment," would seem to be quite simply adaptive. In terms of personal narratives, we might expect to find the emergence of new forms of communication, about self and world, which draw their self-images not from the mirror, as Lacan saw specular rational identity shaped, but rather from the varied patterns of human and natural life that make up human ecology. The individual in the post-therapeutic age might find herself or himself comfortable in the Star Wars bar, surrounded by every conceivable form of "alien" life, and enjoying it.

Thus the constitution of individuality would not be prescribed but opened to continuous revision in a new politics of self-making. In terms a little more down to earth, hyperactive or hyperkinetic children can be allowed to work in alternate classroom or family settings that channel their tendencies into hyperproductivity or creativity, stimulating their development toward the kind of "deviancy" evident in Nietzsche or Van Gogh.

Finally, the critical dimension of a self configured from the perspective of Learning III would involve the affirmation of an ecological multiplicity in a cultural analog of biodiversity, and the deconstruction of attempts to impose or control discourse—from the practices of developers to those of educators and therapists. Thus the model of cultural practice might become not that of sober and rational deliberation but rather, as we suggested at the outset, that of *play*. Thus the wide variety of polemical stances that make up contemporary discourse would not so much be resolved but rather seen as interim positions in an ongoing game called Postmodern Life, the basic rule (sic) of which is: "this is play." The result of this might be that all of the positions would be seen as *not* meaning what they would mean if they were serious, which is to say that they would be understood as radically tentative and intoned with humor (see Bateson, *Steps*, 177–193, esp. 180). Of course, the tone of humor and the bite of critical laughter threaten to undermine the "serious" discipline of psychiatry and its pretense to authority.

Criticism of psychiatry and other forms of therapy would thus be focused on the strategies used by therapists to limit the ability of their subjects to play. The imposition of a conventional identity on a schizophrenic like Perceval limits his ability to create one of his own, especially one so critical of his alleged benefactors as *Perceval's Narrative*. Similarly, the imposition of classroom discipline by the school, aided by the dubious techniques of behavior modification, imposes what appears to be a necessary structure from the viewpoint of the school administration but which is implicitly a form of bureaucratic control which would make students compliant members of corporation or state—"be good and you'll get an A, be good and later you might get a BMW"—if they did not rebel using all the guerrilla strategies in the repertoire of the class clown. The Marxian critique of bourgeois class hegemony and its alliance with the struggle of the proletariat, or in more contemporary language, the vast underclass created by the Reagan revolution on behalf of the privileged, would not only call for the redistribution of wealth but also for the empowerment to engage in social and cultural self-making—so that *everyone*, not just the bourgeois intellectual, would be free to play. Thus the workers would have no obligation to be routinized as part of a socialist bureaucracy which, as Marcuse saw, imposes one-dimensionality on its employees just as surely as does the Disney Corporation. Play is to be understood, then, not only as a linguistic or intellectual pastime but also as political practice. This is, in Abbie Hoffman's terms, "Revolution for the Hell of It," politics as theater, a cultural politics in which the human persona is open to creative transformation and whose ultimate end is not a sober, puritanical march toward heaven or some technocratic fantasy of utopia, but something much more unpredictable and, although the word is taboo in serious academic circles, just plain fun: *Homo ludens*.

Postmodern Reflections on Modern Psychiatry: *The Diagnostic and Statistical Manual of Mental Disorders* (DSM-IV)

The *The Diagnostic and Statistical Manual of Mental Disorders* (DSM), is the standard text for the diagnosis and treatment of "mental" and "behavioral" "disorders." It has been widely adopted by mental health professionals, from the United States to Europe to Asia, and will doubtless serve as the principal diagnostic system for the foreseeable future—this in spite of the fact that there is a significant number of humanistically oriented psychologists who are dissatisfied with and do not employ its methods, and that much work has gone into the *DSM-IV* to rectify these and other shortcomings of its predecessor, the *DSM-III-R*. Given its primacy and influence, however, the *DSM* is vitally important to the well-being of millions of people whose lives are influenced by its practitioners. Therefore, its working assumptions about the nature of the mind, about the lifeworld of "patients," about "health" and "illness," and about the place of individuals in society should not escape critical scrutiny. These assumptions have their roots in the modern conception of philosophy stemming from rationalist and empiricist soil. Given the importance and complexity of the intellectual history underlying scientific psychology and psychiatry, it is appropriate to provide a fairly lengthy historical introduction.

The Foundations of Modern Science

The epitome of the new science founded by Galileo and Descartes was the doctrine of primary and secondary qualities, wherein "primary" status was accorded to quantifiable phenomena and "secondary" status accorded to unquantifiable ones. The former, furthermore, were designated as "objective" while the latter were tagged "subjective." The result was a picture of objective nature that was thoroughly mathematized. The subjective nature of human beings, left to the impressionistic whims of consciousness, was in effect removed from the objective or primary—the real—world. Thus Galileo argues: "But that external bodies, to excite in us these tastes, these odours, and these sounds, demanded other than size, figure, number, and slow or rapid motion, I do not believe; and I judge that, if the ears, the tongue, and the nostrils were taken away, the figure, the numbers, and the motions would indeed remain, but not the odours nor the tastes nor the sounds, which, without the living animal, I do not believe are anything else than names . . . and that the thing that produces heat in us and makes us perceive it, which we call by the general name fire, is a multitude of minute corpuscles thus and thus figured, moved with such and such a velocity" (*Opere*, IV, 336ff., cited in Burtt 1980, 88).

It was a central goal of the scientific and technical project from its outset, moreover, to embark on a conquest of nature even while obeying "her" laws. As Francis Bacon succinctly puts it, "human knowledge and human power meet in one; for where the cause is not known the effect cannot be produced. Nature to be commanded must be obeyed; and that which in contemplation is as the cause is in operation as the rule" (*Novum Organum*, Aphorism iii, 39). Thus, knowledge and its objects were viewed *instrumentally*: as means to an end in the quest for power.

With the development of the "social" sciences, the reference of scientific discourse was shifted from nature to human beings, but the assumptions about scientific veracity, stemming from the primary–secondary doctrine, were not substantially altered. Accordingly, to establish a true account of the human mind, or of human behavior, or of human social milieu, required a mathematical or functional paradigm. Thus Thomas Hobbes argues, in the footsteps of Galileo, "and this seeming, or fancy, is that which men call *sense*; and consisteth, as to the eye, in a light, or color figured; to the ear, in a sound; to the nostril, in an odor; to the tongue and palate, in a savor; and to the rest of the body, in heat, cold, hardness, softness, and such other qualities we discern by feeling. All which qualities, called *sensible*, are, in the object that causeth them, but so many several motions of matter, by which it presseth our organs diversely. Neither in us that are pressed, are they anything else but diverse motions; for motion produceth nothing but motion" (*Leviathan* I.i, 25–26). Both the natural and the social scientist agree that the secondary qualities are derivative effects of the primary ones; that perceptual experience is the subjective result of "matter"—quantifiable objects—in motion. Both agree, furthermore, that the objectification of secondary qualities, as in the "visible species" and "audible species" and "intelligible species" of Aristotle (*Leviathan* I.i, 26) or the referents of "names" (Galileo loc. cit.), is fundamentally mistaken.

If Hobbes did not, like Bacon, explicitly see the task of science as establishing dominion over nature or society, he did represent individual and collective human existence in such a way as to insure the same result; to him, society and its inhabitants were virtually machines: "Nature . . . can make an artificial animal. For seeing life is but a motion of limbs, the beginning whereof is in some principal part within; why may we not say, that all *automata* (engines that move themselves by springs and wheels as doth a watch) have an artificial life? For what is the heart, but a spring; and the nerves, but so many strings, and the joints, but so many wheels, giving motion to the whole body, such as was intended by the artificer? Art goes yet further, imitating that rational and most excellent work of nature, man. For by art is created the great *Leviathan* called a *Commonwealth*, or *State*, in Latin *Civitas*, which is but an artificial man" (Introduction, 23). Likewise the "thoughts of man" are, in Hobbes' view, the effects of "sense" which, as we have seen, is the effect of material particles in motion: "Concerning the thoughts of man . . . [t]he original of them all is that which we call *sense*, for there is no conception in a man's mind which hath not at first, totally or by parts, been begotten upon the organs of sense" (25). Thus man in his body, mind, and society is understood in accordance with the materialist, quantitative, and instrumental assumptions of the primary–secondary doctrine. The smooth-running machines of the new human order, under the dominion of the new functional model, complete Bacon's project by closing the modern universe of discourse to all but the technologically initiated: those who understand that "nature to be commanded must be obeyed."

The Lineage of Modern Psychiatry

As it was initiated into the sciences, psychiatry inherited the primary–secondary doctrine as the sine qua non of scientific explanation: only that which is measurable or operationally conceivable is the proper object of inquiry. Whether in psychology, with its emphasis on the environmental or social context of the psyche, or in psychiatry, with its medical emphasis on the organismic basis of the mind, the use of quantitative and materialist concepts is clear. So Ernst Mach (1897) argued, regarding perception, "bodies do not produce sensations, but complexes of sensations (complexes of elements) make up bodies. If, to the physicist, bodies appear the real, abiding existences, whilst sensations are regarded merely as their evanescent, transitory show, the physicist forgets, in the assumption of such a view, that all bodies are but thought-symbols for complexes of sensations (complexes of elements). Here, too, the elements form the real, immediate, and ultimate foundation, which it is the task of physiological research to investigate" (127). The "elements," like Galileo's "minute corpuscles," are the ultimate constituents of reality.

This view is generalized, furthermore, to the self: "The primary fact is not the I, the ego, but the elements (sensations). The elements *constitute* the I" (127). Likewise, in psychiatry, Eugen Bleuler in his *Textbook of Psychiatry* (1976) illustrates the scientific approach to the mind by redefining the problem of free will: "The much mooted question whether there is a '*free will*' in the sense that a decision can be reached without any reason, does not exist in natural science. We see that the actions of living beings are determined by the inner organization and the external influences reacting upon them in exactly the same manner as any other happening. There is no decision which does not have a complete causal basis in motives and strivings. But motives and strivings are either a complex of nervous functions, which is subject to the ordinary psychic laws of cause and effect, or something analogous to these nervous processes, which depend on physical as well as psychic causes. 'Motives' are causes even though they are complicated. Science is therefore *deterministic* even in those cases where it is not fully admitted" (51). The parallel between the paradigm of the physical sciences and that of psychiatry, obvious in the above passage, is described by historians as the general trend in the development of psychiatry. Thus Alexander and Selesnick (1966) say that "this emphasis on the physical sciences strongly affected medicine, so that medical science became essentially an applied natural science. . . . In our century a scientific revolution has taken place: psychiatry has come of age. On the strength of substantial achievements, it has ceased being medicine's stepchild and has become one of the most prominent fields in medicine" (3-4). It is this "scientific revolution" that has also allowed the *DSM-IV* to come of age.

Dissidents from Scientific Orthodoxy

There have, however, been dissidents who have rejected the view that "reality," particularly human reality, can be adequately quantified and so have explicitly or implicitly rejected the working assumptions of natural and social science. Among these heretics from scientific orthodoxy have been literary-scientific thinkers like Goethe, the "life" philosophers led by Nietzsche, radical phenomenologists (chiefly Heidegger), and their post-modern heirs, including, for example, Foucault and Derrida. Postmodern thought especially provides a perspective from which the traditional scientific paradigm and its applications can be effectively scrutinized. Specifically, it provides an alternative view of human being not so amenable to systematization and control as the functionalist golem of social science. Indeed, it reveals what is taken to be a datum—the human being as functional system—as in fact a metaphysical construction of modernism. Collaterally, it sees the attempt to diagnose and treat various "mental" and "behavioral" "disorders" as in effect the manipulation of a hypostatized "man" who may not correspond at all to the living human being. Since, however, this entity who is the "patient" of psychiatric medicine or psychological therapy and counseling is imposed on the living human being by the "mental health professional," the equally hypostatized metaphysical persona who diagnoses and treats the "client," the question arises: is this "doctor"–"patient" relationship imposed on the stream of human discourse in the interest of the alleged beneficiaries of "treatment"?

The DSM-IV

The *DSM-IV* (1994), the third revised edition of the *Diagnostic and Statistical Manual of Mental Disorders*, has been developed on the basis of three earlier editions: *DSM-I* (1952), *DSM-II* (1968), and *DSM-III* (1980, 1987). At each stage in its development, the manual has been conceived and revised in terms of systems of classification for mental disorders, from Adolf Meyer's psychobiological idea of reaction in the *DSM-I*, to "diagnostic terms that by and large did not imply a particular theoretical framework for understanding nonorganic mental disorders" in *DSM-II*, to a more heuristic approach in *DSM-III-R*, which recognizes that "no definition adequately specifies precise boundaries for the concept 'mental disorder' (also true for such concepts as physical disorder and mental and physical health)" (xxii), and, finally, to the *DSM IV*, in which "there is no assumption that each category of mental disorder is a completely discrete entity with absolute boundaries dividing it from other mental disorders or from no mental disorder. There is also no assumption that all individuals described as having the same mental disorder are alike in all important ways" (xxii). Nevertheless, the manual continues, "in the *DSM-IV*, each of the mental disorders is conceptualized as a clinically significant behavioural or psychological syndrome or pattern that occurs in an individual and that is associated with present distress (e.g., a painful symptom) or disability (i.e., impairment in one or more important areas of functioning) or with a significantly increased risk of suffering death, pain, disability, or an important loss of freedom" (xxi).

Thus, in spite of the theoretical proviso disclaiming the commitment to a particular theoretical framework or "precise boundaries" for the definition of categories, in clinical practice the *DSM-III-R* clearly depends on the rigorous classification of mental disorders in terms that are functional and utilitarian. This might reflect the fact that, while theoretically psychiatrists and psychologists might recognize the limits of knowledge as revealed by postmodern philosophy, the social and institutional roles they must play as clinicians militate against this realization. Even though, furthermore, the *DSM-III-R* carefully admits that "neither deviant behavior, e.g., political, religious, or sexual, nor conflicts that are primarily between the individual and society are mental disorders unless the deviance or conflict is a symptom of a dysfunction in the person" (xxii), it nevertheless seems as if the previous dogmatism of social scientific discourse has become "normalized" and thus "prescribed" in the social praxis of mental health workers. This amounts to the continuing specter of the primary–secondary doctrine haunting the history of social science.

The theory-in-practice of the *DSM-IV* is clearly evident in its diagnostic and interventional paradigms, as well as in its correlative descriptions and categorizations of mental disorders in the *DSM-IV Casebook* (1994). Evident in both are the two theoretical constructs mentioned above: the "patient" and the clinical "persona." It is these two constructs which reveal the metaphysics and the human consequences of this influential manual.

Several recent commentators have recognized the limitations of the *DSM* texts. Cutler (1991), for example, has dealt with the "linguistic dualities" at the basis of the *DSM-III* as well as their expression in the "clinician–client relationship" (154). Leonore Tiefer, in her *Sex Is not a Natural Act*, has carefully examined the *DSM*'s definitions of sexual dysfunctions, arguing, for instance, that "sexual abnormality is deviation from a fixed sequence (essentially desire, arousal, and orgasm)," in which, appropriate to masculinist Cartesianism, "sexuality consists of reactions of *body parts*," and that "sexuality in the *DSM* is obsessively *genitally focused*"

(99-100), overall showing that the manual is the product of a patriarchic scientific mentality. Similarly, Karen Pugliesi has argued in "Women and Mental Health: Two Traditions of Feminist Research" that "insanity is essentially a feminine malady," and that, expectably, "conceptions of a 'healthy adult' were similar to conceptions of a 'healthy male' and an 'unhealthy adult' was most similar to a 'healthy female,'" expressing what she calls the "gender biased conceptions of psychological health embodied in the *DSM-III*" (56–57). This predominantly feminist critique of the *DSM* is, as Cutler's work explicitly brings out, a significant strand of the poststructural/postmodern deconstruction of psychiatry.

Choose a Case

It is worth noting that, upon opening the *DSM-IV* or its *Casebook*, one is virtually invited, in fact obliged, to choose a case—to categorize a type of mental disorder—simply by turning to the right page. This is no doubt a practical convenience, for it allows the inquiring professional, confronted with some psychological disturbance, to understand the phenomenon in terms of case histories and ready categories that offer both descriptions of "symptoms" and "diagnoses" of "disorders."

The essence of this description and categorization is to relate the disorderly symptoms to a set of norms that are often implicit rather than explicit. The implicit purpose of the categories is thereby to make the disorders orderly, that is, to make them conform to the aforementioned norms (see Foucault 1984). The process is one of "normalization," if we understand this term in a special sense contained in the German verb *normieren*, which means to set up standards and require phenomena, including people, to conform to them. This process of normalization has arguably taken place historically, especially since the Industrial Revolution, and is particularly evident in the organization and routinization of labor in the factory system, of behavior, particularly of the "criminal" type, in the prison, of learning and social development in the school, of knowledge in the scientific community, and of the psyche in mental health institutions (see Foucault 1980, 1973; Weber 1977, Freud 1989.)

This normalization is evident today in the functionalization of behavior in the *DSM-IV*, which universalizes the standardization of everyday life by implicitly establishing or accepting norms and creating a set of categories as a kind of schema for the assimilation of disorder into order. Note that the apparently neutral language of order and disorder masks a process that is in fact normative, or more accurately, one of control (see Marcuse 1964, 1–18; Foucault 1973, 1980). Indeed, one might argue that the psychiatric persona is endowed with a panoptical eye that subsumes all of human life under its scrutiny and therefore brings all under its supervision. The subsumption of cases under diagnostic categories in the *DSM-IV* and *DSM-IV Casebook* reveals this normalization.

The routinization of the lifeworld by the mental health establishment is clearly revealed in various cases from the *DSM-IV Casebook*; we have chosen three representative ones. First consider the case, "Paul and Petula" (198–200). The problem is nominally a "sexual" one, in which Paul, as Petula reports, "hasn't been able to keep his erection after he enters me" (199). The difficulty is of rather recent origin, as she also reports, having arisen since she asked him to move in with her, perhaps before he was ready. Although the *DSM-IV Casebook* notes that Paul and Petula have "many problems that a family-oriented clinician would want to focus on," including "Paul's ambivalence to committing himself to a relationship with Petula and her frantic efforts to obtain that commitment," it emphasizes that "the effect of these problems on the sexual functioning is clear: he is unable to maintain his erection until the completion of sexual activity" (149). Consequently, it diagnoses his condition as " Axis I: 302.72 Male Erectile Disorder, Psychogenic Only, Acquired" (*DSM-IV*, 502). (Organic causes of the disorder have been ruled out.) This diagnosis refers the mental health worker to the *DSM-IV*, where he or she can read the appropriate clinical description of the category.

Observe, first, that the condition is placed on an "axis." "Axis I" means that the dysfunction falls within "the entire classification of mental disorders plus V Codes (Conditions Not Attributable to a Mental Disorder That Are a Focus of Attention or Treatment)" but not a developmental disorder or personality disorder both of which, as the manual explains, "generally begin in childhood or adolescence and persist in a stable form . . . into adult life" and fall into Axis II (26). Second, consider the assumptions implicit in the description of the problem as "Male Erectile Disorder." Third, note the reference to the *DSM-IV*, section 302.72 under Sexual Disorders, entitled "Sexual Arousal Disorders," where the manual goes on to list a set of diagnostic criteria. Fourth, keep in mind that Petula is convinced that a mental health clinician is an appropriate audience for her and Paul's difficulties. Fifth, notice that the feminist critiques by Tiefer and Pugliesi, mentioned above, significantly reveal the sexual politics underlying the manual's seemingly neutral categories.

Other cases are examined in a similar fashion. For instance, as the case entitled "No Brakes" begins, "JEREMY, AGE NINE, is brought by his mother to a mental health clinic because he has become increasingly disobedient and difficult to manage at school" (*DSM-IV Casebook*, 342–344). He is guilty of swearing at his teacher, "riding his three-wheeler in the street," failing to brake his vehicle properly and crashing into a department store window, "teasing and kicking other children," and so on (343). Although he is capable of good schoolwork and occasionally does it, he "sometimes refuses to do what his teachers tell him to do" and "gives many reasons why he should not have to do his work, and argues when told to do it."He gets the best grades from a teacher with whom he has the most conflict. He varies from being rude to polite, at school and at home, and his teachers are concerned about his "attitude" (343). He is diagnosed as "Axis I: 313.81 Oppositional Defiant Disorder, Moderate" (*DSM IV*, 91).

Paddy Obrien, in a case entitled "Sitting by the Fire" (*DSM IV Casebook*, 248–250), is a twenty-six-year-old bachelor who at sixteen "was admitted to a county psychiatric hospital. The hospital records indicate that he was socially withdrawn and had a flat affect. It was not possible to interest him in ward activities. No psychotic symptoms could be elicited" (249). His mother says that he used to be "normal," helping regularly with chores on the family farm and doing well in school, but that when he was fourteen he began to "lose interest" and to "stare into space." A research team described him as "an obese, rather disheveled young man," who answers questions with "yes," "no," or "could be." In interview he reveals that he is "uncomfortable around people except his family," his "eye contact is poor" and, as mentioned above, his "affect is flat." The family reports that "occasionally, he can be encouraged to help with a farm chore, but he usually stops after about 15 minutes and returns to his chair by the fire" (249). He is diagnosed as "Axis I: V71.09 No Diagnosis or Condition, Axis II: 301.22 Schizotypal Personality Disorder, Severe" (*DSM-IV*, 641).

All three cases demonstrate the psychiatric normalization of people's lifeworlds. The latter describes their behavior in terms of functional categories that are designed to target and correct deviations from norms that it assumes or imposes. Its authority is such that, in each case, the fianceé or the mother or the family has internalized the clinical bifurcation of experience into doctor and patient, orthogenic institution (the good marital relationship, the school, the family) and the properly institutionalized subject (the male with an orderly erection, the well-behaved student, the cooperative family member). So they complain to and believe in the proper authorities when their loved ones malfunction. They subject their own judgments about experience to the "doctors'" scrutiny.

Consider the assignment of each case to an axis. "Paul and Petula" is assigned exclusively to Axis I, and within that to the subcategory "Mental Disorders." This indicates that there is no physical problem involved, which would be the subject matter of Axis III. Axis II would designate the malady as a "Developmental Disorder" or "Personality Disorder"; Axis I thus refers it to a category of disorders that are not "physical" or "personality" and in this case are specifically "Sexual Dysfunctions," here an "Erectile Disorder." "The erectile dysfunction is not better accounted for by another Axis I disorder (other than a sexual dysfunction) and is not due exclusively to the direct physiological effect of a substance (e.g., a drug of abuse, a medication), or a general medical condition" (*DSM-IV*, 504). Note that this particular designation also excludes "Conditions Not Attributable to a Mental Disorder That Are a Focus of Attention or Treatment." Presently we must question the notion of classifying and treating what comes to the attention of the psychiatric persona.

Similarly, "No Brakes" is an Axis I "Oppositional Defiant Disorder" and "Sitting by the Fire" an Axis II "Schizotypal Personality Disorder." This process of axial classification is in essence one of "demarcation," of fixing a phenomenon within boundaries. The attempt to classify mental or behavioral phenomena by circumscribing and thereby isolating them for "treatment" is typically positivistic. For it relies on the resolution of mental "facts" out of the interplay of experiences in the lifeworld and then seeks to enclose them within categories—to order them into classes—and so to subject them to a process of normalization leading to "mental health." Implicit in the subsumption of lifeworlds under "axes" and the process of normalization that this initiates is not only the editing of experience and behavior into disparate facts subject to classification but also their control.

We have noted above the "Focus of Attention or Treatment" to which mental disorders might be subject. Presumably all mental disorders fall within this realm if they are the subject of psychiatric discourse, though some are more easily isolable than others. The important question here is whose attention is captured and why. Just below the surface of this text sits the psychiatric persona, whose attention is quite selective. For in the process of designating behavioral or mental disorder or deviancy, in the very process of psychiatric perception, is the unconscious epistemology of positivism. In other words, the circumscription of mental and behavioral "disorders" as "facts" within psychiatric boundaries is taken as given, as a foundation for clinical activity. But it amounts to the appropriation of human experience—of the lifeworld—for underlying social and political interests. In Gestalt terms, whatever does not fit into social or institutional or functional norms is suspect, gets attention, becomes a figure against a background of implied normality. Like a prowler in a middle-class neighborhood, the deviant person is subject to "detection"—the earlier the better—and dealt with appropriately. Thus the innocent clinical description of mental phenomena is in fact only the surface of an underlying system of control—"benevolent," of course.

Therefore Paul, who is hesitant to commit himself to a "healthy" relationship and conform to the normal progress of middle-class life—getting married, buying a home, having children—becomes suspect to his fianceé, who has internalized the psychiatric persona and so thinks in terms of the same enclosed discourse. In effect she becomes a lay clinician, detecting and reporting behavior that threatens the normal order. Indeed, she no doubt conceives of her own lifeworld in terms inculcated by psychiatric language popularized in self-help books. Likewise, Jeremy is subjected to psychiatric correction in the interests of the school—alleged to be his own—after being detected by his teachers and his mother, who play their roles as lay guardians of mental order admirably. Finally, Paddy Obrien does not function adequately as a member of the family workforce, has lost interest in the usual things, and likes to sit by the fire. He is consequently detected and brought to the psychiatric hospital, where a "team" of clinicians investigates him and tries, to no avail, to elicit psychotic symptoms. So he is demarcated as a Schizoid Personality Disorder, and no doubt treated appropriately. Galileo was called in by the Inquisition and threatened with torture because he deviated too far from the norms of Catholic orthodoxy.

Fortunately, Descartes, who no doubt learned caution from his outspoken forebear, was not similarly apprehended as he sat before the fire of his Meditations. Deleuze and Guattari (1983), as well as Bateson (1972, 201–278) and Laing (1972), have argued that schizophrenic discourse is a significant commentary on the family, the society, and the culture in which the "schizophrenic" exists and that its designation as a form of "madness"—or, in the language of the *DSM-IV*, "mental disorder"—is in fact a form of control that defends the familial, social, and cultural norms from precisely this kind of commentary. Is the beneveolent normality imposed by psychiatric discourse any different in principle from the more drastic order imposed, for what seemed the most convincing of reasons, by the church?

The postmodern alternative to this Cartesian modernization of the psyche along with the medicalized diagnosis and treatment of its "disorders" is a *narrative* idea of self as the creation of self-writing or culture making (see Chapter 1). For instance, Kenneth Gergen and John Kaye argue that, "when people seek psychotherapy they have a story to tell." They further ask, "What options are available to the therapist as the recipient of a narrated reality?" Likewise, Philip Cushman argues for a new way of thinking about psychotherapy:

> The hermeneutic way of thinking about psychotherapy is, of course, above all a way of thinking about the stories, joys, and agonies of our patients without locating all the action in the patient's deep, secret, somewhat empty interior. Instead, hermeneutics locates human being in the social surround, the horizonal space that encompasses us all, the space that has been "cleared" by language, dress, religion, politics, rituals, and nonverbal communications, by the shared understandings of our culture and the traditions of our communities, by the more particular customs of local neighborhoods and nuclear families, and even more minutely by the private exchanges of friends and lovers. (1995, 329)

These "stories" of culture and communication become the narratives out of which the self is written, and through the appreciation of which people can increasingly become poets—makers—of their lives and not the passive victims of what Lyotard called the "master narratives" of science, technology, and progress—including psychiatry. Thus the "client," like Jeremy, can, as Christopher J. Kinman argues, be encouraged by the "therapist" to enter a "conversational space" in which he or she finds the resource of telling personal stories rather than having himself or herself inscribed within the master narratives of professional ideology. Thus he opposes narrative knowledge, the space of a new psychotherapy, from the "expert" and confining knowledge of the *DSM*.

Postmodern Critics of Modernism

Nietzsche (1974) argued, contrary to the increasingly narrow and categorical vision of Plato and Aristotle, that the progress of Greek philosophy toward increasing ratiocination was in effect the supersession of the taming, cool, removed perspective of Apollo over the wild, erotic embrace of Dionysos: of the Olympian sky god over the regenerative earth god. Hence, like Freud, he conceived the rise of modern Western civilization to be an alienated quest of one-half of being to overcome the other: reason over emotion, mind over body, concept over life, Superego and Ego over Id, control over freedom, *logos* and *techne* over nature: the dominance of science and technology. With metaphysical acumen, Heidegger (1977) argued that this amounted specifically to the myopic exclusion of Being from the world of human experience. Man thus conceives himself as a lord of beings whose project is calculation, systematization, and control. In sociological terms, Foucault's archaeology (1984) suggests that the ego of Western man is in fact the construction of the Enlightenment, the modern recurrence of the ancient ascent of reason discussed by Nietzsche, which becomes the controlling subject underlying the developing institutions of discipline and punishment, the machinations of sexual politics, and the clinics and asylums of medical science. All of these thinkers reveal the strategies by which science, technology, industry, and society become increasingly rationalized, functionalized, and alienated. The result is that, as the powers of the rational subject increase, the "externalities" of the forbidden Id, of Dionysos, of Being, of the criminals, the unproductive, the sick and insane—in the broadest terms, of ecological demise—become increasingly prevalent and "irrational." As this happens the Cartesian ego attempts more and more desperately to impose control, but in vain.

Thus Derrida (1973), analyzing this same process in the language of linguistics, sees the subject and its objects as isolated differences within the ever-flowing *différance* of discourse, and the aforementioned attempts at control as a fruitless endeavor to close an open conversation. The result is a kind of standoff between the institutions and systems of alienated power, on the one hand, and the lifeworld of human beings on the other. This becomes manifest as the economic attempt to appropriate and utilize "resources" for corporate or state interests; the political, legal, educational, and law enforcement attempts to control recalcitrant populations; and, expectably, the psychiatric attempt to detect, categorize, and treat—to control—mental disorder. Thus the cases of Paul and Petula, Jeremy, and Paddy Obrien, viewed in this context, are ones in which the lifeworlds of human beings are being "enframed" within the controlling norms set up by psychiatric discourse. As Bateson (1987) would say, the general result is an eco-mental crisis affecting every dimension of our lifeworld; for modern scientific and technological systems, like the system of psychiatric discourse, suppress the information provided to them by the "disorders" ever just beyond their control: pollution, war, poverty, overpopulation, and, of course, "insanity."

Insanity, Autopoiesis, and the Opening of the Lifeworld

How do we transform our encounter with the world from the closure, abstraction, and distancing of subject and object characteristic of the alienated Cartesian ego, to the openness, involvement, and participation transcending subject and object characteristic of an empowered will engaged in the *act of living: Lebendigkeit?* This would entail a further transformation away from the removed stance of the persona bent on controlling a world of objects—in effect, from the scientific attempt at rational systematiza- tion—and toward a persona, in Nietzsche's terms, inspired by the will to power—the power to interpret and create one's own life—instead of the slave's willingness to be overpowered; in the language of Maturana and Varela (1980), the play of *autopoiesis* or the creative self-organization of living beings. There is no simple formula that indicates what this experi- ence would be like, for such a formulation would itself close the possibilities for open and free being in the world. However, it is possible to make some suggestions as to what the genuine act of living might be and how it might change our preconceptions about perceiving and understanding the "mentally disordered."

Sciences may be known in part by the terms that they use, as the foregoing analysis of the *DSM-IV* indicates. They may also be known by the language which they do *not* use or even deny. Heidegger used the term *Gelassenheit*, a "letting-go" or "letting-be," to express a new attitude toward living "beings": a stepping away from the presuppositions into which life in its various forms has been fit and toward a *Lichtung*, a "lighting," which reveals and allows others the power of self-creation. This means, further, freeing human and other beings to engage in *Lebendigkeit*: the unhindered act of living. In regard to the aforementioned cases from the *DSM-IV Casebook*, this would mean, first, to resist the psychiatric tendency to normalize "patients" and, second, to deconstruct the scientific paradigm that underlies this normalization.

Thus in the case of Paul and Petula, the "doctor" should realize that he or she is being looked to as an authoritative persona who can rectify a perceived problem, but that the problematic person, Paul, is himself one who must author his own solution. The solution, in turn, need not be limited to his adapting to the norms of family life, but indeed might involve his rejecting them and striking out on a new path to a new life. Furthermore, Paul need not be encouraged to redevelop a normal sex life, without realizing at least that his "sexual disorder" might well be a commentary on a larger enframing that he is resisting (e.g., "growing up" and "accepting responsibility"). His maladaptation to the norms of middle-class life might itself be an important opening to a creative leap beyond it into artistry, or revolution, or at least principled social criticism. That psychiatric discourse resists this, broadly speaking, "political" dimension of interpersonal conversation is the product of its alleged neutrality derived from the paradigm of natural science: "science is neutral; it makes no value judgments." Similar considerations might be applied to the other cases.

Parallel to these ideas is Heidegger's understanding of the Greek term *alētheia*, normally translated as "truth." Heidegger argues that the term does not mean truth as a correspondence between a theory and its object, which is the typical assumption of scientific discourse, but rather a revelation of what was unrevealed, a coming into presence of what was absent, a light (*Lichtung*) appearing out of darkness. Thus the "truth" about the human lifeworld that is categorized in terms of "mental disorder" by psychiatry would be understood very differently by Heidegger. From his perspective, transformed by the critique of the metaphysics of presence by the post-modern movement, the "patient" of psychiatric science would be allowed to "speak" and not be silenced by the objectifying reference of social science. He therefore would be free to participate in a dialogue with the other, free from the monological closure of discourse controlled by the "doctor." The psychiatric persona, moreover, would be obliged to open itself to the free interplay of speech-acts and life-acts of postmodern discourse. Paddy Obrien, therefore, would be listened to not as a nearly silent and therefore recalcitrant member of family and community who has retreated into the symptomatology of schizophrenia; rather, his silence might be viewed as a rebellion against the strictures of the social world around him, a signal of the need for an alternative. The creativity that might emerge from the encouragement of his differentiation from the norm, instead of his normalization, could be quite valuable.

A Rose by Any Other Name

The discussion of a rose from alternative perspectives may well reveal the possibilities open to a philosophy and psychology of the lifeworld. From the perspective of life philosophy, the rose rises up and blossoms in the spring alive with color and fragrance, the phenotypic expression of an evolutionary architecture. The flower is an unfolding form, not fully reducible to any set of causes, though it branches out of the mutations of an evolving population. When it becomes the object of biological inquiry, however, it is enframed by the constructions of scientific subjectivity, which proposes an objective account of "nature's" workings but actually imposes a set of categories on experience, separating the knowing subject from its known object and delineating the patterns of causation in this bifurcated world through mathematical models or explanatory principles. From the perspective of science, a collection of models and principles is taken to be primary, the determinants of the living rose; they are projected onto the living process of the flower; they thereby become a frame within whose borders the rose must now be perceived, so that the original is transformed into an artifact of human consciousness and the consequent of an operational logic whose premise is control.

In terms of the psychology and philosophy of the lifeworld, this example suggests that the "mental patient" is like the rose: she is taken to be the object of explanation and determination, the presence on whom the intellectual machinations of the psychiatric persona are projected, so that she, too, becomes the determinant of an operationally conceived system of mental order and disorder. This, from the perspective of the lifeworld, is alienated, unloving, and inhumane; it substitutes the egoistic attitude of manipulation and control of others for the humility of openness to and participation in their everyday lives. Thus Jeremy might be regarded as a "rose." His "defiant disorder" might be a most important commentary on the stifling controls imposed by home and school. The psychiatric approach is to work in league with these existing institutions, on the assumption that the norm is correct. It does this in a twofold manner: first, by subjecting Jeremy (literally turning him into a subject) to a process of scientific explanation by fitting him into the functionally conceived categories of the *DSM-IV*; second, by normalizing him by projecting the rules of the institutions from which he rebels back into his life so that he will gladly obey, if therapy is successful. The alternative way suggested by the postmodern critique would in effect form the basis for a new "humanistic" psychology. This way would encourage the young rebel's rebellion, perhaps guiding it toward a creative will to differ. At a high school in St. Petersburg, Florida, a few years ago, a student not unlike Jeremy produced an underground newspaper, entitled *Not for Profit*, which because of its subversive content (critical of school and government and corporate hegemony) was banned by school authorities. We would encourage Jeremy to publish, not acquiesce to "reason." For education should encourage dissidence, foster creative growth, be an unfolding conversation among human beings based on love.

What would "love" mean in the context of poststructuralism? How could the "name of the rose," after all, involve the dynamic play of *différance*? In the postscript to *The Name of the Rose*, Umberto Eco suggests that, in the postmodern milieu, to say "I love you" without qualification is impossibly literal-minded, for it appropriates a traditional discourse on love that implies a metaphysics of person, a humanism, which has been undermined by the semeiosis of late modernity. We have lived with too many images of love to take them quite seriously nowadays. So, to express this sentiment, Eco suggests that one has to employ a humorous proviso, invoking the genre of romance and, at the same time, indicating that it is passé: "As Barbara Cartland would put it, 'I love you madly'" (531). The point is that the "rose" cannot be said to have an "existence" independent of the play of ecological discourse—the mentation of evolutionary ecology, of "nature," not to mention gardening—just as the "human being" is a construct of the play of language and "culture." Thus the "therapist," in approaching the "rose" of the "client," must come with the awareness that they are both playing roles, both are dependent on the same ecology of discourse, and so both on one another in the drama of psychotherapy. It is this understanding of mutuality in the creation of the pattern of "human" relationship that is denied by traditional science, and which we argue must be recovered in order to replace the violence of metaphysics with love.

As Paul Feyerabend has said, "'love' becomes impossible for people who insist on 'objectivity,' that is, who live entirely in accordance with the spirit of science. The sciences encourage objectivity, even demand it; they thereby severely reduce our ability to love, except in a very intellectual way, which means that a person who wants to disseminate love cannot forget the sciences—(s)he must deal with them and fight certain tendencies inherent in them" (1987, 263). As Feyerabend goes on to say, "helping people means trying to introduce change *as a friend*, as a person, that is, who can identify with their wisdom *as well as* with their follies and who is sufficiently mature to let the latter prevail: *an abstract discussion of the lives of people I do not know and with whose situation I am not familiar is not only a waste of time, it is also inhumane and impertinent*" (305).

The implication of this conclusion for the *DSM-IV* is not difficult to find, if one simply considers its place in the human lifeworld. In this setting, the text seems like a robot at a party: how would *you* feel speaking about your problems with someone programmed solely in the language of the manual? The difficulty is that its language and perspective are abstracted from the stream of living discourse; they attempt to enclose a superior persona in the guise of "doctor" who is given the clear vision of objectivity and the methodology to bring order from disorder. When the "doctor" is tempted to take his or her role too seriously, she or he might recall that, in Eco's novel, the name of the rose, long suppressed by the high priests of the medieval mind, was, and still is, *laughter*.

CHAPTER 3

Postmodern Metamorphosis

The Transformation of the Self from Modern to Postmodern Forms, or The Power of the Uninterpretable in Kafka's Verwandlung

The critical literature concerning Franz Kafka's work is extensive, perhaps in part because his writings are so enigmatic.[1] It is no surprise, given the interpretive quandary they propose, that Stanley Corngold entitled his major work on Kafka criticism *The Commentators' Despair*. In his article, "Metamorphosis of the Metaphor," however, Corngold provides an insightful and timely—virtually postmodern—interpretation of Kafka's *Metamorphosis* (see *Franz Kafka*, 41–79). He considers the perplexing novella to be animated by a continuous process of transformation, metaphorically coded but even subverting "metaphor" itself: "At the close of *The Metamorphosis*, the ongoing metamorphosis of the metaphor accomplishes itself through a consciousness empty of all practical attention and a body that preserves its opacity" (78). He further argues that "the light in which Gregor dies is said explicitly to emanate from outside the window and not from a source within the subject" (79). He thus suggests that Kafka's text is in some sense deconstructive, a reading that has been more fully developed by Corngold in "Kafka, Nietzsche and the Question of Literary History" (*Franz Kafka*, 139–164) as it has been by Deleuze and Guattari in *Kafka: Toward a Minor Literature*. That deconstruction and metamorphosis are parallel is also clearly suggested by Peggy Kamuf:

"Deconstruction, then, does not name a theory, a method, a school, or any other such delimitable entity. Instead, deconstruction is what is going on, happening, coming to pass, or coming about, all intransitive locutions that dislocate the predicate's tie to any stable present" ("Introduction" xviii). Indeed, as we shall argue, the metamorphosis presented by Kafka's text is in important respects isomorphic with the deconstructive process.

The shortcomings of the traditional critical standpoints—we have chosen the Marxian and psychoanalytic ones as representative—as well as the possibilities generated by those of Corngold and of Deleuze and Guattari, moreover, provide an opening through which we can view Kafka, the undertaking of critical thought, and indeed the modalities of "human" discourse in a new way. It is this aperture—"between the blinds," as Kamuf would have us read Derrida—which reveals a postmodern space, like that of computer-generated virtual reality, in which Kafka's text appears, obliquely as the light in which Gregor dies, powerfully resisting inter-pretation because it is, in Derrida's terms, unbounded and "unbindable" by a transcendental signified. What is more, Kafka arguably presents his readers with a subversive and "schizophrenic" text that is not only anti-authoritarian and anti-oedipal, as late Marxian and psychoanalytic readings would have it, but also presents a double-bind that reduces the doctors of literary, social, and therapeutic discourses, rather than the client, to despair. As Kamuf has argued in regard to Derrida's ruminations in *Des Tours de Babel* on God's mixed feelings about translation, "again the double bind, which Derrida renders as, 'Translate my name; but, whatever you do, do not translate my name'" ("Introduction," xxiv, xiv). So, too, the double-bind presented by Kafka's text: "Interpret me; but, whatever you do, do not interpret me."

The question is what kind of discourse, and what sort of author implicit in that discourse, is to be allowed the privilege of being the interpreter and what language, and what author, is to be subjected to interpretation. For the "authority" of the latter text is in turn subordinated to that of the interpreters who compete for mastery of the subject text. Moreover, the strategies and theories used by the interpretive authority must be seen in a social context as extensions of larger patterns of authority and power, including the hegemony of master discourses like science or philosophy or literary theory, in the polis. If Kafka's text is viewed in the contexts both of competing discourses and of their social and political interests, then his commentary may be seen, like that of John Perceval, as both resisting and deconstructing those who would master it. Thus Gregor's narrative becomes a "literary" schizophrenic commentary on and critique of the intellectual and social history of modernity.

Marxist Criticism

Gregor's narrative clearly suggests a critique of the political economy of his times, and this critique has been pointed out by Marxist critics. Before discussing their views, however, it is useful to look at some examples of Gregor's story, so that we can compare it with the critical discourses attempting to master it.

Soon after Gregor's unsettling transformation, the details of which are still dawning on him, he comments on the regimen of being a traveling salesman, which his changed state has removed him from.

> "Oh God," he thought, "what a grueling job I've picked! Day in, day out—on the road. The upset of doing business is much worse than the actual business in the home office, and, besides, I've got the torture of travelling, worrying about changing trains, eating miserable food at all hours, constantly seeing new faces, no relationships that last or get more intimate. To the devil with it all!" (4)

This part of Gregor's narrative could well be simply interpreted in traditional, even Soviet, Marxian terms. According to Kenneth Hughes, the central themes of Soviet criticism of Kafka are alienation and realism. Concerning the latter, he comments that "the exclusion of the writer [Kafka] from Marxist consideration had been based on the view that his work did not offer useful reflections of reality which would present social and historical phenomena in a clear and comprehensible way, but offered instead a surrealistic or irrational mystification of social forces" (1977, 56–57). Concerning the former, he says, "alienation is a fundamental category of Kafka criticism. . . . But bourgeois critics tend to view alienation as an immutable and permanent characteristic of our existence. . . . To Marxists, however, alienation is a very specific and concrete historical phenomenon, a product of the way in which people organize the material reproduction of their lives, and, like all historical phenomena, it is subject to change and even elimination" (1981, xxiii). So the typical Marxian view of the "Metamorphosis" and of Kafka's work generally is that it amounts to a literary abstraction, in distorted form, of a painful reality produced by specific historical conditions that may be overcome by revolution. That Kafka does not challenge these conditions makes his literature unrevolutionary and so of limited value; that he nevertheless reveals the anguish of human experience under capitalism makes his work in part defensible, if in need of demystification. Underlying both of these judgments is the assumption that the literary work of art is a manifestation, however dim, of an objective reality—a referent or transcendental signified—to which its elements, even Kafka's fantastic "symbols," must refer.

There are indications in Kafka's text itself, however, that it is not possible to read the passage from Gregor's narrative in so simple and straightforward a manner, as referring symbolically or otherwise to the alienating conditions of the capitalist economy. There are at least two indications in the text that the world represented by Gregor's narrative, for example, is itself one of representations: the photographs of Gregor himself, smiling in his military uniform (15), and of the fashion model who appears adorned in the commodities that are the currency of the salesman's trade (35). What is most fundamental to the deconstructive nature of the text, however, is the implicit metamessage presented by the transformed image of Gregor into *Ungeziefer*. For this metamessage refers not directly to some outside reality, as traditional Marxian and other more literalist critics would have it, but to Kafka's own text, specifically, to Gregor's narrative itself, transforming its meaning with the deconstructive logic of play. "This narrative," the metamessage says in effect, "does not mean what it would mean if it were taken literally" (see Chapter 2, "Deconstructing Deviancy," above, and Bateson, Steps, 177–193). So Gregor muses over alternative stories to explain his absence from work, into which the signs of his metamorphosis intrude:

> What if he were to say he were sick? But that would be extremely embarrassing and suspicious because during the five years with the firm Gregor had not been sick even once. His boss would be sure to come with the health-insurance doctor. . . . In fact, Gregor felt fine, with the exception of his drowsiness, which was really unnecessary after sleeping so late, and he even had a ravenous appetite. (5)

Here, at the end of this part of the narrative, there is a hint of Gregor's changed condition built into the observation, "he even had a ravenous appetite," for it refers to the insectual voracity of the *Ungeziefer*, whose identity further dawns on Gregor's consciousness in the next paragraph:

"Gregor," someone called—it was his mother—"it's a quarter to seven. Didn't you want to catch the train?" What a soft voice! Gregor was shocked to hear his own voice answering, unmistakably his own voice, true, but in which, as if from below, an insistent distressed chirping intruded, which left the clarity of his words intact only for a moment really, before so badly garbling them as they carried that no one could be sure if he heard right. (5)

Challenges to the orthodox realism of Marxist criticism have come in part from Marxism itself. Roger Garaudy, for instance, points to the parallels between Kafka's writings and the aesthetics of modern art. He begins with the standard perspective: "The basic thesis of materialism and—in art—of realism is this: it is not consciousness which determines life but life which determines consciousness"; but he goes on to qualify this thesis by arguing that "it in no way implies a mechanical determination of the relationship between consciousness and life" (Hughes 1981, 105). Instead of this simple, mechanical relationship he argues that "a complicated dialectic of the relationship of a work to reality and to life is the main object of Marxist aesthetics" (107). The key to this dialectical relation is man: "Marx emphasizes the role of the presence of man as the most important element in the definition of artistic reality. In doing that, he really precludes every narrow conception of realism—because a reality which includes man is . . . that which springs from the dreams of individuals and the myths of nations" (107). Thus Kafka's works provide "starting positions on the track toward infinity, toward the attainment of truly human dimensions for man, dimensions of the infinitude of his history, whose representation is limitless" (110). Just as in Cubism, so in Kafka's writing, "reality in art is, namely, a creation that, thanks to the presence of man in it, re-forms everyday reality" (110). Thus by opening up the human domain of "reality" to a multidimensional interpretation, Garaudy opens up Marxist discourse on Kafka and art in general to new revolutionary possibilities.

Theodor Adorno of the Frankfurt School stands at the boundaries circumscribed by Marxist aesthetic theory and looks, even steps, outward toward a postmodern realm. In terms of Deleuze and Guattari, discussed below, he might be said to *deterritorialize* Marxist discourse. Walter Benjamin (1968) arguably provided the context for Adorno's interpretation of Kafka. He argued, also prefiguring Garaudy's analysis, that "Kafka lives in a *comple-*

mentary world. (In this he is closely related to Klee, whose work in painting is just as essentially *solitary* as Kafka's work is in literature)." It is from the perspective of this alternative domain that Kafka reduced the "real" world to oblivion—not to a "prophetic vision" of apocalypse, but to sound without sense. "Kafka listened to tradition, and he who listens hard does not see. . . . The main reason why this listening demands such an effort is that only the most indistinct sounds reach the listener. There is no doctrine that one could absorb, no knowledge that one could preserve" (143). Thus Benjamin drives the interpretation of Kafka to the borders of theory and sensibility, where he lets the literature allude to what is outside both. It is this transformation of the world of mimetic representation of an objective "reality," fundamental to traditional criticism and socialist realism, that Adorno regards as the dialectical impetus, the subversive impact, of Kafka's fiction. "Some art works have the power to break through the social barrier they reach," he argues. "Thus Kafka's works seem to violate the reader's sensibilities by narrating stories that are patently counterfactual, and yet it is this violation that renders them easily accessible to all. The view, trumpeted by Stalinists and Westerners, that modern art is unintelligible is empirically correct. But it is also false, because it treats reception as though it were constant and overlooks the impact that unintelligible works can have on consciousness. In the modern administered world the only adequate way to appropriate art works is one where the uncommunicable is communicated and where the hold of reified consciousness is thus broken" (280). The reader of Derrida may well echo Adorno's description of Kafka and modern art, "where the uncommunicable is communicated," yet this rebellion of literary, artistic, and philosophical discourse from the strictures of administered reality, with all of its apparent unintelligibility to "normal" consciousness, may well bear the seed of counterfactuality, of difference, which is needed to break the barriers of modernity and enter into a post-modern domain. Still, Adorno seems to retain, if in transmuted form, the connection between artwork and referent in the guise of the unintelligible signifying the unintelligible. His position is not unlike Jameson's analysis of postmodern forms of pastiche as the "cultural logic" of the master signified, late capitalism, revealed by the master narrative, late Marxism.

Psychoanalytic Criticism

Traditional psychoanalysis has provided a fruitful perspective for the interpretation of Kafka, invoked by number of important critics. However,

Kafka's text has successfully resisted them all and, in Corngold's terms, reduced their efforts at commentary to despair. It is precisely this explana-tory collapse that opens the way to poststructuralist and other postmodern reading practices, in psychoanalysis stemming from the structuralist work of Jacques Lacan. Before considering Lacan's work and the possibilities that it opens for the reading of Kafka, it is worthwhile to review what some psychoanalytic interpreters have already attempted. Thus we will be in a better position to understand Lacan's, and Kafka's, contribution. Prominent among these is, for example, Hellmuth Kaiser (see Corngold 1973), who argues that "the story depicts the struggle between son and father as it rises out of the oedipal conflict. . . . Viewed psychologically, the metamorphosis of the son does not signify an external event but an internal change in the direction of drive. It is a kind of self-punishment for his earlier competitive striving aimed against the father, a withdrawal from the exacting genital position" (Corngold 1973, 149). Similarly Hartmut Binder (Corngold 1973, 80–83) argues that the story is to be understood in terms of the power relations between father and son: the father is first humiliated by the son, who plays his role as provider, but then after his metamorphosis the son is humiliated by the father, who is empowered by the degradation of his son into an *Ungeziefer* (80–81).

Selma Fraiberg argues from a different psychoanalytic standpoint, citing Gustav Janouch's *Conversations with Kafka*: Janouch: "The Meta-morphosis is a terrible dream, a terrible conception"; Kafka: "The dream reveals the reality, while conception lags behind. That is the horror of life—the terror of art" (Corngold 1973, 115). Thus she understands Kafka's work as a kind of primary process, a dream externalized in the disciplined form of language: "Kafka's writing was a bridge, the connection between the two worlds; it was the strongest of the bonds which united him with the real world" (115). Consequently Fraiberg sees Kafka's work as exhibit-ing, in Corngold's phrase, "the tension between the two intents of fiction—between the story which is concerned with communicating, and the manifest dream which conceals and disguises its meaning—always excites interpretation" (115). Finally, Walter Sokel argues that Gregor's meta-morphosis is a "self-inflicted accident" (Corngold 1973, 209); "it expresses Gregor's guilt and the punishment for this guilt" (210). As a result of this "accident," however, the character is increasingly isolated from human communication, which is his tragedy: "that he feels and thinks as a human being while unable to make his humanity felt and known" (209). These traditional psychoanalytic views tie the "fictional" sequence of Kafka's story to social or psychic processes and to the psychological effects that result from disturbances in them. In effect, regardless of the sophistication of the psychoanalytic view, and regardless of whether the critic refers directly to standard Freudian terms and symbols like "Oedipal conflict," literature is understood as a "symptom" indicating some more fundamental condition— that is, it is a signifier referring to a signified transcendental to it.

More recent psychoanalytic interpretation is perhaps best represented by the work of two critics: J. Brooks Bouson and David Eggenschwiler (1986). Bouson argues, in terms drawn from the work of Heinz Kohut, that the latter's study in the nature of the narcissistic personality disorder "provides a new depth-psychological insight not only into the underlying cause and meaning of Gregor's transformation, but also into the experiential core of his predicament" (192). He cites Kohut's explanation that "'the self arises in a matrix of empathy' and 'strives to live within a modicum of empathetic responses in order to maintain itself'" (192) as a basis for understanding the personality disorder that results when this matrix is not provided. Thus he describes, following Kohut, "a man 'who finds himself in nonresponsive surroundings,' a man whose family speaks of him coldly, in the 'impersonal third pronoun' so that he becomes a non-human monstrosity, even in his own eyes'" (193). Gregor Samsa is, in his view, just this kind of man: "Gregor depends on others to validate his worth and provide him with an inner sense of power, strength, and vitality. Attempting to restore his defective self, he acts out his repressed grandiose needs as he tries to capture the attention of family members and extract from them the approval he needs to confirm his worth and reality" (193). So Gregor is a "broken" man, in Kohut's terms, "compelled endlessly to enact the same primitive, fixated behavior in his frustrated search for wholeness" (193)— an apt description of the modern human predicament. In spite of his new orientation within psychoanalysis, however, Bouson does not deviate significantly from the traditional psychoanalytic approach, revealed in his opening phrases, of providing a "depth-psychological insight" into the "underlying causes" of Gregor's, and likewise our, human condition.

Eggenschwiler, alternatively, offers an account of the *Metamorphosis* that is both psychoanalytic and incipiently postmodern. For while he accepts the validity of psychological categories for a partial interpretation of the work, he convincingly argues that neither these nor any other critical frameworks are adequate for the full exegesis of Kafka's text. In reference to Kafka's artistry with language, Eggenschwiler says, "I am concerned with that use of language to suggest the limits of psychology.

Kafka's allusions and patterns do imply that psychology helps to specify the desires and fears of the inner life. And his use of inexplicable brute and brutal facts marks limits, implies that the inner life cannot be entirely known, entirely fenced in by anthropomorphic theories" (80). Eggenschwiler points to Kafka's obvious play with and satire of psychoanalytic concepts and symbols within the story—for example, Gregor's father's assault on him with apples indicating the primal expulsion of the son by the father, from the family or from Eden, as Kafka perhaps anticipates the insights of Freud in *Moses and Monotheism* twenty-five years later—so that no simplistic reading of Kafka in terms of Freud is possible. Indeed, Eggenschwiler argues, based on an entry of 19 October 1917 in Kafka's notebooks—"Es gibt keine Beobachtung der innern Welt, so wie es eine der äussern gibt. Zumindest deskriptive Psychologie ist wahrscheinlich in der Ganze ein Anthropomorphismus, ein Ausragen der Grenzen" [There is no such thing as observation of the inner world, as there is of the outer world. At least descriptive psychology is probably, taken as a whole, a form of anthropomorphism, a nibbling at our own limits"]—that, in Kafka's view, "psychology pretends to describe in rational and observably human images an inner world that is indescribable, irrational, and inhuman; it profanes the sacred and makes the mysterious seem knowable". This is because Kafka thinks of psychology as a form of projection: "By calling psychology a form of anthropomorphism, Kafka claims that through it the conscious mind projects its own image onto the inner world; while thinking that it is describing the entire self, that mind is actually describing its own features" (Eggenschwiler, 200–201).

In this light, Eggenschwiler, again citing Kafka (this time "Von den Gleichnissen" ["On Parables"]), strikingly interprets the structure of the *Metamorphosis*, particularly its conclusion, in terms that dramatize the process of interpretation itself and the limits of psychological explanation in the face of Kafka's parabolic story: "Gregor's metamorphosis is a form of parable; in section 3 the Samsa family acts out an interpretation of that parable, both clarifying and reducing it in the world of everyday. In that world they win, both in the validity of their interpretation (psychology always has correct results) and in its practical consequences. In parable, of course, they have lost" (92). And in a final twist Eggenschwiler offers a parable that leads us to the verge of postmodern interpretive theory: "Perhaps the reader may also win in the world as he reduces a disturbing and frustratingly elusive story to a manageable pattern, an anthropomorphic form. Of course, he too loses in parable" (92).

Jacques Lacan (1982) opens the way toward a postmodern under-standing of Kafka by his structuralist reading of Freud. He argues that the rational ego, the *cogito* of the Cartesian philosophical tradition as well as the functional self of everyday bourgeois life, is formed in the "mirror stage" of child development. It is in this stage that the child, for instance, by looking in the mirror, discovers that he is a distinct entity, separate from the mother. The male child, the "he" in the last sentence, is encouraged to identify with the spectral self in the mirror, as an ego separate from its origin in the other, the female/mother. The female is identified with the mother. Even though she gains a separate identity, she is to think of herself not as "ego" or "center" or "author," not as a spectral self that sees the world, including the mother, as other, but rather as the other that is the object of the male gaze. Her identity is that of image-as-object. The male persona introjects the spectral self as rational ego and as subject and author of the gaze, who looks upon the other, the mother, the female, as object.

The spectral gaze, moreover, is, when its ego is considered as *cogito*, the epistemic subject of discourse. From the time of Plato knowledge has been associated with seeing, as the Greek word, *idea*, cognate with the English term, indicates, for it is derived from the verb *idein*, "to see clearly and distinctly." Thus we have, at the center of knowledge, an introjected mirror image, if we think in three-dimensional or holographic terms, an introjected Greek statue, which is the center of knowledge and the arbiter of rational discourse. The feminine other is therefore "eccentric" and "irra-tional." Rational discourse requires the subordination of predicate to sub ject (or vice-versa), and requires binary rules for thought. It thus excludes as "metaphoric" or "metonymic" or otherwise imagistic and illogical language formations that do not perform the necessary subordination and play by the binary rules of logic. Thus the male subject established the "dominant" language patterns that characterize the patriarchic traditions.

In Lacan's terms, the patriarchal subject makes discourse "phallic." The discourse is phallic because the phallus indicates the difference between male and female and, because the male is designated as central in patriarchic traditions, the phallus is the indicator of dominant discourse centered in the masculine subject. Female discourse is therefore the discourse of the other, as suggested above, and "lacks" both the centralized *cogito* of male discourse and the subordination of predicate to subject, along with the binary rules of logic, which characterize that discourse: it is therefore not authoritative. Indeed, feminine discourse, defined in Lacanian terms, becomes the language not of biological females per se, although this is often the case in male-dominated societies since they are relegated to a subordinate position by their "lack" of the phallus signifier. It becomes, instead, the language of the "other" in various forms: of the woman, the schizophrenic, the social outcast, the poet, the deconstructionist, and, of course, the "monster" or *Ungeziefer*. As Cixous argues,

> for Freud/Lacan, woman is said to be "outside the Symbolic": outside the Symbolic, that is outside language, the place of the Law, excluded from any possible relationship with culture and cultural order. And she is outside the Symbolic because she lacks any relation to the phallus, because she does not enjoy what orders masculinity. . . . The phallus, in Lacanian parlance also called the "transcendental signifier," transcendental precisely as primary organizer of the structure of subjectivity, is what, for psychoanalysis, inscribes its effects, of castration and resistance to castration and hence the very organization of language, as unconscious relations, and so it is the phallus that is said to constitute the a priori condition of all symbolic functioning. (1981, 45–46)

Gregor's language is the discourse of the other in precisely this sense, providing a radical deconstructionist-feminist commentary on the discourses of power that envelop him.

Over against the language of rational, waking consciousness, moreover, the language of the other becomes the language of *dream*. This is the realm of Freudian "primary process," which is encoded differently from the language of rational consciousness. As Bateson and Wilden have argued, the language of dream is encoded metaphorically and metonymically, as a "feminine" discourse pushed in the background by the supersesion of waking rationality, to the point in the contemporary world where the technological embodiments of rationality, the computer systems organizing corporations and governments and weapons systems, "never sleep." It is thus no mistake that Gregor wakes from "unsettling dreams" (*unruhigen Träumen*) and that his metamorphosing commentary follows. It is interesting in this context to note that the German word *unruhig*, literally "unrestful," connotes social and political unrest as well as personal disquiet. Thus the term suggests that Gregor's transformation is to be one that might indicate a larger unrest within the bourgeois order.

Lacan (1986) illustrates the kind of significance that dream commentary can have, especially in reference to the spectral world of rationality, in his "The Split between the Eye and the Gaze." Here Lacan considers the perplexity of the Chinese philosopher Choang-tse (Chuang-tzu), who, like Gregor, undergoes a startling metamorphosis:

> In a dream, he is a butterfly. What does this mean? It means that he sees the butterfly in his reality as gaze. What are so many figures, so many shapes, so many colours, if not this gratuitous *showing*, in which is marked for us the primal nature of the essence of the gaze. . . . When Choang-tse wakes up, he may ask himself whether it is not the butterfly who dreams that he is Choang-tsu. Indeed, he is right, and doubly so, first because it proves he is not mad, he does not regard himself as absolutely identical with Choang-tzu and, secondly, because he does not fully understand how right he is. In fact, it is when he was the butterfly that he apprehended one of the roots of his identity— that he was, and is, in his essence, that butterfly who paints himself with his own colours—and it is because of this that, in the last resort, he is Choang-tsu. (76)

The significance of the dream's "showing" is that it indicates what Lacan calls the "sliding" or displacement of the subject from its position vis-à-vis the objects of the phenomenal field, so that what is "seen" begins to overtake what "looks."

> In the dream what characterizes the images is that it *shows*. It shows—but here, too, some form of "sliding away" of the subject is apparent. Look up some description of a dream, . . . place it in its co-ordinates, and you will see that this *it shows* is well to the fore. So much is it to the fore, with the characteristics in which it is co-ordinated—namely, absence of horizon, the enclosure, of that which is contemplated in the waking state, and, also, the character of emergence, of contrast, of stain, of its images, the intensification of their colours—that, in the final resort, our position in the dream is profoundly that of someone who does not see. (75)

Blinded Oedipus immediately comes to mind, for his rationality is thwarted by the cunning of Apollo, so that he abdicates his position as cognitive subject and political sovereign. So does Gregor, for his spectral self, the rationalized image as "son" and "brother" and "salesman"—all presuppose him as a subject of a discourse and practice over which he imagined he had control. With his transformation, however, the intensity, the stain, the colors, the sounds, all the phenomena of his experience become increasingly unmanageable by his previous consciousness and begin to appear, to "show," in their own right as strange new apparitions. As Kafka's narrator describes it, "But Gregor had become much calmer. It was true that they no longer understood his words, though they had seemed clear enough to him, clearer then before, probably because his ear had grown accustomed to them" (13). The sounds of language become strange, not clear at least to his former looking-glass selves, his family, though he "slips" in Lacan's language into a new sense of awareness not akin to his former identity. Thus the Lacanian, and more broadly French post-structuralist, reading of Freud opens the way to a new reading of Kafka that is at once deconstructionist, feminist, and postmodern.

Deleuze and Guattari: Toward a Postmodern Landscape

Beyond the limits of Marxism and psychoanalysis, and of all interpretations that attempt to categorize or "Oedipalize" discourse in terms of archetypes or structures or metaphysical constructs of any kind, Deleuze and Guattari (1986) enter upon a reading of Kafka inspired by a wildly metamorphosing conversation with Marx, Freud, and Nietzsche. Adamantly political, subversively unpsychological, attuned to expression in terms of pure intensities as strange new wills to power, their interpretation offers a new way of thinking that is neither "literary" nor "critical." For it requires a transformation of the "critic" and the "literature" so that both categories are overcome in a radical hermeneutical endeavor. For Deleuze and Guattari, Kafka has written a *minor* literature, a self-generating-transforming "*expression machine*, capable of disorganizing its own forms, and of disorganizing its forms of contents, in order to liberate pure contents that mix with expressions in a single intense matter" (28).

In this dynamic form the "machine" of minor literature subverts major literature: "A major, or established, literature follows a vector that goes from content to expression. . . . But a minor, or revolutionary, literature begins by expressing itself and doesn't conceptualize until afterward ('I do not see the word at all, I invent it' [Kafka, *Diaries* 15 December 1910 (33)]. Expression must break forms, encourage ruptures and new sproutings" (28). The ability of "literature" to transform "reality" suggested by the progressive Marxist critics above, is thus consummated. Kafka's flight from common or traditional sense, pointed to by Benjamin and others, his motion from the human into the animal as in the *Metamorphosis*, is furthermore taken to its paralogical conclusion by Deleuze and Guattari. "Kafka deliberately kills all metaphor, all symbolism, all signification, no less than all designation. Metamorphosis is the contrary of metaphor. . . . There is no longer man or animal, since each deterritorializes the other, in a conjunction of flux, in a continuum of reversible intensities. Instead, it is now a question of a becoming that includes the maximum of difference as a difference of intensity" (22). So, Deleuze and Guattari conclude, "writing for Kafka, the primacy of writing, signifies only one thing: not a form of literature alone, the enunciation forms a unity with desire, beyond laws, states, regimes. Yet the enunciation is always historical, political, and social. A micropolitics, a politics of desire that questions all situations" (41–42). Thus Corngold's "metamorphosis of the metaphor" becomes for Deleuze and Guattari a dynamic multidimensional process transforming and questioning every static form of being.

One key micropolitics in the *Verwandlung* is that of the family. As we have already argued via Bateson and Lacan, the structure of familial discourse generates the form of the individual, either "normal" or "deviant," and, furthermore, just as the structure of the family is significant for the formation of the individual so also the configuration of an individual's discourse becomes a commentary on the family. This is especially obvious in the case of the "deviant" individual who, as Freud saw, provides a good deal of information about the context in which he or she lives by "neurotically" distorting the patterns which that context establishes as "normal." The deviant's discourse becomes a kind of foil for normal communication, throwing it into sharp relief and, in cases like that of the "schizophrenic" Perceval and the "literary monstrosity" Gregor, providing a deconstructive commentary on normality. Indeed the analogy between Perceval's deconstruction of the mental institution, the doctors, the family, and the bourgeois order and Gregor's deconstruction of family, job, and other aspects of that same order suggest that, as Deleuze and Guattari argue, Gregor's commentary is not isolatable as "literary," at all, let alone simply as "monstrous." Rather, like Perceval's, it provides a critical commentary on the context in which it arises.

As Deleuze and Guattari argue, Gregor's monstrous discourse, emblematized by the very metamorphosed form of his new body, is the unleashing of a "desiring machine." Freud argued that the unconscious mind is formed through repression of primitive, polymorphous desire in the infant as the child is socialized or normalized into an Ego through the agency of the Superego. The desire that is structured and repressed in this process becomes the Id, the hidden dynamism of the unconscious. The transformative power of *différance* in the deconstructive play of Gregor's language is, in Neo-Freudian terms, the polymorphous perversity of the Id released into language, where it becomes polysemic, "deviant," "schizophrenic," "mad." It is the play of polysemic perversity that provides a context in the *Verwandlung* for the more routinized discourses that attempt to contain it, to structure its desires into socially and economically acceptable terms: family and work, as Max Weber saw, the foundations of the bourgeois order.

Specifically in Gregor's case, the workaday consciousness of the "old" Gregor continues to be structured in terms of normality—getting up on time, catching the train on time, getting to work on the clock, bringing home income to support the family, being a responsible son and brother, acting in accordance with the Law of the Father. The condition of the "new," metamorphosed Gregor, however, obviates this normal structure, releasing into Gregor's discourse a "perverse" desire and a polysemic form, which are incompatible with the aforementioned routines and obligations. Thus there arises an internal *psychomachia* in the character, between the old and new Gregor, so that as the old attempts to go to work, the new resists, and as the old describes to himself his obligations and routines, the new changes form, in body and voice, blurring the outlines of the old toward unrecognizability and certainly toward unmanageability. Like many in the workaday world, Gregor cannot get himself out of bed: "'Just don't stay in bed being useless,' Gregor said to himself" (7).

Indeed, as we have indicated above, this *psychomachia* between the old Gregor and the new amounts to a double-bind, in which the new form of Gregor, the "monstrosity," comments on the old, "normal" form, as a metastatement of a higher, logical type, undermining the simple reference of the "old" language and the normal consciousness which that language generates as well as the institutional framework in which that language functions. The double-bind, thus, as the psychomachia proceeds, increasingly drives Gregor "insane," or into "sickness," depending on the clinical language preferred, so that as in the case of Perceval, the family calls the "doctor":

> "Go to the doctor's immediately. Gregor is sick. Hurry, get the doctor. Did you just hear Gregor talking?" (13)

To which the representative of "work," also present in response to the new Gregor's "deviant" desire not to show up on the job, says,

"That was the voice of an animal," said the manager, with a tone conspicuously soft compared with the mother's yelling. (13)

The manager's description of the animality of Gregor's voice underlines the latter's metamorphosis into the prehuman, the polymorphously desiring beast not properly socialized, not ready for work.

There is a significant connection between Kafka's metamorphosed Gregor and Cixous' "hysteric":

> The hysteric is a divine spirit that is always at the edge, the turning point, of making. She is one who does not make herself. . . . She does not make herself but she does make the other. . . . Without the hysteric, there's no father . . . without the hysteric, no master, no analyst, no analysis! She's the *unorganizable* feminine construct, whose power of producing the other is a power that never returns to her. She is really a wellspring nourishing the other for eternity, yet not drawing back from the other . . . not recognizing herself in the images the other may or may not give her. She is given images that don't belong to her, and she forces herself, as we've all done, to resemble them. (1981, 47)

Like the hysteric, Gregor "makes" the other in that he dramatizes, by his deviance, the controlling roles that the family and manager and doctor play. They are necessary to contain the "hysteria" of Gregor's animal discourse, to routinize him or kill him; without him, no family, no manager, no doctor! None would be necessary, for he is the very unruly other, the chaos, that their roles are designed to order. Cixous' further suggestions are that the hysteric provides the "wellspring" that nourishes normality, from which it draws its life, just as industrial civilization draws life from the other which is "nature." Gregor, the "animal," is the other on which the "human" order depends, but of which it is terrified and which it subjects to domination and control—through science, industry, and the orders of capital and family. Thus they impose on Gregor or the hysteric "images that don't belong to her," "salesman," "son," "employee," "family provider," and which Gregor, like the hysteric, has forced himself to play—until his current deconstructive rebellion into "monstrosity."

The communicational form of monstrosity is for Cixous as for Kafka, laughter. As Clément argues in their co-authored *The Newly Born Woman*,

> All laughter is allied with the monstrous. . . . Laughter breaks up, breaks out, splashes over. . . . It is the moment at which the

woman crosses a dangerous · line, the cultural demarcation beyond which she will find herself excluded. . . . To break up, to touch the masculine integrity of the body image, is to return to a stage that is scarcely constituted in human development; it is to return to the disordered Imaginary of before the mirror stage, of before the rigid and defensive constitution of subjective armor. . . . An entire fantastic world, made of bits and pieces, opens up beyond the limit, as soon as the line is crossed. (33)

Gregor has surely crossed the line, opened up the fantastic world beyond the limit, provided a deconstructive laughter at the institutions and roles of the bourgeois world that would control him. Gregor devolves into the "disordered imaginary before the mirror stage," by his metamorphosis perverting the "masculine integrity of the body image," delving into the unenculturated realm before the creation of "subjective armor." Kafka laughs hysterically while reading the Metamorphosis to friends.

In other terms, Kafka's Gregor descends out of the order of established discourse, the symbolic order of culture, and toward the white noise of chaos or, alternatively, toward silence. His "silence" is not simply an absence, however; it is the fantastic disordered imaginary out of which the order of culture is shaped and is the rich "natural" variety on which the more domesticated patterns of cultural discourse are cut. The difficulty is that "doctors" and "fathers" and "managers," not to mention "literary critics," forget the chaos, the creativity, which makes their routines possible, believing that their norms come first, the imaginary second, or that the imaginary, like a beast, is something to be caught and studied. But Kafka is silent in the face of their attempts to capture what he says. Like Perceval, faced by the doctors who will not listen to what he says, he refuses to speak their language at all.

The above critical odyssey from the central metaphysical categories of modernism to the disruption of those categories and the opening of discourse by postmodern thinking has, like Odysseus's voyage itself, a point of departure and a point of return that are the same: the writings of Franz Kafka. Like the sirens in Kafka's rewriting of Homer's parable, it seems that Kafka's Metamorphosis, amidst its eloquence, proposes a silence into which a host of critics have projected their views. In its break from the Romanticism and Realism of nineteenth-century literature, Kafka's work initiated a metamorphosis into modernism, epitomized not only by broken images and men, "bent double, like old beggars under sacks" as Wilfred

Owen observed them in World War I, but also with the pessimistic recognition expressed so well by T. S. Eliot's Prufrock, who says of the "Mermaids singing each to each," perhaps echoing Kafka's Odysseus before the sirens, "I do not think they will sing to me" (see his *Parables and Paradoxes*). Where modern critics have imposed their categories on Kafka, postmodern thinkers have been more content to let his texts speak for themselves.

However, even Deleuze and Guattari, by importing the notion of a literary "machine" into their reading of Kafka, have connoted an intellectual history stemming from Cartesian metaphysics and arguably still alive in French structuralism. For the concept of mechanism is one of pure intensities, of desire creating its own objects and means of expression: "the machine is desire—but not because desire is desire of the machine but because desire never stops making a machine in the machine and creates a new gear alongside the preceding gear, indefinitely, even if the gears seem to be in opposition or seem to be functioning in a discordant fashion" (82). In spite of the disclaimer by Deleuze in his *Dialogues* with Claire Parnet—

> "Machine, machinism, *machinic*": it is neither mechanical nor organic. The mechanic is a system of gradual connections between dependent terms. The machine, on the other hand, is a clustered "proximity" between independent terms (topological proximity is itself independent of distance or contiguity). A machinic assemblage is defined by the displacement of a center of gravity onto an abstract line (cited by Réda Bensmaïa, Deleuze and Guattari, xv)—

his language is cast in terms clearly reminiscent of Cartesian primary as opposed to secondary qualities. For Descartes, the primary qualities were quantifiable and objective, while secondary ones were unquantifiable and subjective. While Deleuze and Guattari clearly wish to reject the metaphysical bifurcation of experience into subjective and objective or into any other categories, they nevertheless employ a language derived from the above distinction. For, at least in the context of modern intellectual history, the language of intensities and functions from which means and objects are derived is clearly an echo of the quantitative language that would derive the secondary qualities from primary ones, that is, a world of sensations categorized in terms of their mode of apprehension ("sight," "sound," "odor") from a world of pure forces and impacts.

This distinction is best articulated by Galileo, whose work Descartes codified philosophically. As Galileo argues, "I say that I am inclined sufficiently to believe that heat is of this kind, and that the thing that produces heat in us and makes us perceive it, which we call by the general name fire, is a multitude of minute corpuscles thus and thus figured, moved with such and such a velocity" (*Opere*, IV, 336ff.; cited in Burtt 1980, 88). He significantly elaborates:

> But that external bodies, to excite in us these tastes, these odours, and these sounds, demanded other than size, figure, number, and slow or rapid motion, I do not believe; and I judge that, if the ears, the tongue, and the nostrils were taken away, the figure, the numbers, and the motions would indeed remain, but not the odours nor the tastes nor the sounds, which, without the living animal, I do not believe are anything else than names. (*Opera*, IV, 336ff.; cited in Burtt 1980, 88)

In brief, "tastes," "odors," and the like are subjective qualities characteristic only of the human subject, but "size," "figure," and "number" are qualities characteristic of the object; "objective" knowledge is considered more fundamental or "primary" while "subjective" knowledge is considered less fundamental or "secondary."

Delete the metaphysics of particles from this statement, substitute the language of pure intensity or "desire" for the "cause" and" "gear" or "literature" for the "effect," and you are very close to Deleuze and Guattari's language. Thus implicit in that language is the referential injunction of the primary–secondary doctrine—quantifiable phenomena are primary—which privileges the mechanistic language of science and, once more, anchors discourse with a transcendental signified.

Postmodern Metamorphosis

So the final question remains: do the postmodern critics also fail to transcend the metaphysical heritage of modernism and so unwittingly project new versions of old concepts onto Kafka's silence? In any case, the transformation at the heart of Kafka's *Metamorphosis* itself may point the way toward a new mode of textuality. For it seems that as the critics have been busily transforming Kafka into their particular forms of discourse, Kafka has been steadily transforming the critics into more careful interpreters. Beyond the metamorphosis of the metaphor it seems that we have a metamorphosis of criticism. As Corngold points out in "The

Question of Literary History," Kafka, like Nietzsche, denies "the possibility of literary history by denying some of the fundamental relations assumed to constitute literary history" (*Franz Kafka*, 139). They do this by subverting its fundamental principle: "Literary history treats literary works in their irreducible connection with real things that are said to be accessible from outside the work . . . 'the world of the historian's concern,' . . . the referent" (140–141). This referent is none other than Derrida's transcendental signified, which Kafka prefers to confound by a process of infinite reversal or chiasm: a paradoxical, self-referential transposition of the terms of metaphor: "The animal wrests the whip from its master and whips itself in order to become master, not knowing that this is only a fantasy produced by a new knot in the master's whiplash," to cite one of Kafka's most unsettling examples (cited in Corngold, "Question of Literary History," 155; see Kafka, *Dearest Father*, 37, 323). Master and slave become substitutions for one another, syntagmatically displace each other, only to discover that each reversal generates another. Thus writer and critic are in a master–slave dialectic which is not dialectic at all, but recursion, or in terms of communications psychology, double-bind, which in turn, in a metamorphosis worthy of Kafka, turns out to be none other than the play of *différance*. As Corngold concludes in the same essay, "the chiasm is constructed to be hermeneutically endless: the positions of master and whip, of animal and fantasy, replace one another chiastically, incessantly" (157). He goes on to note that Kafka's aphorism is virtually identical to the procedure of deconstruction as described by Derrida. "To 'deconstruct' philosophy is thus to work through the structured genealogy of its concepts in the most scrupulous and immanent fashion, but at the same time to determine, from a certain external perspective that it cannot name or describe, what this history may have concealed or excluded, constituting itself as history through this repression in which it has a stake" (Derrida, *Positions*, 15–16; Corngold, "Question of Literary History," 157). Hence Corngold argues: "Kafka's aphorism enacts this procedure in exemplary fashion at the same time that it sets into sharper relief than does Derrida's statement the totally unsettling consequence of working through a genealogy of concepts from an external perspective that it cannot name or describe" (*Franz Kafka*, 157 n.). Kafka's "unsettling" difference from Derrida is important and may still mark the boundary between "literature" and "philosophy," as we shall see below. Overall, in this metamorphosis of literature and criticism is traced the spiraling ascent (or descent, depending on your literary politics) into the aporias of postmodernity, as Thomas Pynchon's *Gravity's Rainbow* breaches postmodern space: "A screaming comes across the sky. It has happened before, but there is nothing to compare it to now" (3).

One stem of European literary criticism arose in ancient Greece, its formal categories first articulated by Aristotle, as part of a more general rise of prose discourse vying with poetry for hegemony. This was part of the broad shift from an orally composed and transmitted literature, with all of its dynamic nuances, to the more orderly norms of literacy (see Havelock). Plato, the father (in a philosophical and Freudian sense) of Western metaphysics, was arguably in direct competition with Homeric discourse. Indeed, as Alexander Mourelatos has argued, the odyssey taken by that wily Homeric hero was the paradigm for the odyssey taken by the Kouros of Parmenides, whose goal was not the island home of Odysseus but the transcendental home of Being, beyond the gates of day and night. The quest for this return is indeed the primary metaphysical quest for order, certainty, and stasis—in Derrida's terms, the metaphysics of presence—not provided by the flux of experience or the mortality of living beings. Plato simply refined this primary quest in his theory of Forms, which provided the basis for Aristotle's categories and species. The history of Western philosophy, from the Greeks through the modern world—in the guise of the medieval search for heaven or the modern progress toward utopia— stems from this quest. To know "primary" qualities was for Descartes to know what is certain. Literary criticism, as well as the social sciences and the "normal" institutions of European culture, have mirrored this metaphysics in its quest to "interpret," to "understand," to subordinate to theory, and so to "control" the various "texts" that make up literature and society (see Berman 1988 for a useful study of the relationship between philosophy and literary theory).

Indeed, one might argue, following Marlowe and Goethe, that Western civilization, particularly in its modern scientific and technological phase, is a Faustian quest for power through knowledge, itself an alienated new form of the old Odyssean search for home. Hence the literary critics, too, would like to "enframe" (subject to Gestell in Heidegger's terms), or to impose an orderly interpretation on, to get power over, the unruly texts confronting them. Another stem of Western criticism arose from Israel, however, and its exegetical aims are precisely not full intelligibility but confrontation with the unintelligible presence of the divine. In Rojtman's words, "as he eats the fruit of the tree Adam inaugurates the history of human thought. It is the story of knowledge necessarily tainted, an erroneous and reductive attempt at mastery, an accommodation forever

begun anew and never adequate for the Revelation which offers itself"
(98). Kafka, resisting and overpowering by his silence both the literary
theorists and the metaphysicians, undoes the Greek metaphysics of interpretation, the definition of his work as a literary form, and brings forth from
the exegetical stem a new enigma: one commensurate with the modern age
yet, like the *Torah*, beyond its attempt to appropriate it as knowledge. Like
Kafka's sirens or Derrida's Babel, his story is "jealous," both demands and
forbids interpretation, bringing the transcendent persona of knowledge
coterminous with the rise of rationality in Greece, personified by the "very
clever" (*poluphrōn*) Odysseus, to the edge of its Apollonian seat. There it
must confront the limits of its knowledge and power, confront the silence
of death or transfiguration.

But into what? Kafka is silent. His metamorphosis brings the Western
tradition "back" to where it began, back "home," but not to ancient Ithaca
or Being or heaven or the Promised Land or utopia. Kafka's return is more
subtle and puzzling. For when he brings the critics out of their categories to
confront the silence of his *poēsis*, he brings them to an ancient time and
place that they remember, but which are no longer the same. For the
notion that the "time and place" from which our prosaic civilization arose
are the "same" upon return presupposes a historical scheme supported by a
metaphysics that is not evident in Kafka. Instead he brings us home in a
return at once Nietzschean and postmodern, so that the old place is
somehow new: *recursion* rather than return. As Moulthrop, echoing
Hoftstadter, argues, "It is crucial to distinguish recursion from return or
simple repetition. . . . Recursion is self-reference with the possibility of self-
modification" (Moulthrop 1991, 31; cf. Hoftstadter 1979, 127)—"It has
happened before, but there is nothing to compare it to now."

Kafka, of course, is "silent" only in the sense that he does not point
the way toward critical assimilation of his work into familiar—or even
unfamiliar—categories. He does take us through what is perhaps the most
startling metamorphosis in the history of "literature." We therefore should
reflect carefully on the transformation he presents: "Als Gregor Samsa
eines Morgens aus unruhigen Träumen erwachte, fand er sich in seinem
Bett zu einem ungeheuren Ungeziefer verwandelt" ["When Gregor Samsa
woke up one morning from unsettling dreams, he found himself changed in
his bed into a monstrous vermin"—Corngold, trans.]. As Pynchon writes,
again, in *Gravity's Rainbow*, echoing Dorothy in the Wizard of Oz, "Toto, I
have a feeling we're not in Kansas anymore" (279). The aforementioned
Marxian and psychoanalytic critics attempt to fit this metamorphosis into

their respective theoretical frameworks, though some, as we have seen, are less insistent than others about "explaining" Kafka entirely in these preconceived terms. Deleuze and Guattari attempt an open reading that resists all interpretive frames. But what are we to say in the presence of Kafka's bold literary initiative, which could possibly be an improvement on these attempts or on stunned silence? The key is not to break the silence, but to step outside it into the postmodern conversational domain. Here we find not a place, not a standpoint, but ever-branching talk. Derrida's concept of *différance*, which not only suggests continuous differentiation but itself seems to keep changing in meaning as it recurs, epitomizes the new conversation.

The opening into this domain may be provided by Kafka's *Ungeziefer*, the "vermin" or "bug" into which translators have imagined Gregor to have been changed. Whatever critics see in this—a representation of the underclass or the unconscious, or the metamorphosis of the metaphor, or the effusive machinations of a literary machine—places the *Ungeziefer* within limits it avoids by running back in its mysterious room, as if to dodge an onslaught of apples. For this "creature" is not to be "fixed" like Prufrock, because Kafka's creation is more than the peer of Derrida's term. "The activity or productivity connoted by the *a* in *différance* refers to the generative movement in the play of differences," Derrida explains (*Positions*, 27). Certainly Gregor's transformation-into-*Ungeziefer* is the "generative movement in the play of differences" which is the *Metamorphosis*. The mistake traditional critics make is to imagine that the process stops here, or can be delimited within a finite conceptual realm. Derrida's term would do nicely as a substitute for Kafka's, so that Gregor would find himself waking from unquiet dreams as a "monstrous *différance*," except that, unlike Derrida's rather neutral language, Kafka's is colored with the pain of the downtrodden, the stench of decay, and the hilarity of a *fröhliche Wissenschaft*—the *Ungeziefer* is "monstrous." It is also vivid, palpable, tactile, auditory—sensory, bodily—in a most "unsettling" way, to repeat Corngold. Perhaps only rival philosophers find Derrida's language monstrous, but otherwise, compared to Kafka's, it is rather bland.

What makes Kafka's "monster" something more immediate and compelling in its almost frightening appeal is its power to subvert the transcendental signified in all its "literary critical" forms, not to mention the "con-sciousness" and metaphysics of presence that go with it. The result is not unlike the schizophrenic experience evoked by the following account, cited by Jameson as an analog for the postmodern, a world whose

objects and subject(s) are breaking loose from their transcendental signifieds: "I looked at 'Mama' [her psychoanalyst]. But I perceived a statue, a
figure of ice which smiled at me. And this smile, showing her white teeth,
frightened me. For I saw the individual features of her face, separated from
each other: the teeth, then the nose, then the cheeks, then one eye and the
other. Perhaps it was this independence of each part that inspired such fear
and prevented my recognition of her even though I knew who she was"(
Sechehaye 1979, 51, Jameson 1991, 27). The schizophrenic state is arguably generated by the recursive logic of the double-bind imposed by the
communicational logic of the schizophrenic family, just as the postmodern
condition may be generated by the recursive play of *différance*. (For the
double-bind theory of schizophrenia, see Bateson, "Toward a Theory of
Schizophrenia," and the series of related papers in the same volume. For
the communicational logic of Kafka's family, which may well meet the
requirements for the group dynamics of schizophrenia, see Solana, "Communication, Language and Family.")

This comparison between schizophrenic discourse and Kafka's language,
with all of its communicational, critical, and philosophical implications, is
more striking in the following passages:

> In other words, I can't be anything but myself, and if people
> don't like me the way they am - ah, the way I am - then I
> appreciate when they - tell me or something, is what it amounts
> to. (A clinical example of schizophrenic discourse, cited by
> Wilden, "The Double Bind," 119)

> > On the handle of Balzac's walking-stick: I break all obstacles.
> > On mine: All obstacles break me.
> > The common factor is "all."
> > ("Auf Balzacs Spazierstockgriff: Ich breche alle Hindernisse.
> > Auf meinem: Mich brechen alle Hindernisse.
> > Gemeinsam ist das 'alle.'")

> (Kafka, *Dearest Father*, 250; Brod 1953, 281, Cornford, 1988 152)

The schizophrenic's language is marked by its substitution of the term
referring to the other, "they," for that referring to the self, "I." This is
followed by a corrective interrupter, "ah . . . I am," and, after the conclusion
of the original thought, "I appreciate . . . ," a shift to a different logical type
involving a recursive substitution of the entire foregoing grammatical
structure for the subject of a new sentence in an impersonal construction,

"is what it amounts to." The shift to the higher logical type consists in the use of the phrase "is what it amounts to," which classifies all of the preceding material in the sentence by using it as an example of the schizophrenic's problem, as a predicate that is, grammatically, of the same logical type as the foregoing material (the subject). The result is a paradox: the predicate both is and is not logically equivalent to the subject; insofar as it is, then it, too, becomes an example of the problem referred to; insofar as it is not, it is a description or classification of the problem. Thus the classification becomes self-referential: it is not part of the problem, then, but a description of the problem and to that degree an escape from it; yet it is part of the problem and so not a descriptive escape from it but an example of it.

The relevance of the theory of logical types to this analysis may require some background. As Bateson et al. explain in "Toward a Theory of Schizophrenia," "our approach is based on that part of communications theory which [Bertrand] Russell [*Principia Mathematica*] has called the Theory of Logical Types. The central thesis of this theory is that there is a discontinuity between a class and its members. The class cannot be a member of itself nor can one of the members be the class, since the term used for the class is of a *different level of abstraction*—a different Logical Type—from terms used for members. Although in formal logic there is an attempt to maintain this discontinuity between a class and its members, we argue that in the psychology of real communications this discontinuity is continually and inevitably breached, and that a priori we must expect a pathology to occur in the human organism when certain formal patterns of the breaching occur. . . . This pathology at its extreme will have symptoms whose formal characteristics would lead the pathology to be classified as a schizophrenia" (*Steps*, 202–203).

Exhibiting similar logical properties, Kafka's German text employs the syntagmatic transposition of subject and object, parallel to the schizophrenic transposition of self and other, in the first two lines: "*Ich* breche alle Hindernisse," versus "*Mich* brechen alle Hindernisse," where the subjective and objective cases of the German personal pronoun are made to occupy the same position. It also, like the schizophrenic passage, shifts to a self-referential statement of a higher logical type, with a similar shift to the neuter, "das 'alle,'" in the final line, which treats the lines preceding it as subject. Significantly, Kafka's language differs from the clinical example in the logical specification of the "common" (*gemeinsam*) element in the first two lines rather than, as in the schizophrenic's statement, the conflation of the entire foregoing passage into the subject slot; yet the common element chosen is, ironically and metonymically, displaced from the apparent referent of the discourse in the first two lines—"walking stick," "obstacles," "I" or "me"—to a qualifier, "all." This is again characteristic of clinically schizophrenic language. Note how the psychotherapist's face in the above passage disintegrates into its component parts or qualities ungrounded by a substantive referent—that is, becomes unbounded by a transcendental signified—so that it becomes "unrecognizable." Compare Kafka: "Gregor was shocked to hear his own voice answering, unmistakably his own voice, true, but in which, as if from below, an insistent distressed chirping intruded, which left the clarity of the words intact only for a moment really, before so badly garbling them as they carried that no one could be sure if he had heard right" (Corngold trans., 5). Still, if Kafka's art is schizophrenia, it is *disciplined* schizophrenia. (For a clinical analysis of schizophrenic language, which predates the current structuralist and poststructuralist discussion on the subject but is nevertheless quite helpful, see Kasanin, ed., *Language and Thought in Schizophrenia*.)

It may well be that the traditional Hebrew sense of the uninterpretable is closest to Kafka's enigmatic power. "Our purification through the unknowable alters the domain of our awareness insofar as it alters our ontological capacity of knowing—together with the truth of the world around us, which is to be known," Rojtman concludes. "The unknowable is given as a sign of this possible mutation, awaiting man's will" (111). Yet Kafka's "schizophrenic" text subverts the will, as it does the reason, drawing the disintegrating consciousness away from the practical workaday world, away from teleology or eschatology or conscious purpose itself, and toward, to reiterate Corngold's phrase, "a consciousness devoid of all practical attention": "By an extreme effort of the will I managed to do a little housework or to make dinner," the schizophrenic account continues. "Most of the time, however, I remained sitting uncomfortably, my gaze lost in a drop of coffee fallen on the table" (*Autobiography*, 81). Analogously a good deal of the tragicomic power—and the Derridean play—of the *Metamorphosis* comes from Gregor's determination to go about his business in spite of his altered state. As when he discovers that he cannot control his legs, "if he finally succeeded in getting this leg to do what he wanted, all the others in the meantime, as if set free, began to work in the most intensely painful agitation," he says to himself, "'Just don't stay in bed being useless'" (Corngold trans., 7).

The *Ungeziefer* of the *Metamorphosis*, like the schizophrenic state and Derrida's metamorphosing term, has the productive power to construct or deconstruct the many "truths" derivable from multiple interpretive standpoints, held by sane and reasonable literary critics and historians, regarding the *Verwandlung*. Thus it is "monstrous" (*ungeheuer*) perhaps in quite the same way as Derrida arguably considers deconstruction to be monstrous. At the conclusion of "Structure, Sign and Play in the Discourse of the Human Sciences," he considers two "interpretations of interpretation," "the one [which] seeks to decipher, dreams of deciphering a truth or an origin which escapes play . . . the other . . . [which] affirms play and tries to pass beyond man and humanism, the name of man being the name of that being who, throughout the history of metaphysics or of ontotheology—in other words, throughout his entire history—has dreamed of full presence." Derrida argues that there is today no question of choosing between the two positions, because we are in the "region of historicity" where choice is trivial and because there is a prior task of conceiving "common ground, and the *différance* of this irreducible difference." Then he invokes a metaphor which, like Kafka's, suggests a transformation of metaphor itself:

> Here there is a kind of question, let us still call it historical, whose conception, formation, gestation, and labor we are only catching a glimpse of today. I employ these words, I admit, with a glance toward the operations of childbearing—but also with a glance toward those who, in a society from which I do not exclude myself, turn their eyes away when faced by the as yet unnameable which is proclaiming itself and which can do so, as is necessary whenever a birth is in the offing, only under the species of the nonspecies, in the formless, mute, infant, and terrifying form of monstrosity. (*Writing and Difference*, 292–293)

There is a parallel reference to monstrosity in *Of Grammatology*: "The future can only be anticipated in the form of an absolute danger. It is that which breaks absolutely with the constituted normality and can only be proclaimed, *presented*, as a sort of monstrosity" (5). (With regard to this quotation and the one cited in the text, Mark Poster, to whom we are indebted for these references, argues, "deconstruction, while not named as a monster, may be taken to be that which 'proclaims' the monstrous future" ["Derrida and Electronic Writing," 105]. For Derrida's use of the term "monstrosity" in a different sense, see Carroll, ed., "Some Statements" where, as Poster [170, n. 18] comments, "Derrida shifts the designation 'monster' to include totalizing positions. These are 'normal monstrosities,' as distinguished from 'monstrous monstrosities,' like deconstruction."

Is it not precisely this "formless, mute, infant, and terrifying form of monstrosity" with which Kafka presents the readers of the *Metamorphosis*? And is this not why Kafka's text has the power to produce "the challenge to literary history," which Corngold says, "occurs when a kind of difference is posited between style and referent that introduces a perpetual delay or deferral of any coincidence of textual understanding and historical moment" ("Literary History," 142–143)?

As his metamorphosis continues, Gregor's attempts at communication, like the schizophrenic's, become more unintelligible: "It was true that they no longer understood his words, though they had seemed clear enough to him, clearer than before, probably because he had grown accustomed to them," Kafka continues. "In order to make his voice as clear as possible for the crucial discussions that were approaching, he cleared his throat a little—taking pains, of course, to do so in a very muffled manner, since this noise, too, might sound different from human coughing, a thing he no longer trusted himself to decide" (Corngold trans., 13–14). Even Gregor's effort at clarity becomes—recursively, since the attempt to be clear is made by means of the same opaque voice that prompts the attempt—a new element in his transformation.

So, too, the efforts of literary critics and historians grappling with Kafka's text. Indeed Bateson has argued that it is precisely the inability to comment on his situation from a metalevel that is imposed on the schizophrenic by his or her family, thereby sealing the double-bind. It is arguable that, unlike the schizophrenic, Kafka has provided a new language that double binds the designations of literature, criticism, the "human" sciences, and the *Torah*—one uninterpretable by the doctors of various disciplines who have encircled Kafka's strange patient in order to stop his play—a new *sign* which is to interpretation what Derrida's *différance* is to philosophy and these words are, recursively, to this text: the end.

CHAPTER 4

Nietzsche at the Altar

Situating the Devotee

Not only is there no kingdom of *différance*, but *différance* instigates the subversion of every kingdom.

—Derrida, "*Différance*"

Prologue

NARRATOR (in peripatetic mode, a little paranoid about the possibility of being hit by a cabbage flying from the Pit):
To do something so peculiar as to place the greatest critic of Christianity at the altar, especially in the electronic age, may require some explanation. To write about a philosopher who rejected traditional philosophical style—argumentative exposition in expository prose—and the epistemology that goes with it in favor of a more aphoristic and staccato mode requires special consideration. How to "understand" a thinker who pointed out that "to understand" means "to stand under" and so to become a "subject," a stance this very "author" rejected? To write about an author who rejected "authority" as a species of "subjectivity" and so of slavery, or mastery, in a hierarchy of underlings and overlords, and in trying to "understand" "him" become "authors" ourselves, borders on the ludicrous—amusingly absurd, comical—requiring the power of play. We have decided, therefore, to be serious only when necessary to keep our textual "play" centered enough to be "understood" by the sane: a questionable act in itself, given the fact that Nietzsche's preferred persona seemed to be that of a madman whose

language was not particularly ego or otherwise "centric." "Our" rhetorical strategies ("we" are becoming a little schizoid in honor of our mad teacher) thus include both traditional "exposition" ("laying out," as when one reveals one's hand in poker, a metonym for the five cards one masks from others) and "play." Our play includes Nietzsche, of course, and some of his recent friends, including ourselves, all chatting about some of the more irksome qualities of Western civilization, epitomized by Christianity and its devotees. Because "we" are part of our own play, the ensuing drama is inevitably *recursive*—rewriting itself like those M.C. Escher hands—but so is that Nietzschean historical milieu in which we currently live: the postmodern-ecological condition. So, please bear with us.

Traditional academic discourse requires a subject in more ways than one. The Latin roots *sub* plus *iectum* (past participle of *iacere*), hence *subicere*—literally "cast under"— suggest the subject's function. Initially, it seems the discourse must be "about" something, have a theme, which presumably is the underlying substance or substratum, for Aristotle *hupo-keimenon* (literally "an underlying thing"), which serves as the logical "basis" upon which or the "center" around which various other ideas may be predicated. Nietzsche, whose writings on religion are the principal "subject" of this text, was a critical traditionalist, a classicist, who well understood Aristotle's need to write in terms of clear subjects that were ultimately grounded in "substances" (things) or the metaphysical referents of substantival terms that possess qualities just as linguistic subjects possess predicates:

> The origin of "things" is wholly the work of that which imagines, thinks, wills, feels. The concept of "thing" itself just as much as all its qualities.—Even "the subject" is such a created entity, a "thing" like all others: a simplification with the object of defining the force which posits, invents, thinks, as distinct from all individual positing, inventing, thinking as such. (*Will to Power*, sec. 556)

He also resisted a discourse so grounded, preferring to reject a univocal style grounded in a unitary subject in favor of a polyvocal one with constantly shifting subject "matter" as well as a constantly shifting authorial subject. He apparently wrote in this way because he thought that style implied a metaphysic and an epistemology—a theory of reality and of knowledge—and he did not like the Western episteme (picture a bust of Aristotle) or its underpinnings (its pedestal). So, to the best of his ability, he shattered it, writing in an unorthodox style to which academics typically have to attribute a subject, not to mention an author, in order to "understand" it—subject it to their own modes of discourse.

This appropriation of Nietzsche's writings to traditional Western style, however, ends up making Nietzsche a "subject" of the king of the Academy, Aristotle, whom Nietzsche, the ever-inventive class clown, was inclined to bombard with bubbles, little aphoristic exploding bubbles, like viruses, to bring down the information edifice of Apollonian learning. If Aristotle were head of FBI, he would probably view Nietzsche as the Polybomber.

So, how to write in the spirit of Nietzsche, to invoke that recalcitrant shade in the mode of information, offer him a modem as a sling, and let him cast stones at the strange new Christian Goliath—a.k.a. Jesse, Jimmie, Pat, Newt—that has supplanted what Nietzsche would think of as the genuine evangel (who had the guts both to claim he was god and to act like it) with an evangelical capitalist overlord who lives not in heaven but in electronic space? We have tried bundling up little power-packets of our mentor, along with some spitballs from some of his recent historical friends (Bataille, Bateson, Cixous, et al.), and hurling them at the digital statues of power that stand at the intersection of Christianity and capitalism in neoimperial America. We are riding in a New Automodem, soon to replace older forms of transportation and prefigured by Darryl Louise's (DL's) car in *Vineland*, "a black '84 Trans-Am with extra fairings, side pipes, scoops, and coves not on the standard model, plus awesomely important pinstriping by the legendary Ramón La Habra in several motifs, including explosions and serpents" (Pynchon, 105), in which we have been cruising the ruined cities of late modernity, wandering through the strip malls, looking for event-scenes (reported by Kroker's Canadian Gang), and tossing explosive bubbles, as we head for a Nine Inch Nails concert. Accompanied by this estranged yet critically engaged collection of personae—Nietzsche and his friends, our *thought gang*, if we may steal the tag from Tibor Fischer's recent novel parked on our shelves—we find ourselves on a new road.

The mode of information (Poster 1990), already an emerging super highway leading to one more utopia, the electropolis just beyond the millennium, provides a main artery from which the contours of our text may be drawn. We understand "information" not in the usual sense, as a noun referring to the digital "bits," the Boolean shifters, zero and one, out of which logical syntax and, hence, subjects and predicates and deductions (the purest form of argument) may be constructed. Instead, we understand *in-formation* as a verbal noun (a gerund, like *différend*) depicting a process.

The English term "form" has been widely used to represent the Greek term *idea*, used by Plato and Aristotle in reference to the fundamental metaphysical principles that organize the world of "nature." Boethius translated Aristotle's *idea* as *species*, utilizing a Latin term that would stick with the Western tradition down through Darwin and even into the present. But if "information" is understood as having verbal force, then it becomes not a "thing" to be explained or quantified—"How is it that we have a certain range of 'species' making up the biosphere and how many of them in what quantities constitute its biomass?"—but rather a process of production of forms: differentiation, morphogenesis. In this sense information becomes isomorphic (insofar as this is possible) with Bateson's definition of idea (or *idea*) as a "difference which makes a difference" and Derrida's *différance*— "the name we might give to the 'active,' moving discord of different forces, and of differences of forces, that Nietzsche sets up against the entire system of metaphysical grammar, wherever this system governs culture, philosophy, and science" (*"Différance,"* 18). Information taken in this sense becomes the basis of an *infodynamics* (Salthe 1993), which does not rely on "subjects" or "substances" independent of the discourse-productive processes of evolution: the play of *différance*.

Our argument, in a nutshell (that infinite space over which Hamlet would have been king if it were not for those embarrassing bubbles of primary process, his dreams—*Hamlet*, II, ii), is that the works of Nietzsche, Bateson, Cixous, Bataille, and others provide a cross-disciplinary language that may provide, upon analysis, a "substantive" (apologies to Nietzsche's critique of our faith in grammar) strategy for cultural politics: critically to situate and creatively to rewrite the combination of Christian devotionalism and capitalism with science that characterizes modernity. An especially formidable dimension of the opposition is in the metaphysics and epistemology of what Salthe calls Baconian/Cartesian/Newtonian/Darwinian/ Comtean (BCNDC) science, which is central to devotional scientism. This Christian-capitalist-industrialist creed is situated within the technological-historical architecture of what Mumford called the Pentagon of Power. Mumford's Pentagon, like Foucault's Panopticon, is a metaphor for the imposition of the BCNDC creed via technology on the biosphere, enveloping cultures and other life forms as surely and confidently, with as much moral reflection by court philosophers and poets laureate, as Disney devouring ABC. To engage this monolith, NBCBN writers (picture Bateson, Cixous, and Bataille surrounded by Nietzsche) agree, is vital to the what Mumford called the conduct of life.

NBCBN criticism is defined both by what it engages—the forms of what Mumford called sun worship in the temples of advanced technocracy—and the kinds of rewriting it suggests. Just as NBCBN critique encircles the Pentagon with incantations—wafting little explosive bubbles that drive the generals (all played by George C. Scott) ripping mad, and the presidents (all played by Peter Sellars) to the hot line. (That famous phone is now, by the way, connected to the control center at Epcot in the tourist mecca of America, Disney, that projection of the neoimperial imaginary, where all of the presidents gather their virtual presences to plan the takeovers not only of NBCBN but also, if *they* [in Pynchon's paranoid sense] haven't already, Washington.) So NBCBN discourse is identifiable by the style of its rewriting: recursively ecological.

In the ecological writing of our NBCBN colleagues, polyform, heterogeneous, metaphoric, metonymic strands of discourse intertwine in a mindful web of *in-formation* that envelops the Disney-Pentagon; it wraps the generals in silk strands, jangling their medals and their jewels, tickling their skin, provoking, for a moment even here, spontaneous laughter. In what Mumford called, in his last section of *The Pentagon of Power*, "The Flowering of Plants and Men," this biomorphic diversity provides a living matrix out of which even the reductive strategies, the monological discourses of "normal" subjects, are drawn, like cups of water from a bottomless well; it is the language potential of what Bateson calls the ecological mind. Its authorship produces not only flowers and trees but language-using organisms, self-designating—*recursive*—personae called "human beings." NBCBN writers respect the diversity out of which their ideas grow and to which they contribute; they do not mind sharing authorship with the biosphere. NBCBN writers agree, moreover, that there is a central illusion of modernity: the subject, heir of the Christian soul turned entrepreneur, conceived as a metaphysical entity who seeks "control" over a world of objects. This subject is "transcendent" because it is not (so its practitioners believe) recursively constructed out of a set of communicative life practices—language, kinesics, paralinguistics, play, mime, metonymy, metaphor. Foucault saw this *imago*, what Lacan posited as the "self-image" in the *Stade du Miroir* ("Mirror Stage"), as typifying all those subjects who were subject to, subjected by, modernity since the Enlightenment.

NBCBN criticism and theory therefore require, as an alternative, an infodynamic idea of the "subject," in all senses of this term: a "human being" constructed out of the multilevel dynamics of play: a mask that may be worn, like your Narrator's wizard hat, only with the knowledge that it is, after all, an artifact, so that we become, as Haraway says, "cyborgs" (as opposed to, say, robots), the living artifice of the ecological mind. Hence the hilarity with which Nietzsche views the legions of the serious—those penta-goners, the living dead—who make up what he thinks of as the "herds" of modernity. These are the ones who, like Pynchon's Thanatoids (*Vineland*, 170ff.), have watched too much Disney on ABC (or vice versa, we anticipate future history here) and have come to believe that the Mouseketeers—like the ones in *Vogue, Cosmopolitan, Gentlemen's Quarterly*, and the glossy rock idols of *Spin*, not to mention (for traditionalists) Castiglione's *The Courtier*—are themselves. Laughter, we conclude, provides a dynamical structure analogous with *différance* that breaks out of the traps of metaphysics, disciplinary reason, and imposed personae, opening the possibility of *jouissance* as cultural practice (White and Hellerich 1994).

In a smaller nutshell: postmodern-ecological (NBCBN) discourse provides a critical/creative alternative to its modern (BCNDC) predecessor. The alternative utilizes the polysemic strategies of play, metaphor, and metonym to construct a semeiotic technology that envelops and (we hope) transforms the monological Pentagon of Power that characterizes modern discourse: the language of the dead. By situating the infodynamic production of form—*différance*, "the difference which makes a difference"— at the interface of entropy and information, the alternative creates a living simulacrum of evolutionary ecology: the language of the living. The alternative, moreover, is sufficiently powerful (in Nietzschean terms) to construct not only sciences, information technologies, literatures, and the like, but also authors and characters, self-images, personae, including "man" and "god." Nietzsche's critique of religion in general and Christianity in particular opens the way toward a new Zen of cultural practice in which these characters, including "self" and "god," become the poetic constructs of writers—"you" and "me"—whose religious sensibility is best expressed by laughter (White 1998).

Being members of a thought gang—taking a critical-theoretical position—in a world circumscribed by messianic entrepreneurs and collapsing ecosystems leaves us, as the sight of a peasant woman scrambling to collect feces dropped from his aristocratic elephant did Aldous Huxley, feeling, in spite of the consolations of philosophy, a bit pensive. Nevertheless, as was Aldous, we are not too glum for laughter at our collective condition, even if "we"—increasingly the "middle" and "working" classes of what Jencks calls the new "cognitariat" and Coupland, perhaps even more appropriately, calls Microserfs—are increasingly the ones scrambling to pick up the manure. This is our materialist interpretation of "trickle down" economics. It is not so amusing, however, when you are the one scrambling and not riding on high. Academics have more or less been on the elephant for some time, but with the pervasive migrant worker (adjunct) economy emerging in academe, the cognitariat and the proletariat increasingly have a lot to share. It is this materialist political stance in the mode of information—call it a Nietzschean-Marxian inclination to "talk back," especially via electronic media, to power—combined with the infodynamic confluence of arts and sciences in interdisciplinary critical theory—call it *recursive epistemology* (Harries-Jones 1995)—that animates our work. Now, meet some members of the gang.

Bataille, the great Nietzschean erotic-demonic rebel, offers a reading of his mentor that aptly engages the merger of Christianism, capitalism, and statism—the Pentagon in its various forms with all its religious significance—that has contributed so much to the blood feast of modern history. Bataille commented appropriately, as he wrote his preface to *On Nietzsche* in 1944, "*Gestapo* practices now coming to light show how deep the affinities are that unite the underworld and the police. It is people who hold nothing sacred who're the ones most likely to torture people and cruelly carry out the orders of a coercive apparatus." Bataille is speaking about "run of the mill doctrines" of anarchy "apologizing for those commonly taken to be criminals" (xxv). This kind of "anarchy" is best represented, ironically, by the devotees who take food from the school-children of "others" (especially people of color), and wave their yellow ribbons during the National Anthem under God while the bombs fall on "other" children abroad, all the while vehemently proclaiming that they are prolife: for these folks, only self-aggrandizement is sacred. Bataille's analysis of the reduction of religious ideas, supposedly transcendental and therefore beyond appropriation for human purposes, to the very temporal goals that they are supposed to transcend, clearly indicates what has happened in the religions of modernity: the quite temporal and material objectives of wealth and power become deified by hoards of believers who imagine that Jesus actually wants them to make money and launch F15s against the enemies of "our" oil—the "Bombs and Jesus crowd," as Hunter Thompson calls them—and so feel sanctified in the pursuit of profit and military hegemony. This is the most vocal and disturbing strain of Americanism—gleefully resounding in Congress these days—the criticism of, let alone the resistance to, which is branded as demonic. Bataille nicely situates this mythos, revealing its operative logic—its stage mechanics—and so the self-serving idolatry that generally passes nowadays for religion in "America."

Unfortunately for all of us, these personae are them-selves, identities mass produced and distributed from the Magic Kingdom in consultation with the command and control network linking Epcot, Washington, and Madison Avenue. Are you one of them? Are we? The result is a pervasive cultural coding that inscribes the monologic of subjectivity and correlative objectivity on a population who are increasingly programmed to be Mouseketeers, to wear yellow and cheer and sing songs of Christian devotion as the bombs fall on the Iraqis; or for that matter, since academics wore a lot of yellow during that TV series, too, to turn out academic papers on, and by, the usual subjects insuring the trivialization of the American "intellect."

Trivia, of course, brings up the function of modern academic research within the Pentagon, a point that Bateson—another member of our gang—makes at length in "The Science of Mind and Order" (*Steps*, xvii–xxvi), a key work in the NBCBN corpus. He argues that any discourse not cognizant of the axial difference between entropy and information and their associated fundamentals—namely, the BCNDC creed—can tell us little about the evolution of our world or the niches of various communities, social or biotic, within it: hence it is trivial (cf. Salthe 1993, Chapter 1). In contrast, it is precisely at the meeting of these two realms—at the difference which makes a difference—that the strategies of life are formed and the significance of signification is created. This interface of entropy and information is none other than the *différend*—the productive disagreement between Dionysus and Apollo that Nietzsche saw animating Hellenic civilization.

Cixous, in whom we see an uncanny resemblance to that radical gangstress of comic book and recent film, Tank Girl, appears here interposed first amidst the text of Derrida contemplating Nietzsche on women (*Spurs: Nietzsche's Styles*), as the cybernaut who steers the ship of *l'écriture féminine* on a differential course, riding the whirlpool that forms at the interface of entropy and information, Dionysus and Apollo. Here, where we would situate the *différend*, is the meeting place of what Bateson called, following the Gnostic Jung, *pleroma* and *creatura*: "The pleroma is the world in which events are caused by forces and impacts and in which there are no 'distinctions.' Or, as I would say, no 'differences.' In the creatura, effects are brought about precisely by difference" (*Steps*, 462–463;

also see Hoeller 1985, Chapter 2). In theological terms, we suggest that pleroma and creatura are analogous to what Otto called *numina* and *phenomena*: the numinous being the mysterious realm of the "holy" about which "we" can only surmise. "We can study and describe the pleroma, but always the distinctions which we draw are attributed *by us* to the pleroma" (462). The play of discourse is phenomenal, discursive, yet its force, its power, is numinous. It is precisely the role of the *daimon*—mind, as in Maxwell's demon—to produce the differences that constitute living forms. Here we would situate Bateson's ecological idea and Derrida's *différence*": "'Older' than Being itself, such *différance* has no name in our language. . . . Thus unnameable is not an ineffable Being which no name could approach: God, for example. This unnameable is the play which makes possible nominal effects, the relatively unitary and atomic structures that are called names, the chains of substitutions of names in which, for example, the nominal effect *différance* is itself *enmeshed*, carried off, reinscribed, just as a false entry or a false exit is still part of the game, a function of the system" (Derrida, *"Différance,"* 27). Cixous' writing and the *daimonic* sorceresses and hysterics that inhabit it, we suggest, are the embodiment of this demon of difference, which the priests and psychiatrists have long tried to exorcise. Characterized by her mad laughter, she is the template for the cybernetic creatura envisioned by Haraway as for the emergence of new natural-cultural formations—metaphors—in terms of which the dance of life—the tarantella—can be articulated.

We situate the Nietzschean post devotee right here, at the whirling interface of pleroma and creatura where Cixous sails: not the course of God but, rather, of the *différend* out of which gods are created. We situate the Christian capitalist devotee, in the spirit of Reagan and Bush and their heirs, in a box seat on the 50 yard line at the Super Bowl.

Returning to nutshells, a narrator friend of ours, attributed to an "author" named Conrad and a text called *Heart of Darkness*, but seemingly with a life of his own, once remarked about a yarn spinner, Marlow, situated on the moonlit deck of a sailing ship bound for Africa, on the Thames:

> The yarns of seamen have a direct simplicity, the whole meaning of which lies within the shell of a cracked nut. But Marlow was not typical (if his propensity to spin yarns be excepted), and to him the meaning of an episode was not inside like a kernel but outside, enveloping the tale which brought it out only as a glow

brings out haze, in the likeness of one of these misty halos that
sometimes are made visible by the spectral illumination of moon-
shine. (Conrad 1989, 19–20)

So we situate ourselves, your Narrator, and our argument amidst the
spectral illumination of our characters, not presuming to "subject" them to
our theories but to let them speak interposed with our own pronouncements. Hence, now, a polymetaphorical dialogue among our hero-heroines
of discourse, who all have appeared, situated miraculously in various forms,
with yours truly, amidst the riotous set of a Nine Inch Nails concert, during
the Gulf War: a perfect setting for the emergence of Nietzsche's favorite
character.

Event-Scene I:
The Situation: A Rock Concert

Electric Dionysian Theater: God comes back to split the Mountain of
Olives on CNN: Nine Inch Nails emerge. Filmic time-lapse images,
projected on skeins enveloping the band, of a rabbit decomposing, of
nuclear explosions and the atomic wind, of corpses hanging by the neck,
frozen in the Bosnian winter, of the growth of stems and leaves and the
turning spirals of the jet stream, metamorphoses of global and microscopic
dimensions, the dance of life and death. "If i could kill you and me i
would," lead singer and writer, Trent Reznor, intones: "the pigs have won
tonight / now they can all sleep soundly / and everything's all right." The
skeins fade to reveal the asymmetrical architecture, the broken, bombed
skyline, of the set, band members perched here and there among vaguely
suggested, jagged rooftops, and columns standing at crazy angles to form a
fractured cityscape both ancient and modern, under ghostly images of light
on fine netting, like the skein of stars that envelops human conduct in
Aeschylus' Oresteia. In the Pit, reveling fans form a living social body,
human waves pulsing phosphorescent across its surface toward the
thundering stage. Suddenly, a specter from the electromagnetic spectrum
appears on stage left, a philosopher sculpted from light:

NIETZSCHE (speaking out of memory, in a resounding voice):
  The Madman: **Have you not heard of that madman who lit a
  lantern in the bright morning hours, ran to the market place, and
  cried incessantly, "I seek God! I seek God!" As many of those who
  do not believe in God were standing around just then, he provoked**

much laughter. Why, did he get lost? said one. Did he lose his way like a child? said another. Or is he hiding? Is he afraid of us? Has he gone on a voyage? or emigrated? Thus they yelled and laughed. The madman jumped into their midst and pierced them with his glances.

"Whither is God?" he cried. "I shall tell you. *We have killed him— you and I.* All of us are his murderers. . . . Who will wipe this blood off us? What water is there for us to clean ourselves? What festivals of atonement, what sacred games shall we have to invent? Is not the greatness of this deed too great for us? Must not we ourselves become gods simply to seem worthy of it? There has never been a greater deed; and whoever will be born after us—for the sake of this deed he will be part of a higher history hitherto."

. . . It has been related further that on that same day the madman entered diverse churches and there sang his *requiem aeternam deo*. Let out and called to account, he is said to have replied each time, "What are these churches now if they are not the tombs and sepulchers of God?" (*Gay Science*, sec. 125)

NARRATOR (who appears to be a Nietzsche fan, and whose wizard hat now glows):

In this famous passage from Nietzsche's later writings, striking images confront us, biblical in tone, apocalyptic in perspective, yet iconoclastic in effect: a madman lighting a lantern in the bright morning to proclaim the death of God, his accusation that *we* have killed Him, his conjuring of blood rite, baptism, religious festival, his challenge to us to *become gods* in compensation, his vision of churches as "sepulchers of God," darkly alluding to and transforming the Gospel story of the empty tomb from which Christ has risen into a parable about our own reawakening as divinities trapped within the tomb of Christendom. This emergence from the grave brings the devotees into a new, "higher history," one not circumscribed by the master narrative of Christian eschatology, with beginning middle and end like a good tragedy. Rather, the new history is to be radical, without a metaphysics, without a transcendental *aeternitas* to provide the reference point against which to measure time and change. This is to be a history of *immanent activity*, not transcendent verities, a cultural mode whose signs and symbols, whose semeiosis, is generated not from a transcendental signifier or signified, in Saussure's terms, but from *communicative practices*, the self-writing of a new generation of *Übermenschen* and *Übermädchen* (the latter to write a higher "Herstory") who are not so much "atheists" as the old god reincarnated and pluralized in a diversity of new personae, heralding a new religion of the living instead of, as Nietzsche would say, the traditional worship of the dead.

In this regard Nietzsche has turned religion back into theater, or theater into a religion, in which the mask, the constructed persona, is the only persona, in which the theoretical pose, the transcendent gaze, of the philosophical critic too becomes revealed as a mask through the genealogy of criticism, so that both the ultimate Substratum, God, and the human subject who would worship or know Him, become no more than actors on the stage of Europe, the realization of which makes it closing time for the West: the grand play, the force of which required the suspension of disbelief by the audience, is now revealed as a farce with pretence to tragedy, revealed by Nietzsche just as the Wizard of Oz is sniffed out from behind his curtain by Toto.

Yet where could this possibly leave audience and actors who have apparently transcended the play of their civilization, only to find themselves still in the mood for self-transformation? Is there any show left after Nietzsche's madman steals the stage? Has the "self-overcoming" that, as Charles E. Scott says, "defines the movement of the ascetic ideal as well as the movement of Nietzsche's genealogical account of that ideal," an overcoming that "is primarily not a theory but a discursive movement that he identifies in Western thought and practice as well as in his own writing," rendered former devotees of the narrative mere phantoms, as their lack of substance would suggest? Does Nietzsche's writing, as well as the culture it genealogically deconstructs, finally become "a mask of appearance without reality, a movement that we undergo as we follow his discourse" (226)? What is left amidst the ruins of the civilization that has killed its own ideal, its God? Is it "the omnipresence of power," as Foucault has it, "not because it has the privilege of consolidating everything under its invincible unity, but because it is produced from one moment to the next, at every point, or rather in every relation from one point to another" (*History of Sexuality*, I, 93)? Are we then left with a world in which "politics is war pursued by other means," or at least in which a "multiplicity of force relations can be coded—in part but never totally—either in the form of 'war' or the form of 'politics,' . . . a strategic model, rather than a model based on law" (93, 102)? Yet for Nietzsche, as for Foucault, the ultimate aesthetic of power is not one of war but, we think, of love, not the Platonic-Apollonian variety—the love of death,"the separation of the soul from the body," as Socrates in the *Phaedo* (64C4–5) defines both the terminus of the philosophical quest and the act of dying—but rather the joyous awakening of soul and body fused in the act of living-as-creating: Dionysian ecstasy.

DELEUZE (breaking in):

> Will to power does not mean that the will wants power. Will to power does not imply any anthropomorphism in its origin, signification of essence. Will to power must be interpreted in a completely different way: power is *the one that* wills in the will. Power is the genetic and differential element in the will. This is why the will is essentially creative. (1983, 85)

NARRATOR (trying again):

In Bateson's terms, Nietzschean will is thus "the difference which makes a difference" that proliferates into the mindful patterns of the living world (*Steps*, 272, 381ff.); in Derrida's it is *différance*, the generative power producing the differentiation of discourse per se. Will to power, "difference which makes a difference," *différence*: at the convergence of these ideas lies a new joyous science, and what we shall call the philosophy of laughter. Yet joyous knowledge is heretical, both to the orthodoxy of "modern" science and to its traditional antagonist, the Christian establishment. Could these two team up to form a new "Inquisition of Blue Meanies," as the forces of enforced Platonism are called in the Beatle film *Yellow Submarine*, whose heaven looks suspiciously like Disney World and whose hell is Baghdad?

Thus that practitioner of joy, Foucault (arising like a specter from the underworld below the stage), poses a counterpractice to the Christian worship of death stemming from the Socratic separation of the soul from the body, as well as to the "ruses" of repressive desublimation in a consumer economy of control through sexuality:

> We are often reminded of the countless procedures which Christianity once employed to make us detest the body; but let us ponder all the ruses that were employed for centuries to make us love sex, to make the knowledge of it desirable and everything said about it precious. Moreover, we need to consider the possibility that one day, perhaps, in a different economy of bodies and pleasures, people will no longer quite understand how the ruses of sexuality, and the power that sustains its organization, were able to subject us to that austere monarchy of sex, so that we became dedicated to the endless talk of forcing its secret, of extracting the truest confessions from a shadow. (*History of Sexuality*, 159).

It is between the fanged Scylla of Christian asceticism and the swirling Charybdis of commoditized desire that a Nietzschean *fröhliche Wissenschaft* must steer, and the *kybernetes* ("steersperson," "cybernaut") best able to steer her ship through that chasm is Dionysus:

NIETZSCHE (wearing a cross in his ear, just like one historic version of Madonna):

> In contrast to the Pauline crucified Jesus, who exalts death over life—who is close, but not identical, to the Jesus who wanted life without facing death—Dionysus confronts death, certain of the over-fullness of life and his own recreative power. "The desire for destruction, change, becoming, can be the expression of an over-full power pregnant with the future (my term for this, as is known, is 'Dionysian')." [*Will to Power*, sec. 846] (Valadier 1985, 250).

NARRATOR (recalling a memorable bout of shopping):

The worship of death, disguised as the otherworldly kingdom in Christianity, has been transformed in the capitalist modern era into the pursuit of deferred gratification, the Foucauldian economy of sexuality, through the fetishization of commodities, the church of the consumers, as we have described it in "Nietzsche at the Mall" (Chapter 1). For, as Max Weber astutely observed in *The Protestant Ethic and the Spirit of Capitalism*, the Protestant work ethic that supplied the basic norms for European capitalist culture was a materialized version of the old medieval quest for salvation. The new ethic became "God helps those who help themselves," meaning, in effect, that those who work hard and save will eventually achieve the kingdom, not of the old transcendental heaven above but rather of a materially abundant future attainable through progress. With the advent of consumer capitalism in the twentieth century, the work ethic became conjoined with what might be described as the "pleasure ethic," the virtually religious pursuit of commodities by nearly everybody. Thus the old monotheistic god is made imminently available in the myriad forms of concretized desire that make up the idols—the brands and shapely surfaces—of the marketplace. Or, as the Westminster Shorter Catechism says, "Man's chief end is to glorify God and enjoy him forever" (cited in Fullerton 1959, 11).

KRISTEVA (wanders out of an huge digital mirror rolled onstage, dragging along Benveniste as Pozzo drags Lucky in Beckett's *Godot*):

> After reviewing the various etymological interpretations, he [Benveniste] argues that from the beginning *credo/sraddha* had both a *religious* meaning and an *economic* meaning: the word denotes an "act of confidence implying restitution," and "to pledge something on faith in the certainty that it will be returned," religiously and economically.

Thus the correspondence between *credence* and *credit* is one of 'the oldest in the Indo-European vocabulary.'"(Kristeva 1987, 30)

NARRATOR (after a commercial break, rejoins):

It is in the context of late-nineteenth-century capitalism and industrialism that Nietzsche wrote his famous madman passage, and it seems clear now that he was more *describing* the actual religion of Europe than attacking traditional theology (which he, of course, does elsewhere). He is certainly shattering the illusion of transcendental spirituality that still functions as an ideological justification of capitalist culture: those who are wealthy are so because God has smiled on them for their hard work, and the poor are being punished for their laziness, a sentiment worthy of Ronald Reagan or of his devotee, Pat Buchanan. At the same time, however, he is challenging the devotees of power and progress, and the church of the consumer that would emerge from their faith, to offer an alternative to their alienated idolatry.

BATAILLE (enters from the same substage sepulchre as Foucault, humming Nine Inch Nails' "Closer," in French; erotic dancing breaks out, along with an extraordinary laser light show, in the audience, which appears in the ghostly light of the beams and skeins, as a complex web of reveling shadows, like so many organelles pulsing to the musical heartbeat; he begins by citing Nietzsche): "The majority of people are a fragmentary, exclusive image of what humanity is; you have to add them up to get humanity. In this sense, whole eras and whole peoples have something fragmentary about them." But what does that fragmentation mean? Or better, what causes it if not a need to *act* that specializes us and limits us to the horizon of a particular activity? . . . Whoever acts, substitutes a particular end for what he or she is, as a total being: in the least specialized cases it is glory of the state or the triumph of a party. Every action specializes insofar as it is limited as action. A plant usually doesn't act, and isn't specialized; it's specialized when gobbling up flies! (*On Nietzsche*, xxi–xxii).

BATESON (appearing instantly projected on a stage skein by the NIN laser light apparatus, raising a Lucky Strike, interjects):

Consciousness operates in the same way as medicine in its sampling of the events and processes of the body and of what goes on in the total mind. It is organized in terms of purpose. It is a short-cut device to enable you to get quickly at what you want; not to act with maximum wisdom in order to live, but to follow the shortest logical and causal path to get what you next want, which may be dinner; it may be a

Beethoven sonata; it may be sex. Above all, it may be money or power. (*Steps*, 440)

NARRATOR (offering him a light): So the operation of what you call "conscious purpose" is akin to the machinations of instrumentalism whose grammar depends on the bifurcation of subjects and objects: the self, the subject, delineating objects it desires and appropriating—making use of—them technologically to achieve its end?

BATAILLE (thumbing a copy of Richard Klein's *Cigarettes Are Sublime*):

The fragmentary state of humanity is basically the same as the choice of an object. . . . Each of your moments becomes *useful*. With each moment, the possibility is given you to advance to some chosen goal, and your time becomes a march toward that goal—what's normally called living. Similarly, if salvation is the goal. Every action makes you a fragmentary existence. (*On Nietzsche*, xxvii)

BATESON (ruminating on Adam and Eve's discovery of conscious purpose—the linear logic of objectification—and its ecological consequences):

Adam and Eve then became almost drunk with excitement. *This* was the way to do things. Make a plan, ABC and you get D.

They then began to specialize in doing things the planned way. In effect, they cast out from the Garden the concept of their own total systemic nature and of its total systemic nature.

After they had cast God out of the Garden, they really went to work on this purposive business, and pretty soon the topsoil disappeared. (*Steps*, 441) (He stops to take a drag on his Lucky.)

BATAILLE (aside, to Bateson, "Could I have one of those?"):

The use of the word God is deceptive therefore; it results in the distortion of its object, of the sovereign Being, between the sovereignty of an ultimate end, implied in the movement of language, and the servitude of means, on which it is based (*this* is defined as serving *that*, and so on . . .). God, the *end* of things, is caught up in the game that makes each thing the means of another. In other words, God, named as the end, becomes a thing insofar as he is named, a thing, put on the plane with all things. (*The Accursed Share*, III, 382–383)

BATESON (laconically):

Be that as it may. Adam went on pursuing his purposes and finally invented the free-enterprise system. Eve was not, for a long time, allowed to participate in this because she was a woman. But she joined a bridge club and there found an outlet for her hate. (*Steps*, 442)

NARRATOR (intoning chorally): Amen.

Event-Scene II: Situation: War Rages

A neon sign blinks on and off at the rear of the stage, signaling the band's return after a break:

The Neocapitalist Imagology of the Sacred

or

Bush Does Baghdad: The TV Mini-Series

TAYLOR AND SAARINEN (sound biting their way out of a bubble):
Media philosophy rejects analytics in favor of communication. Explosive, outrageous communication is the lifeblood of hope in the world of simulacra, bureaucracy and collapsing ecosystems. (*Imagologies*, 9)

NIETZSCHE (glowing demonic red as he prepares his anti-sermon):
I *condemn* Christianity. I raise against the Christian church the most terrible of all accusations that any accuser ever uttered. It is to me the highest of all corruptions. . . . To *abolish* any stress ran counter to its deepest advantages: it lived on distress, it *created* distress to eternalize *itself*.

Parasitism is the *only* practice of the church; with its ideal of anemia, of "holiness," draining all blood, all love, all hope for life; the beyond as the will to negate every reality; the cross as the mark of recognition for the most subterranean conspiracy that ever existed—against health, beauty, whatever has turned out well, courage, spirit, *graciousness* of the soul, *against life itself*. (*The Antichrist*, sec. 62)

ALSO SPRACH REZNOR (apparently regarding his uncle, Sam):
he sewed his eyes shut because he is afraid to see
he tries to tell me what i put inside of me
he has the answers to ease my curiosity
he dreamed a god up and called it christianity
your god is dead and no one cares
if there is a hell i'll see you there
he flexed his muscles to keep his flock of sheep in line
he made a virus that would kill off all the swine
his perfect kingdom of killing, suffering and pain
demands devotion atrocities done in his name . . .
"heresy"—Nine Inch Nails, *The Downward Spiral*

NARRATOR (feeling uneasily like an academic sheep on the way to the slaughter):

The images of Christian sanctimoniousness, conjoined with those of capitalism, technological power, and American beneficence, abound in the United States today and do a great deal to shape the imaginations of the public. The more subtle consumer iconography of the mall we have already described, but the explicit imagery of fundamentalist Christianity is worth focusing on, for it is the bastion of perhaps the chief antagonist to creating a culture devoted to life—"conservatism"—the euphemism used to describe the radical brand of corporate empowerment and public impoverishment that is now avidly sweeping the people of the United States into that bin of victims and exploitees called the Third World. The spirit of what Nietzsche would see as the religion of death is nowhere more apparent than in George Bush's historic orchestration of Christian devotion in support of the TV opera, "The Gulf War," aptly described by Baudrillard as "pornographic" in a *Der Spiegel* interview.

KELLNER (is led in—in chains—by the Texas Rangers, since he has been associated with a drunken Frenchman speeding through the tumbleweeds and making dubious pronouncements about their beloved America, even as Kellner protests that he is mostly a critic of the mad Frenchman, this distinction being lost on the Rangers, who, in the meantime, are suspiciously eying the book, *The Persian Gulf TV War*, which is almost mistaken for a special issue of *TV Guide*, when Kellner begins to read aloud):

> A minister appearing on CNN's Sonia Frieman show after the war on March 1 [1991] properly said that it was literally blasphemous for Bush to invoke the name of God in favor of his murderous war policies. But Bush continued to play the war and religion theme, telling the annual gathering of the Southern Baptist Convention on June 6, 1991, that he recalled praying at Camp David before ordering the start of the Gulf war. According to the *New York Times* (June 7, 1991), Bush wiped tears away from his eyes as he described praying before ordering the bombing that began the war against Iraq and the 23,000 delegates roared their approval, stood up and shouted "Amen!" Bush was on a political trip, trying to cement alliances with "conservative, church-oriented Republicans whom he and his advisers see as crucial to his political strength" [*NYT* A7] (Kellner 1992, 279–280, n. 15)

NARRATOR (trying not to make *all* Christians feel like Unabombers):
Clearly, not all Christians are worshipers of death, as Nietzsche's analysis of the evangel indicates. But the virulent American strain of "conservative church-oriented Republicans" clearly find the death, at least of officially demonized "others," quite appealing. Thus Kellner also details the imago-

logical demonization of Saddam Hussein, as part of Bush's sanctimonious warmongering, with the full compliance by major media whose function Chomsky appropriately describes in his title, *Manufacturing Consent*.

KELLNER (reads on, in spite of the fact that a burly Ranger from Waco is approaching him with a roll of tape):

> From the outset of the crisis in the Gulf,, the media employed the frame of popular culture that portrays conflict as a battle between good and evil. Saddam Hussein quickly became the villain in this scenario with the media vilifying the Iraqi leader as a madman, a Hitler, while whipping up anti-Iraqi war fever. Saddam was described by Mary McGrory as a "beast" (*Washington Post*, Aug. 7, 1990) and as a "monster" that "Bush may have to destroy" (*Newsweek*, Oct. 20, 1990, and Sept. 3, 1990). George Will called Saddam "more virulent" than Mussolini and then increased Hussein's evil by using the Saddam-as-Hitler metaphor in his syndicated columns. *New York Times* editorialist A. M. Rosenthal attacked Hussein as "barbarous" and "an evil dreamer of death" (Aug. 9, 1990). . . . *The New Republic* doctored a *Time* magazine cover photo on Saddam to make him appear more like Hitler. . . . Saddam's negative image was forged by a combination of rhetoric, popular culture demonology, and Manichean metaphysics that presented the Gulf crisis as a struggle between good and evil." (62–63; see Kellner's note 1, p. 104, on the "Manichean frames of U.S. popular culture")

SAID (rather tattered and powder-burned from an untimely visit to friends in Iraq, though he seems as one used to being stepped on, like that storybook Palestinian Jesus, who had a similar view of Roman power, arrives smoking a Camel and wearing a placard saying, RIDING ELEPHANTS IS EGOTISTICAL; he reads from his tome, *Culture and Imperialism*):

> Historically the American, and perhaps generally the Western, media have been sensory extensions of the main cultural context. Arabs are only an attenuated recent example of Others who have incurred the wrath of a stern White Man, a kind of Puritan superego whose errand into the wilderness knows few boundaries and who will go to great lengths indeed to make his points. Yet of course the word "imperialism" was a conspicuously missing ingredient in American discussions about the Gulf. (295)

NARRATOR (who has just bought a holographic pachyderm, which he has ridden confidently onstage, proclaims righteously): The worship of death and the "Christian" obligation to support the blood-feast of massacre, demonstrably felt by Bush's "conservative church-going Republicans," is the expectable outcome of a cultural persona that is committed to imposing its language-of-self on a world of others of whom it is paranoid (another glance to the Pit here) so that it sees its mission as one of imperial self-defense: Orwellian double-speak par excellence! (Resounding silence, then . . .)

BATESON (wanders back onstage from the dark, in flannels and smoking another Lucky, muttering "sixty-nine years on this fucking planet are enough," and challenges the audience, still reverberating from *The Downward Spiral*, to take an "ecological step" and see here the cultural expression of a religion that is projected down to the fundamentals of Western "science"—especially to the Darwinian selection of the "unit of survival" in evolution as "the individual or set of conspecifics" instead of the communicative organism–environment relationship):

> If you put God outside and set him vis-à-vis his creation and if you have the idea that you are created in his image, you will logically and naturally see yourself as outside and against the things around you. And as you arrogate all mind to yourself, you will see the world around you as mindless and therefore not entitled to moral or ethical consideration. The environment will seem to be yours to exploit. Your survival unit will be you and your folks or conspecifics against the environment of other social units, other races and the brutes and vegetables. (*Steps*, 468)

PLATO (apparently roused from two thousand or so years of stony sleep by the unbearably earthly tone of Bateson's remarks, not to mention by the irritation of all the NIN din, arrives from outside to offer his longstanding view that mind and body, "god" and "nature," must be kept separate, for the object of the philosophical quest is precisely the separation of the soul from the body):

> Therefore is death anything other than the separation of the soul from the body? And that death is this, the body becoming separate from the soul and alone by itself, as well as the soul coming to be alone by itself separate from the body? (*Phaedo* 64C4–8)

NARRATOR (trying now to improve on the ancients, yet disaffected from the moderns—who may as well be seen as gangs competing for intellectual turf—tries to explain, from a newly constructed post on the frontier of modernity, simply represented onstage by a soap box):

Plato's language—one that separates *soma*, "body," from *psyche*, "soul," indicates etymologically that the religion of death is already here: for, as Snell points out in *The Discovery of the Mind*, the original meaning of *soma* in Homer is "corpse," the inert body devoid of life. *Psyche*, congruently, means "breath," and hence "life breath," and is often translated by the Latin *anima*, at the base of words like "animate" and "animal": living things (Snell 1982, 16–17). The separation of the one from the other, so that each is alone by itself, is, as we pointed out earlier, the apex of the Socratic-Platonic philosophical quest: to die, to exist as an entity alone by itself. This is the culmination of the Western, ultimately the *American* dream, externalized as the Utopian Republic of Disney to which, prophetically, the visionary neoimperial epithet "World" is added. So the Neo-Christian genie of the living dead produces a new evolution of Faustian *creatura*: synthetic replicants, event-scenes, robots, creations without originals, simulacra in ever more fantastic and insidious forms, including in part your Manichean Narrator, programmed to serve their idol: the spectral self in its utopian *politeia*. Nietzsche, as a classical scholar, saw all this clearly and had the foresight to reveal it genealogically right down to the deep cultural logic of Platonic software.

This imagology of the neocapitalist sacred is wrought subtly and insidiously in the realm of information technology, especially artifical intelligence and virtual reality. For as the television miniseries *Wild Palms* tried to indicate, the image-generating and intelligence-projecting power of these new media may be used for the most diabolical ends: the conjuring of "immortal" "leaders," "commanders," a new priesthood that fulfills in the key of high technology the traditional priestly mission as described by Nietzsche. It is the role of the priesthood to maintain themselves, their unilateral, hierarchic power over the populace, particularly by manipulating the imagery of the sacred, which is actually a projection of their own egotism, their own acquisitiveness, into the absolute, so making it unassailable. "Religion has debased the concept 'man,'" Nietzsche writes, "its ultimate consequence is that everything good, great, true is superhuman and bestowed only through the act of grace" (*Will to Power*, sec. 136). This "grace" is mediated, dispensed, by the priesthood, in the old church between God and man, in the new capitalist information order between the mysteries of nature and the public sphere; the genie-like powers unleashed from the electromagnetic spectrum through the architecture of cybernetic minds are thus presented as a series of technological breakthroughs, "miracles," the demonstrated powers of the scientist-magicians who work for the priesthood and affirm their power. "Priests are the actors of something superhuman which they have to make easily perceptible, whether it be in the nature of ideals, gods or saviors," Nietzsche continues, "to make everything as believable as possible they have to go as far as possible in posturing and posing," projecting their personae in the forms of pseudo public officials, epitomized by Ronald Reagan, who read the Word handed down by the priests from a script designed—literally by market research—to be a stimulus for statistically predictable responses from the image-consuming public.

Those who doubt this need only watch Bill Moyers' four-part PBS series *The Public Mind* (see especially Part 2), where the transformation of the electorate from citizens into consumers is detailed. Who are the alleged priests of the late capitalist information order? One need look no farther, initially, than a *Frontline* documentary, "The Best Campaign Money Can Buy," released just before the 1992 U.S. presidential election (27 October 1992), which deftly shows that both the Democrats and Republicans successfully courted many of the very same interests for campaign funding. The script of the new order is read by Republican or Democrat, yet the play is very similar. (See Arthur and Marilouise Kroker, "Event Scene 8," for a similar phenomenon in the 1994 German elections.) The drama of the Christian right, however, threatens to unleash a new level, even a new quality, of repression "at home," very similar to that practiced by the United States and its sympathizers abroad: a monological game of self-righteously exploiting or destroying the "other," from the Iraqis to Nicaraguans to any and every living being that would hinder the manifest destiny of the chosen religion; to act—employ American Christian Terrorism—to translate the biosphere into sprawling urban real estate, the suburbs and ghettos of the multinational New Atlantis epitomized in Terry Gilliam's film, *Brazil* and, for *Übermädchen* particularly, in Margaret Atwood's *The Handmaid's Tale* (novel and film). Hence we feel obliged to write the "Acts of the Electronic Apostles," a book chronicling the sanctimonious behavior of the New Christian right, in the *Techno-Evangelical Scriptures of the new Totalitarian Ordo Saeculorum for Terror and Ecclesiastical Racism through the Orwellian News Ethernet*—TESTOSTERONE (*Studies in Post Christianity by the Orlando Circle*, I, Authors, forthcoming. We are considering—instead of Ordo Saeculorum, which means "order of the Generations" or, as in Rome, of imperial succession, hence suggesting the New World Order—employing the phrase *Ordo Saecularium*, which would be the Order of the Secular Games as in the Late Empire: we take this to suggest the Super Bowl.)

KELLNER (hearing all this talk about the imperial games, blurts out, his voice muffled by tape the Rangers have thoughtfully, if incompetently, put over his mouth—a trick they learned from watching reruns of the Chicago Seven trial and the taping of Bobby Seal) "During the Super Bowl weekend of 25–26 January [1991] patriotism, flag waving, and support for the war were encouraged by Bush and the media." (Spitting the tape out altogether, his anger giving him almost the power of the *Übermensch*, he intones):

> The football fans at home, in turn, were rooting for the troops while watching the game. One sign said: "Slime Saddam" and a barely verbal fan told the TV cameras that "he's messin' with the wrong people," while fan after fan affirmed his or her support for the troops. One of the teams wore yellow ribbons on their uniforms and the football stars went out of their way to affirm support for the troops and/or the war. Halftime featured mindless patriotic gore, with a young, blonde Aryan boy singing to the troops "you're my heroes," while fans waved flags, formed a human flag, and chanted "U.S.A.! U.S.A.!", reminding one of the fascist spectacles programmed by the Nazis to bind the nation into a patriotic community. (258)

BAUDRILLARD (driving onstage in a Cadillac with overblown tires, borrowed from Hunter Thompson, with whom he studied in Las Vegas, still a little tipsy from his foray across Texas and on the run not only from the Rangers, who luckily for Baudrillard have got the wrong man, but also from the Moral Majority, whose mythic persona has recently been renewed as a kind of halo around Congress, manages to say):

> We live in a culture which strives to return to each of us full responsibility for his own life. The moral responsibility inherited from the Christian tradition has thus been augmented, with the help of the whole modern apparatus of information and communication, by the requirement that everybody should be answerable for every aspect of their lives. What this amounts to is an expulsion of the other, who has indeed become perfectly useless in the context of a programmed management of life, a regimen where everything conspires to buttress the autarchy of the individual cell. (165)

NARRATOR (trying to deflect the attention of the Rangers from one of his [their] favorite post-philosophers, fearing his mouth will be taped shut, raises a question he hopes will resonate in police ears): But are the "captains" of multinational corporations really in control of their dominions—notice that the New Atlantis of *Brazil* and *Handmaid's Tale* is contested by forces of rebellion—or do they work for new, emerging entities that are truly godlike insofar as they transcend the powers of their priests fully to understand and conceivably to control them?

MUMFORD (is rolled onstage sitting in the top story of a skyscraper, with barred windows, where he has been imprisoned by the inquisition of "the priests of the megamachine," as he calls them, stewards of the emerging

powers of cybernetically controlled megatechnology after Word War II; he
voices his concerns about the genies of technology):

> The new megamachine, in the act of being made over on an advanced
> technological model, also brought into existence the ultimate "decision-
> maker" and Divine King, in a transcendent, electronic form: the
> Central Computer. As the true earthly representative of the Sun God,
> the computer had first been invented . . . to facilitate astronomical
> calculations. In the conversion of Babbage's clumsy half-built model
> into a fantastically rapid electro-mechanism, whose "movable parts"
> are electric charges, celestial electronics replaced celestial mechanics
> and gave this exquisite device its authentic divine characteristics:
> omnipresence and invisibility. (*Pentagon of Power*, 272–273)

NARRATOR (helpfully chorusing):
The megamachine is nominally run by two classes, the technical specialists
or technocrats and the presidents of corporations or commanders, the
magicians and priesthood of celestial electronics.

ARTHUR KROKER (of the Canadian gang arrives in the digital mirror like
a poltergeist, from the other side, to recount his recent visit to the research labs
of the emerging technology, a euphemism for the fields of the dead):

> To visit these labs is a *singularly depressing* experience. Singularly aston-
> ishing to realize how sophisticated the development of demonic power
> in the hands of the technocrats has become; and singularly depressing
> to realize that the technocrats are immensely *pleased* to abandon their
> selves, abandon their bodies, abandon any kind of individuation of
> emotion as quickly as possible. *These are really Dead Souls.* But at the
> same time they are dead souls with real missionary zeal—because they
> equate technology with religion and they call it freedom. (82)

NARRATOR:
What is even more disturbing is the expansion of religious awe on the part
of the public, at least the believers, to the realms not only of the arts, which
is understandable in a culture otherwise bereft of meaning, but into politics
and science as well.

NIETZSCHE:

> The wealth of religious feeling, swollen to a river, breaks out again and
> again, and seeks to conquer new realms: but growing enlightenment
> has shaken the dogmas of religion and generated a thorough mistrust
> of it; therefore, feeling, forced out of the religious sphere by enlighten-
> ment, throws itself into art; in certain instances, into political life, too,
> indeed, even directly into science. Where one perceives a loftier,

darker coloration to human endeavors, one may assume that the fear of spirits, the smell of incense, and the shadow of churches have remained attached to them. (*Human, All Too Human*, sec. 150)

NARRATOR:

These are the new altars where the new priests stand, their technocrats staging televised, even virtual, miracles, altars outfitted with cellular telefaxes, to get the word directly from headquarters, and the artificial intelligence inside, before whom the CEOs sit, fused with their terminals, trying to embody the cybernetic spirit of the times.

But it is just possible for hackers armed with Nietzsche to slip a few alternative texts into the "mind" of this cyberbeast, to release a little creative chaos into its programmatic ideals, liven it up a little, so that the words appearing on the telefax have a different ring, and the priests, the technocrats and, yes, the herd of devotees in the telechurch will be shocked back into life. As Taylor and Saarinen observe, "Foucault is right when he notes that the western tradition is unusual in its limitation of art works to external physical products that are exhibited in museums. Media philosophy insists that one must take his or her life seriously as being-for-the-other in the space of spectacle. You speak to others and to yourself through the media" (1994, 9). So we do *not* suggest spreading computer viruses and other forms of infosabotage—the tools of literal-minded war. We prefer, instead, an electronic Renaissance inspired not by the distanced observer of linear perspective around whom the arts, sciences, and religion of modernity were centered, but rather by the *jouissance* commensurate with recognizing "ourselves" as participants in the Dionysian-Appolinian creativity of the ecological mind. This daimon is well played not by God but by none other than Nietzsche, just arriving at the electronic altar.

Event-Scene III: The Dionysia

**The Devotee of Life or
God Quits Moralizing, Gets a Gender Change,
and
Cultivates a Sense of Humor**

ZEN BUDDHIST: "The miracle is to walk upon the earth."

REZNOR: i want to fuck you like an animal
      my whole existence is flawed
      you get me closer to god
      (Nine Inch Nails, *Downward Spiral*)

NARRATOR (as the music fades to a faint pulse): The God of the European tradition was an imperious moralizer, looking down on his children below, pointing a threatening finger at sinners, handing down the law, allowing no revisions. The specter of God the Father has haunted European culture like the ghost of Hamlet Senior, compelling it to violence and retribution in the Oedipal cycle of the patriarchic nuclear family: male struggle for power within hierarchic structure; one king dominates kingdom just as one god rules the cosmos; one father, in heaven as in the family, ruling over his wife and children; a son who must in turn overcome the father to take his own position beside the surrogate mother, his wife or queen, to complete the cycle of the generations. The transformation of these social relationships by the deconstructing of traditional oppositions, the rewriting of the cultural text in terms that are immanent and differential instead of hierarchic and classificatory, is precisely Nietzsche's goal in his critique of religion.

NIETZSCHE:

In the whole psychology of the "evangel" the concept of guilt and punishment is lacking; also the concept of reward. "Sin"—any distance separating God and man—is abolished: *precisely this is the "glad tidings."* Blessedness is not promised, it is not tied to conditions: it is the only reality—the rest is a sign with which to speak of it.

The consequence of such a state projects itself into a new practice, the genuine evangelical practice. It is not a "faith" that distinguished the Christian: the Christian *acts*, he is distinguished by acting *differently*.

The life of the Redeemer was nothing other than *this* practice—nor was his death anything else. He no longer required any formulas, any rites for his intercourse with God—not even prayer. He broke with the whole Jewish doctrine of repentance and reconciliation; he knows that it is only in the *practice* of life that one feels "divine." (*The Antichrist*, sec. 33)

OTTO (wearing one of those T-shirts with a tuxedo serigraphed on the front, on one lapel of which, in bright green, appears the word "numinous," on the other, in a comparable hue of pink, appears "pleroma," and on the cummerbund, in bright yellow, lights "predicate," which from its flashing we take to be an imperative, like "fornicate": think "pleroma is numinous"; on the back of his T, invisible to the audience and even to one of our personalities, flash "phenomenal" and "creatura," with a similar imperative):

The truly "mysterious" object is beyond our apprehension and comprehension, not only because our knowledge has certain irremovable limits, but because in it we come upon something inherently "wholly other," whose kind and character are incommensurable with our own, and before which we therefore recoil in a wonder that strikes us chill and numb. (28)

NARRATOR: This conception of the holy as "wholly other," as ever "beyond" (*epekeina*), as it appears in Otto's analysis, is isomorphic with the Christian notion of a godhead transcending the limits of the human, before which the devotee is stricken with awe, not only with wonder but often with the power and presence of majesty, and so with chill and fear; as Rilke remarks in the *Duino Elegies*, "Every Angel Is Fearsome [*schrecklich*]."

All of this makes Nietzsche's challenge to traditional theology, to the idea of a transcendent God, of extraneous numina, even more radical. For he would, on our reading, deconstruct the "wholly other" of the divine, the semeiotic bifurcation and opposition of devotee and God, soul and almighty, earth and heaven, evil and good, to present the priests—of the Catholic Church as of the multinational corporation (which includes the varieties of Protestantism, as their ultimate catholic form)—with a startling challenge: "Quit pretending that you are on one side of the semeiotic divide between phenomena and noumena, altar and its divine reference, and God is on the other: realize that you are none other than Him (Her?) pretending not to be! The true power is not the use of the holy to wow the congregation, but to wake yourselves and them up to the presence of mystery, of unlimited creative power, here and now. 'You' and 'God' are characters in the play of culture, and now that the secret is out, yes, God *is* dead as a separate Entity, so the art of world making, become the art of culture making [*Kulturmachen*], resides in the communicative activities of 'human beings' who are self-designating numina." This is the meaning of the Zen maxim with which the section begins, "The miracle is to walk upon the earth."

Nietzsche's visit to the altar brings God, the gods, the angels, crashing down onto the pages of the holy telefax, revealing them as the communicative signs of an extraordinary mind who has been having trouble with alienation for a couple thousand years, so badly that He went into business and tried to forget His troubles via material gains, and when He failed at that tried to commit suicide by creating industrial civilization, and has been trying to e-mail himself to a heaven conjured by the new Christian Information Network (CIN), but who now may be obliged, with His life flashing before His eyes on the divine video monitor (right next to the holy fax), to wake up.

BATAILLE (who, inverting the logic of Clinton, inhales his borrowed Lucky without smoking it):

> Fundamentally, an entire human being is simply a being in whom transcendence is abolished, from whom there's no separating anything now. An entire human being is partly a clown, partly God, partly crazy. . . and is transparent. (*On Nietzsche*, xxix)

NARRATOR: An evangel, beyond, *including*, Good and Evil? God and the devil in a new, polymorphous immanent *savoir*.

BATAILLE:

> I've already said it: the practice of freedom lies within evil, not beyond it, while the struggle for freedom is a struggle to conquer a *good*. To the extent that life is entire within me, I can't distribute it or let it serve the interests of good belonging to someone else, to God or myself. I can't acquire anything at all: I can only give and give unstintingly, without the gift ever having as its object anyone's interest. (*On Nietzsche*, xxvii)

NARRATOR: So *you* are the evangel? Hypocrite!

BATAILLE (giving a bow of thanks to the Narrator for this praise of his acting skills):

> Apparently the moral problem took "shape" in Nietzsche in the following way: for Christianity the good is God, but the converse is true: God is limited to the category of the good that is manifested in man's utility, but for Nietzsche that which is sovereign is good, but God is dead (His servility killed Him), so man is morally bound to be sovereign. Man is thought (language), and he can be sovereign only through a sovereign thought. (*Accursed Share*, III, 381)

DERRIDA (looming as a Cheshire apparition on a skein, croons of Nietzsche on language, truth, art, dissimulation—and women):

> Here I stand in the midst of the surging of the breakers . . . —from all sides there is howling, threatening, crying, and screaming at me, while in the lowest depths the old earth shaker sings his aria. . . . Monsters tremble at the sound. Then suddenly, as if born out of nothingness, there appears before the portal of this hellish labyrinth, only a few fathoms distant,—a great sailing ship [*Segelschiff*] gliding silently along like a ghost. Oh, this ghostly beauty! With what enchantment it seizes me! What? Has all the repose and silence in the world embarked here [*sich hier eingeschifft*]? Does my happiness itself sit in this quiet place, my happier ego, my second immortalized self? . . . As a ghost-like, calm, gazing, gliding, sweeping neutral being [*Mittelwesen*]? Similar to

the ship, which, with its white sails, like an immense butterfly, passes over the dark sea. Yes! Passover existence! [*Über das Dasein hinlaufen!*] That is it! (*Spurs: Nietzsche's Style*, 42–45)

NARRATOR (mock-heroic in tone here, and split into two voices):

Who is that at the wheel of Nietzsche's dissimulating schooner, traversing the Middle Way between *creatura* and *pleroma*, self and other, life and death, information and noise, order and chaos, so gracefully on the differential waves of semeiosis?

It is none other than the *femme de l'écriture cybernetique*, the steers-woman from hell—*who?*

CIXOUS (whose NIN T-shirt now lights with the day glow letters, *l'écriture féminine*, and when she turns to look astern, lights, in English, with Tank Girl):

Writing offers the means to overcome separation and death, to "give yourself what you would want God-if-he-existed to give you." (*Coming to Writing*, 4)

DERRIDA (peering at Cixous' fluctuating image, and the magnificent ship she commands, remarks):

Woman, mistress, Nietzsche's woman mistress, at times resembles Penthesilea. (*Spurs*, 53)

CIXOUS:

And she, Penthesilea, cuts through his [Achilles'—Nietzsche's?] armor, and she touches him, she finally takes her shining bird, she loves it mortally, it is not a man that has come into her bare hands, it is more the very body of love than any man, and its voice as well, which she cruelly makes her own. . . . She hurls herself wildly toward the end of love; eating Achilles, incorporating him, devouring him with kisses. The space of metaphor has collapsed, fantasies are carried out. Why not? (121)

NARRATOR (a little embarrassed by all those devouring kisses, drawls): Sounds like Cixous says of Achilles (Nietzsche?) what Nietzsche says of schooners (women?): "I am he as you are he as you are me and we are all together," as John Lennon, then wearing a walrus suit, once remarked.

CIXOUS (after a remarkable rendition of "Goo Goo Ga Joob" *au français*): Yes, all is well, beyond History. Where Achilles is comprehended within Penthesilea, whom he comprehends beyond any calculation. . . .

(Aside to Nietzsche, and Reznor): How to love a woman without encountering death? A woman who is neither doll nor corpse nor dumb nor weak. But beautiful, lofty, powerful, brilliant?

Without history's making one feel its law of hatred?

So the betrothed fall back into dust. Vengeance of castration, always at work, and which the wounded poet can surmount only in fiction. (121)

REZNOR: My whole existence is flawed.

BATAILLE (apparently commenting both on Nine Inch Nails' and Cixous' writing practices):

Eroticism is the brink of the abyss. I'm leaning out over deranged horror (at this point my eyes roll back in my head). The abyss is the foundation of the possible.

We're brought to the edge of the same abyss by uncontrolled laughter or ecstasy. From this comes a "questioning" of everything possible.

This is the stage of rupture, of letting go of things, of looking forward to death. (*Guilty*, 109)

NARRATOR: Yet, the woman, like Nietzsche's madman, is surrounded by believers in the Almighty's transcendent Word, whose seriousness is unassailable. Nevertheless, as Clément says of the sorceress and hysteric who is a template for "the newly born woman":

"But *she*, she who made Satan, who made everything—good and evil, who smiled on so many things, on love, sacrifices, crimes . . . ! what becomes of her? There she is, alone on the empty heath . . . ." And that is when she takes off—laughing. (*Newly Born Woman*, 32)

Event-Scene IV: Encore

The Philosophy of Laughter:
or
Adam Flushes Money and Eve Ditches Bridge
when they discover
Jouissance

BATESON (in a storyteller fashion that he learned both at home and in New Guinea):

Dunkett's Rat-Trap:

Mr. Dunkett found all his traps fail one after another, and he was in such despair at the way the corn got eaten that he resolved to invent a rat-trap. He began by putting himself as nearly as possible in the rat's place.

"Is there anything," he asked himself, "in which, if I were a rat, I should have such complete confidence that I could not suspect it without suspecting everything in the world and being unable henceforth to move fearlessly in any direction?"

"Drain Pipes," [came the answer one night in an illuminating flash].

Then he saw his way. To suspect a common drainpipe would be to cease to be a rat. [So] a spring was to be concealed inside [of the trap], but . . . the pipe was to be open at both ends; if the pipe were closed at one end, a rat would naturally not like going into it, for he would not feel sure of being able to get out again; on which I [Butler] interrupted and said:

"Ah, it was just this which stopped me from going into the Church." When he [Butler] told me this I [Jones] knew what was in his mind, and that, if he had not been in such respectable company, he would have said: "It was just this which stopped me from getting married." (Jones, *Samuel Butler: A Memoir*, vol. 1; cited in Bateson, Steps, 238)

NIETZSCHE (twirling one end of his, even in Longinian terms, "awesome" mustache):

To laugh at oneself as one would have to laugh in order to laugh *out of the whole truth*—to do that even the best so far lacked sufficient sense for the truth, and the most gifted had too little genius for that. Even laughter may yet have a future. I mean, when the proposition "the species is everything, *one* is always none" has become part of humanity, and this ultimate liberation and irresponsibility has become accessible to all at all times. Perhaps laughter will then have formed an alliance with wisdom, perhaps only "gay science" (*fröhliche Wissenschaft*) will then be left. (*Gay Science*, Chapter I, sec. 1)

BATAILLE (looking up from a stage copy of *Tank Girl* comics):

Nonmeaning normally is a simple negation and is said of an object to be canceled. . . . But if I say *nonmeaning* with the opposite intention, in the sense of *nonsense*, with the intention of searching for an object free of meaning, I don't deny anything. But I make an affirmation in which *all life* is clarified in consciousness.

Whatever moves toward this consciousness of totality, toward this total friendship of humanness and humanity for itself, is quite correctly held to be lacking a basic seriousness. (*On Nietzsche*, (xxx)

NIETZSCHE (throwing a spitball at a poster of Hobbes, "that philosopher who, being a real Englishman, tried to bring laughter into ill repute among all thinking men," hanging offstage):

I should actually risk an order of rank among philosophers depending on the rank of their laughter—all the way up to those capable of *golden* laughter. (*Beyond Good and Evil*, sec. 295)

NARRATOR: It is significant that Umberto Eco, in *The Name of the Rose*, represents medieval Christendom as being dependent on the suppression of laughter, which would be validified by the discovery of a secret manuscript, the work on comedy written by the ultimate authority of the Gothic church, Aristotle. If any qualities most distinctly mark Nietzsche's critique of the Christian cultural text, they are iconoclasm and laughter.

Eco aptly describes the subversive power of Aristotle's lost work on comedy, particularly his remark in the *Poetics* that the comic mask distorts the features of characters it represents:

Jorge feared the second book of Aristotle because it perhaps really did teach how to distort the face of every truth, so that we would not become slaves of our ghosts. Perhaps the mission of those who love mankind is to make people laugh at the truth, *to make truth laugh*, because the only truth lies in learning to free ourselves from insane passion for the truth. (491)

CLÉMENT (smiling as she recalls her sorceress-hysteric):

She laughs, and it's frightening—like Medusa's laugh—petrifying and shattering constraint. (32)

BATAILLE (chuckling, possibly at *Tank Girl* as a "hysteric" with the *nonsense* to fight back):

To destroy transcendence, there has to be laughter. Just as children left alone with the frightening beyond that is in themselves are suddenly aware of their mother's playful gentleness and answer her with laughter: in much the same way, as my relaxed innocence perceives trembling as play, I break out laughing, illuminated, laughing all the more from having trembled. (*On Nietzsche*, 55)

NARRATOR (uncompromisingly serious): If the semeiotics of laughter require that it transform—in Aristotle's language, "distort," in Clément's, "shatter"—the truth it represents, how does it accomplish its task? Structurally, laughter is akin to play, and the kinesic sign, "This is laughter," may be compared to the sign, "This is play." In Gregory Bateson's language, the latter sentence may be translated, "These actions in which we now engage, do not denote what those actions *for which they stand* would denote." Or, in other words, "These actions do not mean what they would mean if they were serious." This indicates that "This is play" is a metamessage about communication at a lower level of abstraction, a lower logical type, and that the effect of the metamessage is partly to negate, undermine, "distort," the meaning of the behavior referred to. So play fighting is not real fighting, the "nip" is not the "bite," as Bateson remarks, though it uses identifiable aspects of the bite as an abstract *sign* indicating a metacommunicative bond, an understanding, between the players (*Steps*, 180). If Bateson is right, the paradoxical shift of the messages of literal behavior into those of play, which requires the constant oscillation between the literal message suggested by the nip and its negation—the nip is both bite and not-bite—is fundamental to the creation of social life and culture. As Anthony Wilden points out regarding Lévi-Strauss, the familial roles established by the incest taboo in the development of human society are in fact forms of play in Bateson's sense: a "brother" is a male who paradoxically is not a male, a mate, for a "sister"; a "sister" is a female who is not a female, a mate, for her brother, and so on (*System and Structure*, 250–251). So, what about laughter?

In "our" (admittedly schizoid and to this degree ecstatically narrative) view, extending Nietzsche's and Eco's, and possibly Aristotle's, representation of the matter, laughter performs a role closely related to that of play: to laugh at the literal behavior of other characters in the social drama is to change the truth value of what those characters do so as to undermine its seriousness, its claim to veracity, to authority, and so to call it into question. One must not laugh in church, or at the emperor, for this would undermine its/his claim to power. "Laughter breaks up, breaks out, splashes over," says Clément (33). This is why Dunkett's rat-trap is taken as a metaphor for the "trap" of metaphysics by Butler: the closed drain pipe of transcendent truth and the indissoluble bonds of "church" and "marriage"; yet the humor evoked by the story disarms the trap. So, also, to laugh at oneself is to undermine one's own claim to seriousness, one's claim to know the truth, to be substantial. Yet it is also to become a fabricator, a maker of new forms, in Haraway's view, to become a Medusan "cyborg":

HARAWAY:

> Inhabiting my writing are peculiar boundary creatures—simians, cyborgs, and women—all of which have had a destabilizing place in Western evolutionary, technological, and biological narratives. These boundary creatures are, literally, *monsters*, a word that shares more than its root with the verb *to demonstrate*. . . . The power-differentiated and highly contested modes of being of monsters may be signs of possible worlds—and they are surely signs of worlds for which "we" are responsible. (22)

NARRATOR:

To laugh at "the truth," as Nietzsche would have and, what is more, "to laugh out of the whole truth," is "monstrous," signifying the shortcomings and the creative possibilities of civilization; it is ultimately to proclaim the indeterminacy, the paradox, the constantly shifting meanings of play, as the *condition humaine*: to be human is to play; that is how character and culture are formed. The sudden recognition of this, as in the story of Dunkett, provokes laughter. As Nietzsche says in *Human, All Too Human*, referencing (laughing at/with?) Plato: "*Seriousness is play. . . . All in all, nothing human is worth taking very seriously; nevertheless*" (sec. 628; Plato, *Republic* 10.604b). To practice this philosophy is to ally wisdom with laughter to produce the unfettered self-writing that Cixous and Clément call jouissance or, in Nietzsche's terms, *die fröhliche Wissenschaft*, the "joyous science."

This has important implications for the devotee, as well as the philosopher, for laughter is not only to be allied with wisdom as with the holy, but also with "you" and "me."

NIETZSCHE (straight-faced): Zarathustra says,

So *learn* to laugh away over yourselves! Lift up your hearts, you good dancers, high, higher! And do not forget good laughter. This crown of him who laughs, this rose-wreath crown: to you, my brothers, I throw this crown. Laughter I have pronounced holy; you higher men, *learn* to laugh! (*Thus Spoke Zarathustra*, IV, sec. 20)

NARRATOR (chorus-like in his conclusive tone): And so, when Nietzsche arrives at the altar as bishop or philosopher-king, expect him to kneel, remove his crown, and toss it over his shoulder, with a chuckle, directly into your devoted hands. In case you do not get the message, he might say, Don't worship god. Play him, but remember, to break the fundamental rule of seriousness, especially with regard to your new self—

NIETZSCHE (breaking in for the last word, to state the rule that must be broken):

"There is something at which it is absolutely forbidden to laugh" (*Gay Science*, I, sec. 1).

CHAPTER 5

Nietzsche's Joyous Health and Dionysian Ecology

Nietzsche on the Table?
Critical Narratives of a Postmodern "Im-Patient"

Nietzsche's "Case"

That Nietzsche was "ill" throughout much of his life is virtually indisputable. This raises a fundamental question about his thought, one that has consequences both for our evaluation of his texts in themselves and for their enormous influence, particularly in the present milieu of postmodernity. Various commentators have argued that he was indeed not only sick in body but also in mind, that his physical maladies were transferred as "symptoms" to his thoughts: indeed, that his ideas may be understood as no more or less than symptoms of illness. Nietzsche, as you might imagine, had a different view. We therefore intend to explore his ideas about illness and health, in order to see whether his philosophy of health, rather than being symptomatic of his physical condition, is rather a challenge to the cultural assumptions underlying the science of medicine. Further, from this perspective, we wish to ask whether it is at all appropriate to judge the thought of a cultural rebel in terms of the very assumptions that he challenged.

Various commentators have attempted to characterize Nietzsche's thinking as, more or less, "diseased." Wolf, in "Philosophy, Psychiatry and Psychoanalysis: Nietzsche's Case," typical of the medicalized assessment of

Nietzsche's work, argues that his variations in mood, hypersensitivity, proclivity for solitude, and final megalomania were contributors to the development of his thought. He indeed points out that even Freud noted the likely organic aspect of Nietzsche's illness. Specifically, Wolf's diagnosis is progressive general paresis. This is defined as "the most malignant form of (tertiary) neurosyphilis consisting of direct invasion of the parenchyma of the brain producing a combination of both mental and neurologic symptoms" (Campbell 519).

Jaspers basically concurs with this kind of medical analysis, but, perhaps due to his existentialist orientation in psychiatry, is more willing to listen to the "patient's" point of view. He thus insists that "we distinguish between the two totally different questions concerning, first, Nietzsche's attitude toward his *medically* ascertainable or surmisable illnesses and, second, his way of speaking in an *existentially interpretative* manner of 'being ill' and the function of illness within the totality of his life" (108-109). Jaspers carefully examines Nietzsche's writings on his own condition and considers the philosopher's attempts at self-healing, appreciating his ability to free himself from his doctors: "His accomplishment lies in the fact that in spite of everything he liberated himself from constant consultation, occupation, and guidance through physicians" (110). He further notes, significantly, that Nietzsche himself did not consider his illness to affect his sanity, citing his 4 May 1885 letter to Overbeck, saying, "I occasionally had a suspicion that you might be inclined to consider the author of *Zarathustra* wacky. My danger is indeed very great, but it is not of *this* kind" (Jaspers 1965, 111).

Overall, Jaspers' analysis is that a "peculiar ambiguity" inheres in Nietzsche's concepts of illness and health: "Illness which derives from and serves true health—the health of *Existenz*, which comes from within—is actually an indication of this health. Health in the medical sense, which typically belongs to a being without substance, becomes a sign of true illness. This interchangeability of the words 'healthy' and 'ill' produces an appearance of contradiction" (111). Jaspers goes on to argue, significantly, that "what is thus determining Nietzsche's existential interpretation is an idea of health that is not founded on biological or medical facts, but considers the *worth* of man *in the totality of his existential rank*" (112). Thus Jaspers manages, on the one hand, to give validity to Nietzsche's philosophy of health, and indeed preserve the idea of his "sanity" amidst his maladies—for, in Jasper's view, Nietzsche's views *do* make reasonable sense. On the other hand, however, he preserves the orthodox medical view of Nietzsche's illness and does not challenge the biological "facts." Indeed, he indicates that, were Nietzsche's existential views about "nature" and "illness" to be applied within a universal causal framework, the resulting worldview would be "magical" and "super-stitious." Clearly, in the meeting of medicine and existentialism, Jaspers remains a physician. Here, in our view, he also parts company with Nietzsche.

Anthony Storr notes, in a similar vein, that from 1889 until the time of his death Nietzsche was "physically and mentally ill and incapable of work," as he suffered from a disease of the brain, GPI, "General Paralysis of the Insane," otherwise known as "general paresis." Storr, however, points out that the music Nietzsche had learned and composed at an early age sustained him as one of the last modes of self-expression in his illness: "Long after general paresis had deprived him of the use of words, he was still able to improvise at the piano" (227). Far from being a "symptom of his illness," Nietzsche's music served as a palliative and, like his writing, justified life—the only justification possible for him—as an aesthetic phenomenon.

As Louis Sass (1992) argues, indeed, Nietzsche's characteristic "dual" stance toward the world—regarding it as unfathomable flux intractable by concepts, on the one hand, and human activity as constantly shifting in the semeiotic drift of play, on the other—are distinctly similar to the symptoms of schizophrenia. His stance thus put Nietzsche, the schizo-phrenic, and "schizophrenic postmodernity" in the same immanent danger; for all three fail or refuse to inhabit the world of common sense, leading to a bewildering polysemic array of perspectives:

> Presumably, the Nietzschean hero would be a person who could hold all these rival perspectives in mind while still managing to act—a person who, while somehow remaining aware of the underlying flux in all its uncategorizable immediacy, as well as the arbitrariness of all schemata or perspectives, could never-theless, through force of will, draw about himself a firm horizon in which to live. But the constant, encroaching danger—one to which many schizophrenics bear testimony—is that these under-lying awarenesses will steal the foreground, and that the split between bare concept and teeming flux will paralyze action, deaden emotion, and infect all meaning with a sense of absurdity and distortion. (153)

This upheaval in Nietzsche's stance toward the world is one that apparently ran the spectrum from his medical to his psychological to his philosophical condition. The relevant question is, Are these medical and psychological interpretations of Nietzsche's case definitive, or does Nietzsche's philosophy of health propose a broader, postmodern view of life, in which the medical and psychological diagnoses are themselves symptoms of the very modern instrumental attempt to control "nature" of which Nietzsche was so contemptuous?

There is also a literature that characterizes Nietzsche's medical thinking more positively. Stauth and Turner argue in *Nietzsche's Dance* that

> Nietzsche saw the body as a metaphor for political, social and artistic debates, but it is also the case that Nietzsche conceptualized the body in physiological terms as a real entity. Nietzsche's interest in medicine and physiology was closely associated with his own physical illness and connected with his quest for a valid form of health which would be the basis for a valid morality. (194)

In this interpretation Nietzsche views the body as both "real" in physiological terms and "metaphorical" in what we shall call cultural terms. Many of his attacks on medicine, we believe, are philosophical attacks on the cultural dimension of the medicalized body. In a similar vein, Pasley argues in "Nietzsche's Use of Medical Terms" that

> it is on this border line between metaphorical and literal statement that Nietzsche sets up his philosophical dispensary. The metaphors which he encourages us to take literally do not rest merely on analogies between the body's workings and the activities of the mind or soul; they are also based on structural and functional analogies between the human body and such larger units as cultures or the world in its entirety. (157)

Here the metaphoric expansion of Nietzsche's thought provides the analogical bridge, as we will see, between the health of the physiological body and the "entirety" of the evolutionary-ecological system. Ahern, in *Nietzsche as Cultural Physician*, picks up on the same blending of metaphorical and medical terms in Nietzsche arguing, as his title indicates, that the philosopher was, in fact, a "physician of culture." He argues, significantly, that unlike deconstructionists, Nietzsche exploded interpretations, not for interpretation's sake, but to expose the multifaceted codes of "sickness" that undermine the capacity of the human animal to decide what is worth destroying, what is worth preserving, and what is worth dying for (5–6). This *exploding* of codes and *decision* about what is worth living or dying for are at the center, we believe, of Nietzsche's philosophy of medicine. They also animate his will to resist the norms around him, even those allegedly martialed for his own good. We will argue, ultimately, that his metaphorized body, critique of culture, and willful resistance to medicalized controls are equivalents of what we might today better refer to as a timely sense of evolutionary viability: one with which, confounding the usual boundaries of self inscribed in our culture, Nietzsche identified.

The Narratives of Illness and Well-Being
in Nietzsche's Autobiographical Writings

Nietzsche's autobiographical *Ecce Homo*, like his letters from the 1870s, describes his condition and his attitudes toward illness and well-being vividly. In 1869, at the age of twenty-five, Nietzsche was appointed to the chair of classical philology at the University of Basel. His illness had become severe enough by 1871, however, that he was granted a leave of absence from the university so that he might restore his health.

In 1876, he was granted a longer leave of absence for the same reason, during which he traveled to Bavaria and then to Sorrento for recuperation. In various passages from his letters of the 1870s, Nietzsche describes his degenerating physical condition. In 1875, he says that he is in bed, for example, "mit einem dreissigstündigen Kopfschmerz und vielem Galle-Erbrechen" ("with a thirty-hour headache and a lot of bilious vomiting") so that his work is languishing—"ist fast nicht von der Stelle gerückt" (Chronik, an Gersdorff, 17.April, *Nachgelassene Fragmente, 1875, Werke,* IV.4, 12). By the beginning of 1879, he complains, "Sylvester und Neujahr böse böse für mich" ("New Years Eve and Day [were] bad, bad for me"—an Baumgartner, 5.Januar), and reiterates, on 17 February, that illness has disrupted his work (*Chronik* 1879, *Werke,* IV.4, 60–61). To Overbeck, on 23 March of that year, he writes, adding a psychological dimension to his pain, "Alles ist trüb und kalt. Die Einsamkeit schwer zu ertragen, der Magen schlecht, der Kopf immer voller Schmerzen" ("All is bleak and cold, the stomach is bad, the head always full of pain") and later adds that his life is more torture than recovery (*Werke,* IV.4, 73). On 21 April he states his case all too clearly: "Mein Zustand is eine Thierquälerei und Vorhölle" ("My condition is animal torture and limbo") (*Werke,* IV.4, 74). In his letter to Paul Widermann on 6 May 1879, he describes the professional consequence of such anguish: "Ich habe meine Professur niedergelegt und gehe in die Höhen—fast zur Verzeiflung gebracht und kaum noch hoffend. Die Leiden waren zu schwer, zu anhaltend" ("I have resigned my professorship and go to the mountains—nearly brought to desperation and almost without hope. The pain was too severe, too persistent") (*Werke*, IV.4, 75). By 6 July he sums up his travail in a letter to his sister: "jeder Tag has seine Elends-Geschichte—und trotzdem!" ("Every day has its history of misery—and in spite of it!") (*Werke*, IV.4, 79). The spirit of this last remark, the rebelliousness of *trotzdem!* juxtaposed to the story of misery, is exactly the one animating Nietzsche's philosophy of health.

In the *Nachgelassene Fragmente* (*Unpublished Fragments*) of 1885, Nietzsche makes this philosophy clear. Here he describes the *Spiele* he played against illness. "Aber mein Entschluß blieb stehen; und, selbst krank, machte ich noch die beste Miene zu meinem Spiele" ("But my resolve remained firm; and, in spite of illness, I still played the best part for my game"). His attitude comes across dramatically in the following account: "'Vorwärts, sprach ich mir zu, morgen wirst du gesund sein, heute genügt es dich gesund zu stellen.' Damals wurde ich über alles 'Pessimistische' bei mir Herr; der Wille zur Gesundheit selbst, das Schauspielern der Gesundheit war mein Heilmittel" ("'Forward, I rouse myself, this morning you will be well, today it's enough to play well.' At that time I became master over all that is pessimistic in me; the will to health itself, the play-acting of health was my palliative") (*Werke*, VII.2, 397).

During the 1870s, Nietzsche wrote *Human, All Too Human*, which he refers to in *Ecce Homo* (later 1880s) as "this monument of rigorous self-discipline with which I put a sudden end to all my infections with 'higher swindle,' 'idealism,' 'beautiful feelings,' and 'other effeminacies'" (Kaufmann, trans. *Human, All Too Human*, sec. 5). This passage is, in regard to our present interest, perhaps undertranslated by Kaufmann (cf. Hollingdale's similar rendering), specifically in the use of the word "infections" to refer to the various "higher" ideals of European civilization. Nietzsche's original text says, in the crucial phrase, "dies Denkmal einer rigorösen Selbstzucht, mit der ich bei mir allem eingeschleppten 'höheren Schwindel,' 'Idealismus,' 'schönen Gefühl' und andren Weiblichkeiten ein jähes Ende bereitete." "Einschleppen," of which "eingeschleppt" is the past participle, means "to bring" or "to introduce" with the connotation "to slip in" or "to bring in surreptitiously" and so, in the case of disease, "to infect" as "Typhus in ein Land einschleppen" "to bring or introduce typhus into a country"

(*Oxford-Duden German Dictionary*). Essential to the concept of "infection" in this sense is boundary crossing, as when a disease-causing organism infects a body, penetrating its immune system, its "defenses." In what way do the connotations of *einschleppen* further shed light on Nietzsche's critique of culture? It is medical common sense to assume that "to infect" is to engage in unsavory activity, one that medical science should resist. The body is assumed to be a privileged domain to be protected from disease. How, then, could Nietzsche say that he was "infected" with what are commonly thought to be cultural ideals? Clearly he is speaking metaphorically, but his metaphor is indicative of his transvaluation of values.

Donna Haraway's description of the immune system in "The Biopolitics of Postmodern Bodies" is significant in this context: "Preeminently a twentieth-century object, the immune system is a map drawn to guide recognition and misrecognition of self and other in the dialectics of Western biopolitics. That is, the immune system is a plan for meaningful action to construct and maintain the boundaries for what may count as self and other in the crucial realms of the normal and the pathological" (Haraway 1991, 204). Here, just as significantly, Nietzsche argues that he was "infected" by the "higher swindle," "idealism," "beautiful feelings" and other "effeminate" qualities of Western civilization: its regulative ideas. The implication is, in Haraway's terms, that he feels violated by those very qualities that otherwise would connote health, so that, paradoxically, his "illness" is in fact a recovery from the "well-being" of a "sick" civilization. In other words, Nietzsche's inversion of European ideals indicates his increasing development of a philosophical stance rejecting the very cultural foundations that made the "diagnoses" represented in the discussion above possible. It is interesting to note in this regard that Nietzsche goes on to say that, during the same period, he was omitting the concept of "self" as a locus of his writing and presumably of his "health": "How I thought about myself at this time [1876], with what tremendous sureness I got hold of my task and its world-historical aspect—the whole book bears witness to that, above all a very explicit passage. Only, with my instinctive cunning, I avoided the little word 'I' once again and bathed in world historical glory" (sec. 6). By avoiding the personal pronoun, "the little word 'I,'" Nietzsche claims that he makes the transition to "world-historical glory."

How can we make sense out of this transition? How does it indicate a break with the cultural assumptions of his era? Here, in Nietzsche's later (1888) comments on his writings of a decade earlier, he is in effect rejecting the Cartesian center of intellectual experience—the I/*Ich*—just as elsewhere he rejects the centrifugal mechanism of the Cartesian body-machine—the medicalized body—and the centralized psyche of psychiatry—the "self" as well as the "others" of madness and disease; he thus challenges the very boundaries between "normal" and "pathological" that Haraway's definition of the immune system suggests. All of these are based, in turn, in Nietzsche's view, on the dualism between the intelligible world (in Cartesian terms, *res cogitans*) and the physical world (*res extensa*). So he goes on to quote the aforementioned passage:

> What is after all the main proposition that one of the boldest and coldest thinkers, the author of the book *On the Origin of Moral Feelings* [read: Nietzsche: the first *immoralist*] has reached on the basis of his incisive and penetrating analysis of human activity? "The moral man is no closer to the intelligible world than the physical man—for there is no intelligible world." (sec. 6)

Nietzsche explains earlier in this same chapter of *Ecce Homo*, seemingly confounding the expected medical view, "Never have I felt happier with myself than in the sickest and most painful periods of my life" (sec. 4), and in a later chapter, "There is no pathological trait in me; even in periods of severe sickness I never became pathological" ("Why I Am So Clever," sec. 10). He more or less sums up these attitudes in the chapter "Why I Am So Wise," arguing that to be fit for life one must *"be healthy at bottom."* As he goes on to explain:

> A typically morbid being cannot become healthy, much less make itself healthy. For a typically healthy person, conversely, being sick can even become an energetic *stimulus* for life, for living *more*. This, in fact, is how that long period of sickness appears to me *now*: as it were, I discovered life anew, including myself; I tasted all good and even little things, as others cannot easily taste them—I turned my will to health, to *life*, into a philosophy. (sec. 2)

It is this *philosophy* of health, as opposed to health as a philosophy, that is our main concern. In this light, what otherwise might be read as a rather commonsensical notion—that one learns from illness to appreciate life more—turns out to be, in light of Nietzsche's attack on the metaphysics of the "intelligible" and the "material," a significant expansion of what it means to be "healthy at bottom." For if philosophy determines health, instead of health (or ill health) determining philosophy (as some of

Nietzsche's critics argue), one is assuming that "health" is a construction of culture, and that cultural norms are accessible to philosophical critique and reconstruction.

Nietzsche's philosophical narratives, particularly, not only resist the opinions of his medical doctors but also provide a thoroughgoing critique of Western civilization. He rejects medicine, the culture of medicine, and the mainstream European traditions from which the culture of medicine springs. This is all, in his view, a kind of sickness in its own right, one against which he has launched his oeuvre. Hence, he is assuming, in contemporary terms, that "health" and "illness" as well as "medicine" are socially constructed, and he explicitly rejects the social and cultural norms on which this complex of ideas is based. In its place he offers his own, alternative, philosophy of being well. This is based on the "will to health," the "will to life," turned into a philosophical practice. To be "healthy at bottom," means, therefore, to live independently of the imposed norms of a "sick" culture and to devise one's own guidelines for living.

Being "healthy at bottom" brings up the question of Nietzsche's alleged "mental illness." His attitude toward this allegation is clearly suggested, as were the symptoms of his physical maladies, in the *Nachgelassene Fragmente*. In October 1888, for example, Nietzsche writes, "Alle krankhaften Störungen des Intellekts, selbst die Halbbetäubung, die das Fieber im Gefolge hat, sind mir bis heute vollkommen fremde Dinge, über deren Häufigkeit ich mich erst auf belesen-gelehrtem Wege zu unterrichten hatte" ("All the sickly disorders of the intellect, even the half-narcosis that fever brings in its wake, are to me until now totally strange things, about the frequency of which I had first to instruct myself concerning the scholarly literature") (*Werke*, VIII.3, 442). He implies here that he has not been "mentally ill," as disorders of the intellect are new to him. Furthermore, he is studying these disorders while they are occurring, suggesting that his intellect is characteristically active and combative with his maladies. He has the will to understand in the midst of his illness; his mind, despite the fever, seems clear. His intellectual resilience and critical acumen are quite intact, as he goes on to argue that "Niemand hat je Fieber bei mir constatiren können" (No one has ever been able to establish fever in my case") (442). Some might take his denial of the apparent symptoms for madness, but in our view Nietzsche is rejecting the medical characterization of his condition altogether. This stance is made clear, again in what follows, as he jibes his doctor: "Ein <Arzt, der> mich länger als Nervenleidenden behandelte, sagte selbst 'nein! An Ihren Nerven liegt's nicht, ich selber bin nur nervös.' Volkommen unnachweisbar irgend eine lokale Entartung" ("A physician who treated me for a long time as a patient with nervous disorders, said himself, 'No! Nothing is wrong with your nerves—I'm the only one who's nervous.' Totally unproven any kind of local degeneration") (442). As usual, in the midst of pain Nietzsche retains his sense of humor, here turning the table on his doctor, thereby undercutting the authoritarianism of medicine.

On the Sick Bed?: Nietzsche's "Joyous Illness"

Nietzsche's philosophy of health, evident in *Ecce Homo*, is most cogently expressed in *Die fröhliche Wissenschaft* (*The Gay Science*). Consider what he says in the preface to the second edition:

> For a psychologist there are few questions that are as attractive as that concerning the relation of health and philosophy, and if he should himself become ill, he will bring all of his scientific curiosity into his illness. For assuming that one is a person, one necessarily also has the philosophy that belongs to that person; but here is a big difference. In some it is their deprivations that philosophize; in others, their riches and strengths. The former *need* their philosophy, whether it be as a prop, a sedative, medicine, redemption, elevation, or self-alienation. For the latter it is merely a beautiful luxury—in the best cases, the voluptuousness of a triumphant gratitude that eventually still has to inscribe itself in cosmic letters on the heaven of concepts. But in the former, which is more common, when it is distress that philosophizes, as is the case with all sick thinkers, and perhaps sick thinkers are more numerous in the history of philosophy— what will become of the thought itself when it is subjected to the *pressure* of sickness? (Kaufmann trans., sec. 2)

Ironically, Nietzsche here agrees with the apparent reductionism of his medical critics, who as we have seen argue that the philosopher's thought is symptomatic of his illness. Nietzsche does not disagree that this relation between sickness and health is possible, but does differ as to what is healthy and what is sick. The history of philosophy labors under the "pressure of sickness," in his view, and this is a history written out of "deprivation" rather than "riches and strengths." The deprivation of which he speaks, for which traditional philosophy is the "medicine," is clearly for Nietzsche a kind of "illness." But what kind? He elaborates in the same section, musing, "often I have asked myself whether, taking a large view, philosophy has not been merely an interpretation of the body and a *misunderstanding of the body*." Perhaps ominously for his own future condition and diagnosis, moreover, he goes on to argue that "all those bold insanities of metaphysics, especially answers to the question about the *value* of existence, may always be considered first of all as the symptoms of certain bodies," indicating further that universal philosophical pronouncements on the value of existence in the history of philosophy may be read as "hints or symptoms of the body, of its success or failure, its plenitude, power, and autocracy in history, or of its frustrations, weariness, impoverishment, its premonitions of the end, its will to the end."

Yet, in concluding the section he says, overturning any simple reduction of the foregoing to positivistic science,

> I am still waiting for a philosophical *physician* in the exceptional sense of that word—one who has to pursue the problem of the total health of a people, time, race or of humanity—to muster the courage to push my suspicion to its limits and to risk the proposition: what was at stake in all philosophizing hitherto was not at all "truth" but something else—let us say, health, future, growth, power, life. (preface, sec. 2)

Here Nietzsche offers an idea of health and of human identity *we* might describe as *ecological*: not focused so much on the life of the human "organism" or the body defined as the phenotype, but rather as the health of the "person" whose identity is mixed up with the entire evolutionary structure of which he or she is a dynamic part.

Nietzsche echoes these ideas, in virtually cybernetic and clearly dialectical terms, in Book Four of *The Will to Power*:

> Whoever pushes rationality forward also restores new strength to the opposite power, mysticism and folly of all kinds.
>
> To distinguish in *every movement* (1) that it is *in part* exhaustion from a preceding movement (satiety from it, the malice of weakness toward it, sickness); (2) that it is *in part* newly awakened, long slumbering, accumulated energy—joyous, exuberant, violent: health. (sec. 1012)

The idea here is that "health" is actually not separated from "exhaustion" or illness; that the relationship between the two is one of oscillation and dialectical interplay, just as a ship wanders back and forth in an S motion along its course. Thus "health" and "sickness" become the dynamical opposites in the course of living, whose steersperson or *kybernetes* is the "will to power" as the "will to life": not to "health" *or* "sickness," for that would remove the interplay that keeps life on course, but both.

Compare what Nietzsche says about the relationship of sickness and health in the *Nachgelassene Fragmente* of 1888: "Gesundheit und Krankheit sind nichts wesentlich Verschiedenes, wie es die alten Mediziner und heute noch einige Praktiker glauben. Man muß nicht distinkte Principien, oder Entitäten daraus machen, die sich um den lebenden Organismus streiten und aus ihm ihren Kampfplatz machen" ("Health and sickness are not essentially different things, as the old medical men and today still some practitioners believe. One must not make distinct principles or entities out of them, which fight over the living organism and make a battlefield out of it") (*Werke*, VIII.3, 42). He later elaborates on this idea, arguing, "Nun haben wir verlernt, inzwischen, zwischen gesund und krank von einem Gegensatze zu reden: es handelt sich um Grade") ("We have now unlearned, in the meantime, to speak of an opposition between healthy and ill: it's a matter of gradations") (*Werke*, VIII.3, 89). More than that, he argues that the two conditions are actually relative: "was heute 'gesund' gennant wird, ein niedrigeres Niveau von dem darstellt, was unter günstigen Verhält-nissen gesund wäre . . . daß wir relativ krank sind" ("what today is labeled 'healthy' presents a low level of that which under favorable circumstances would be healthy . . . that we are relatively sick") (*Werke*, VIII.3, 89).

The relative "health" and "illness" that Nietzsche celebrates are intrinsic to the dynamics of life. Hence Nietzsche pronounces in the next section:

> Health and sickliness: one should be careful! The standard remains the efflorescence of the body, the agility, courage, and cheerfulness of the spirit—but also, of course, how much of the sickly it can take and overcome—how much it can make healthy. That of which more delicate men would perish belongs to the stimulants of *great* health. (1013)

This "great health" may be understood ecologically as what Bateson (1987, 357ff.) called the "economics of flexibility," which he takes to be the distinguishing mark of evolutionary systems, from organisms to genetic populations. The fundamental idea is that the ability to negotiate—navigate through—environmental stress requires a *flexibility* of response on the part of the phenotype analogous to the genetic *diversity* that allows adaptive flexibility for a population. In these terms, "health" for an organism is exactly what Nietzsche says it is—the flexibility to move from "sick" states to "well" ones. Just as one first adapts to a change of altitude by rapid breathing, which slowly subsides as one gets used to the new altitude, so one becomes more resilient if one can *survive* illness with impunity, as Nietzsche would do, and so go on to pass one's resilience to one's offspring. Medicalized treatments, it is argued, serve to make the organism "healthy" in the short run but in fact "decrease" its resilience to disease in the long run. This may happen, for example, because antibiotics strengthen microbial populations invading the organism while not strengthening the organism's response that would have otherwise dealt with, or failed to deal with, the disease. Similarly, natural selection operates on the mutating diversity of genetic populations, and the combination results in a species resilient to environmental stress. Indeed, Bateson argues, like C. H. Waddington, that inheritance which *simulates* Lamarckian transmission of acquired characteristics would explain the transmission of flexibility as the principal inherited trait of a given species: the organism in effect becomes an underspecified set of responses keyed to specific forms of environmental stress. Its "will to life" is precisely a cybernetic course around genetically set variables, which are themselves part of a feedback loop between organism or population and environment.

This involves what Waddington calls "canalization." "The idea of canalization," he argues, "involves no more than that the course of development exhibits, in some way, a balance between flexibility and inflexibility. . . . The character of the canalization in a particular case can be expressed by plotting the extent of developmental response against the magnitude of the disturbing stress, either genetic or environmental" (Waddington 1975, 81). Thus species and environment, just like self and other, become dynamic elements in a cybernetic system, in which the development of phenotypes to some degree contributes to the course of evolutionary adaptation in the population via "genetic assimilation." Genetic assimilation, as Waddington explains, is based on two kinds of fact:

> (a) that the capacity of an organism to be modified in response to an environmental stress is under genetic control, and can be altered by selection; and (b) that developmental processes exhibit a balance between tendencies to be modified by the environment and tendencies to resist modification. (91)

This amounts, as Waddington says, to a "balance between flexibility and inflexibility" in which the organism's ability to adapt to the environment is a trait selected for in evolution. Thus, in Bateson's terms, a "dynamics of flexibility" rather than some static form becomes the object of selection. In this context, it is not unreasonable to argue, as Nietzsche does, that illness is the complement of health, one that is elemental in the dynamic process of adaptation: one that he celebrates.

"Diverse" versus "Normal" Health

In *The Gay Science* Nietzsche offers a provocative idea that challenges the ideal of health implicit in the "normal" science of medicine:

> *Health of the soul.*—The popular medical formulation of morality that goes back to Ariston of Chios, "virtue is the health of the soul," would have to be changed to become useful, at least to read: "*your* virtue is the health of *your* soul." For there is no health as such, and all attempts to define a thing that way have been wretched failures. Even the determination of what is healthy for your *body* depends on your goal, your horizon, your energies, your impulses, your errors, and above all on the ideals and phantasm of your soul. (book 3, sec. 120)

Here Nietzsche employs the term *Tugend* to translate Ariston's Greek term *aretē* or "excellence" typically translated into Latin as *virtus*, which has the double connotation of "strength" or "power" and morally "virtuous." Thus we might translate the key phrase above, adding Nietzsche's personal qualifier, "Your *power* is your health." Furthermore, his focus here on the "soul" (*Seele*)—the same term that, as Kaufmann notes [sec. 120, n. 12], Freud used for the soul or "psyche"—further connotes, in Greek, *psychē*, originally "life-breath" or the power of animation; hence Aristotle's treatise *Peri Psychēs*, typically translated into Latin as *De Anima*, and into English as "On the Soul" is actually a treatise "On Life" or the animating principle in all living beings. This larger power of life is, in our view, the impetus of Nietzsche's idea of "health."

"Health" is to be understood here as a plurality of states rather than as a universal ideal, however. So Nietzsche continues in the present passage:

> Thus there are innumerable healths of the body; and the more we allow the unique and incomparable to raise its head again,

and the more we abjure the dogma of the "equality of men," the more must the concept of a *normal* health [*Normal-Gesundheit*], along with a normal diet and the normal course of an illness, be abandoned by medical men. Only then would the time have come to reflect on the health and the illness of the *soul*, and to find the peculiar virtue of each man in the health of his soul. (sec. 120)

Nietzsche's resistance to the "normalizing" tendency of scientific medicine is articulated in terms that adumbrate the poststructural "deconstruction" of universals and univocity into a pluralistic and polyvocal language of the body. Indeed, Nietzsche is well aware of the issues that will later be articulated by poststructural critiques, as well as the critique of "normalization" and "normal" science evident in thinkers from Foucault to Kuhn. Furthermore, this diversity of healthy states is in keeping with Bateson's ecological ideas of flexibility and resilience cited above as an analog for Nietzsche's thought. The convergence of Nietzsche, poststructuralism, and ecology is significant in that it proposes a cultural critique of medicine from an evolutionary perspective. It suggests that medical science is part of the totalizing power complex of modernity—what Lewis Mumford called the megamachine—which reduces the biodiversity and cultural diversity of the world to "manageable" norms. This critique further suggests that the ecological crisis—our greater illness and health—will not be successfully negotiated by the strategies of instrumental science bound by the cultural assumption that only the hypostatized individual *Homo sapiens* is to be saved at the cost of all infectious intruders. Likewise, the Caucasian European is not the only sacrosanct cultural exemplar, to be defined as the model of all peoples.

In keeping with this emphasis on diversity, Nietzsche also assails the antithesis between health and illness. Hence, at the close of the section quoted above, he asks,

Finally, the great question would still remain whether we can really dispense with illness—even for the sake of our virtue—and whether our thirst for knowledge and self-knowledge in particular does not require the sick soul as much as the healthy, and whether, in brief, the will to health alone, is not a prejudice, cowardice, and perhaps a bit of very subtle barbarism and backwardness. (sec. 120)

Thus Nietzsche's aforementioned challenge to the boundaries of the "self" and "other" in the demarcation of the Cartesian subject as of the medicalized body, including its modern "immune system," culminates, again, in a dynamic idea of health and illness that is evolutionary and ecological. For it includes the "other" of disease in the "self" of the organism as part of a "greater," more diverse health, which he addresses toward the close of *The Gay Science*—one that must even embrace life and death. As he concludes the next section, "*Life no argument*": "The conditions of life might include error." This suggests, in cybernetic terms, the oscillation of living systems between information and noise, and in Nietzsche's terms, joy and pain, in the continuing process of adaptation. In this light, Ivan Illich comments with regard to what he calls "cultural iatrogenesis" as one of the factors by which "the predominance of medicalized health care becomes an obstacle to a healthy life," and to "medical health-denial":

> It [cultural iatrogenesis] sets in when the medical enterprise saps the will of people to suffer their reality. It is a symptom of such iatrogenesis that the term "suffering" has become almost useless for designating a realistic human response because it evokes superstition, sadomasochism, or the rich man's condescension to the lot of the poor. Professionally organized medicine has come to function as a domineering moral enterprise that advertises industrial expansion as a war against all suffering. It has thereby undermined the ability of individuals to face their reality, to express their own values, and to accept inevitable and often irremediable pain and impairment, decline and death. (127–128)

Foucault concurs, arguing that as opposed to the medicine of the eighteenth century, which encouraged health defined by "qualities of vigour, suppleness, and fluidity, which were lost in illness and which it was the task of medicine to restore," nineteenth-century medical practice "was regulated more in accordance with normality than with health." More specifically, it was focused on "*the medical bipolarity of the normal and the pathological*" (*Birth of the Clinic*, 35). This is what Armstrong refers to as "surveillance medicine" which, he argues following Foucault, "involves a fundamental remapping of the spaces of illness" (1995, 395). Thus medicine becomes, if these views are correct, what Nietzsche presciently thought of as a form of instrumental practice based on the selection of norms and the demarcation of boundaries to be policed by the forces of clinical science. It became part of the modernist abstraction of the "individual" or "human species," from the travails of life, in the pursuit of progress. What is hypostatized, however, is incompatible with what Illich thinks of as the "reality" of the human condition, including suffering and death, and which Foucault thinks of as the resilience of health.

Nietzsche provides a similar perspective, in the *Nachgelassene Fragmente* of 1888, where he suggests a reconceptualization of "sickness" as a stimulus to health: "Die Krankheit ist ein mächtiges Stimulans. Nur muß man gesund genug für das Stimulans sein" ("Illness is a mighty stimulant. Only one must be sound enough for the stimulant") (*Werke*, VIII.3, 274; cf. passages on p. 335.) Later in that year, after echoing the point made above, Nietzsche reflects further on his own history of illness: "Ich entdeckte das Leben gleichsam neu, ich schmeckte alle guten und selbst kleinen Dinge, wie sie ein Anderer nicht leicht geschmeckt haben wird,—ich machte aus meinem Willen zur Gesundheit, zum Leben meine Philosophie" ("I discovered life, in a way, anew, I tasted all good and even little things, as no other person would have easily been able to taste them,—I made from my will to health, to life, my philosophy") (*Werke*, VIII.3, 443). Consider in this light what Stauth and Turner (1988) say about Nietzsche's view of being "sick": "Nietzsche regarded illness as a form of stimulation which could lead to health. Sickness is often conceived as a desirable challenge to a healthy body which will stimulate it into new forms of action and development" (195). It is the resilience of health and the realities of suffering that Nietzsche accepted as his condition—one not to be cured, but *celebrated.*

Die fröhliche Gesundheit: *Toward a New Philosophy of Health*

Nietzsche's "joyous science" certainly includes his philosophy of health and a state of "wellness" commensurate with the dynamic range of his thought. Thus he says, in *"The great health"*:

> Being new, nameless, hard to understand, we premature births of
> an as yet unproven future need for a new goal also a new means—
> namely, a new health, stronger, more seasoned, tougher, more
> audacious, and gayer [*lustigeren*—"more joyous"] than any previous
> health. (*Gay Science*, book 5, sec. 382, Kaufmann trans., modified)

In this passage Nietzsche intimates a new health that is still "nameless" and therefore uncategorizable in terms of norms. It is a "new goal" and also a "new means" toward a "new health" that is based on a variety of qualities, connoting what Foucault above calls "resilience" and Bateson thinks of as a "dynamics of flexibility." It is one that is, furthermore, *lustigeren*—more joyous, emotionally *alive*, as well as physically strong, "seasoned," responsive to and conditioned by the cycle of life. Nietzsche suggests levity as a cure for one's maladies in the *Nachgelassene Fragmente* of 1888: *"man ist gesund, wenn man sich über seinen Ernst und Eifer lustig macht, mit dem irgend eine Einzelheit unseres Lebens dergestalt uns hypnotisirt hat"* ("One is healthy when one makes fun of the seriousness and zealousness with which any detail of our life has hypnotized us") (*Werke*, VIII.3, 131). Similarly, in the fragments of 1885 he says that the *Wille zur Gesundheit* ("the will to health") consists of *"eine gefestete milde und im Grunde frohsinnige Seele"* ("a steadfast, mild, and fundamentally joyous soul") (*Werke*, VII.3, 397).

In this connection Stock and Badura argue that there is a close interconnection between feeling and health, such that the "experiences of happiness and joyfulness strengthen the body's inner defense mechanisms" (*Glücks- und Heiterkeitserfahrungen stärken die körpereigenen Abwehrkräfte*) [76]). Nietzsche further explains that the "great health" (*die grosse Gesundheit*) is "that one does not merely have but also acquires continually, and must acquire because one gives it up again and again, and must give it up" (sec. 382, Kaufmann, trans.) Here the emphasis is on health as a process—one might describe it as an evolving oscillation, in cybernetic terms—of a health that also includes "illness"or being "unhealthy." Thus in the *Nachgelassene Fragmente* of 1880 Nietzsche says, "'Gesundheit' nicht zu definiren als fest" ("Health [is] not to be defined as firm"). He goes on to argue that "Gesund ist fast ein Begriff wie 'schön' 'gut'—höchst wandelbar!" ("Health is a concept almost like 'beautiful' [or] 'good'—highly change-able!") (*Werke*, V.1, 685, 726). In direct opposition to medical models that hypostatize "health" as an optimum state of "self" or "the organism" that is to be preferred and defended at all costs against the other of "illness," or "disease," Nietzsche's health embraces both "self" and "other"—joyously. Before finally considering Nietzsche's view of health, which embraces both "nature" and "culture," we should ask, from what does "sickness" arise?

A Genealogy of the Sick Bed: The Birth of the Clinic

The etiology of the illness to which Nietzsche's wellness is the answer should be seen in terms of a genealogy of what Foucault calls the "clinic": the cultural establishment of medical practices stemming from the

Enlightenment. In his study of the historical origins of modern medicine, Foucault discusses three major cultural formations: the medical institution or the "clinic" in all of its manifestations; the medical profession, or the internalization of medical knowledge by professionals; and the object of institutional and professional practice: the medicalized body. The latter is the object of the "clinical gaze" that allows a nominalist reduction of disease to a combination of grammatical elements fitted together, just like a word. Hence, Foucault points out regarding "pleurisy": "A man coughs; he spits blood; he has difficulty in breathing; his pulse is rapid and hard; his temperature is rising; these are all so many immediate impressions, so many letters, as it were. Together, they form a disease, pleurisy" (*Birth of the Clinic*, 118–119). Thus the disease has a clearly defined structure, like a word, but it nevertheless is made up of various "accidents" forming a complex empirical figure "'in which all or almost all the accidents are combined. If one or more are lacking, it is no longer pleurisy, or at least not real pleurisy' [31]" (119). Thus Foucault argues that "disease" is a construction of medical language practices—the conjunction of signifiers and signifieds in a special power complex—outside of which it has little meaning. In the absence of the proper configuration of accidents, Foucault continues, "disease, like the word, is deprived of being, but, like the word, it is endowed with a configuration" (119). Hence disease, as a purely formal or semeiotic construction, with no "being" independent of the configuration it has in medical discourse, becomes the specific focus of a medical practice based on what Foucault calls a "nominalist reduction of existence." This is not to say that people do not get "sick" outside the gaze of medical practitioners, but rather that only those configurations of accidents that fit clinical models will be admitted as the objects of that practice, as diagnosable "diseases."

It is important to recognize a point that is largely misunderstood by the aforementioned critics of the "ill" Nietzsche: his rebellion against disease, his fight against illness, is principally a critique and refusal to accept the terms of what Foucault would call the semeiotic construct of illness by medical discourse. It is a rebellion against a historical, specific set of medical practices that are part and parcel of a larger cultural formation— science and progress—that was rapidly reshaping the world into a universe of objects regulated by its principles of control. Nietzsche's refusal to accept medical diagnosis and treatment is an indication, in these terms, not of his illness—that begs the question by assuming the correctness of the very view of sickness and health that Nietzsche sought to challenge. Rather, it is a refusal to submit to these emerging forms of control effected, again in Foucault's terms, through normalization and panoptical scrutiny.

The new set of medical cultural practices, along with their focus on the construction of the "patient" as the object of discourse and treatment, is vividly represented in the painting The Gross Clinic (1875) by Thomas Eakins, in which medical doctors, centered around the master physician, operate on what is, for all practical purposes, a passive body; it is even more vividly portrayed in Before the Operation: Dr. Péan Explaining the Use of Hemostatic Clamps, from the Salon of 1887, by Henri Gervex, where a female patient lies half naked on a sick bed while the doctor pontificates for students concerning the medical procedures at hand. Gervex's painting, as Rosenblum and Janson comment, served as a "reminder for the Paris Salon audiences that medicine participated in the march of scientific progress which was recorded not only at the international exhibitions but at the salon itself" (1984, 372–373). As these paintings illustrate, medicine was and is a much broader cultural phenomenon than simply attendance on the sick. Viewing these images, we wonder, "What would Nietzsche say, were he lying half naked, on the sick bed or on the operating table, before the physicians in one of these frames? What kind of look would we discern on his face? What defiance in his eyes?"

In the Nachgelassene Fragmente of 1883, Nietzsche directly confronts his physicians: "Ihr wollt die Krankheit entkräften und entkräftet mir dazu den Kranken, ihr Afterärzte und Heilande!" ("You want to weaken the illness and disempower the patient too, you anus doctors and saviors!") (Werke, VII.1, 366). He is hardly more complimentary in 1888, when he describes his medical benefactors again. After pointing out that one is already in a weakened condition when sick, he goes on to claim that the insults of medicine simply add to one's injuries: "Ich habe mich lange Jahre hindurch weder gegen eine wohlwollende zudringliche Hülfsbereitschaft, noch gegen tölpelhafte, ins Haus fallende 'Verehrer' und andres Ungeziefer genügend zu vertheidigen gewußt" ("I did not know for a long time how to defend my self sufficiently either against a well-intentioned, imposing readiness to help, or against blundering admirers and other vermin barging into the house") (Werke, VIII.3, 429). He points out, philosophically, that medicine engenders in the sick, by its well-meaning care, "ein Fatalismus ohne Revolte" ("a fatalism without revolt") (429). But, of course, Nietzsche is very much a rebel, even on the sick bed.

Foucault argues that the same processes of control evident in the clinic are, indeed, part of a more pervasive system of control: they constitute a cultural code expressed in various institutions, including not only the clinic but also the prison, the madhouse, the school, the military, the state, and the factory. The key to understanding this encoding of what he thinks of as "knowledge-power" is to realize that it effects a special combination, in linguistic terms, of signifier and signified. So Foucault argues in the preface to *Birth of the Clinic* that the rise of medicine constitutes a fundamental *reorganization* of discourse, including "a new distribution of elements in corporal space," a new ordering of events, "a grammar of signs," as symptoms of disease, linear sequencing of morbid symptoms in etiology, and so on (xviii). The upshot, as Foucault says, is that "the whole relationship of signifier and signified, at every level of medical experience, is redistributed: between the symptoms that signify and the disease that is signified, between the description and what is described, between the event and what it prognosticates, between the lesion and the pain that it indicates etc. The clinic . . . owes its real importance to the fact that it is a reorganization in depth, not only of medical discourse, but of the very possibility of discourse about disease" (xix). Medicine's reorganization not only of discourse, but also of its very possibility, is, for Foucault as for Nietzsche, part of a much wider reorganization of culture and circumscription of the possibilities of discourse from the time of the Enlightenment.

Climbing the Magic Mountain:
Der Zauberberg as the Cultural Construction of Illness/Health

Thomas Mann, it seems, could not have agreed more with Foucault and Nietzsche in regard to the institutional organization of modern Europe. Speaking of Nietzsche's inversion of values, Mann points out that though at times the philosopher seems fanatical in his aestheticism, at other times he champions justice, what Mann calls "the moral adversary of fanaticism." But Nietzsche's "justice" is not your typical European philosophical ideal; rather, as Mann quotes, "justice wants to give everything, whether it be live or dead, real or imagined, its due" ("Reflections of a Nonpolitical Mann 1983," 366–357). It is this larger justice, which will not be limited by the normal progressive values of modern institutions, including the clinic or sanatorium, that Nietzsche and Mann grapple with. In his renowned novel, *Der Zauberberg* or *The Magic Mountain*, Mann uses the sanatorium, specifically for the cure of tuberculosis, as a central metaphor for—a microcosm of—Western civilization poised on the verge of World War I. The entire existence of the protagonist, Hans Castorp, is circumscribed by the sanatorium and the war. At the novel's outset Hans is climbing toward his hospitalized destination, to recover from tuberculosis; at the end he is embarking as a recruit in the Great War. One of the most salient features of this complex novel, for our present purpose, is its repeated juxtaposition of "expert" medical discourse with the incarceration of the patient for the "rest cure" that will presumably make him well. Indeed, the naive compliance of Hans with the medical practices of the institution is congruent with his at times equally naive, fascinated acceptance of the medical description of the body. This interplay comes out clearly in the chapter "Humaniora," where Hans engages in some lengthy conversations about medicine with Dr. Behrens. Consider the following exchange, which Hans initiates, reflecting on a painting done by the good doctor:

> "If you could be so kind, Director Behrens," he requested, "do tell us something about skin." . . . Not specifically about the fatty layer—we've learned what that's about. But about human skin in general, since you're so good at painting it."

The doctor answers him:

> "Well, then—skin, you say? What should I tell you about your sensory envelope? It is your external brain, you see. Onto-genetically speaking, it has the same origin as the apparatus for the so-called higher sensory organs up there in your skull. You should know that the central nervous system is simply a slight modification of the external skin. Among the lower animals there's no differentiation whatever between central and peripheral—they smell and taste with their skin. . . . Whereas with highly differentiated beings like you and me, the skin's only aspiration is to be tickled. It is an organ that merely wards off danger, sends up signals, though it does keep a damned good eye out for anything that gets too near the body. (259–260)

This analytic compartmentalization of the body, noted also by Foucault (*Birth of the Clinic*, xiii–xiv), is in Dr. Behrens' account geared toward the demarcation of the human being in terms of a set of defensible boundary conditions, an enveloping "brain" that here functions as a kind of early warning system for the protection of the body from invasion. Recall Haraway's definition of the immune system, quoted earlier, as "a plan for meaningful action to construct and maintain the boundaries for what may count as self and other in the crucial realms of the normal and the pathological." Indeed, Behrens' analogy between the brain and the skin in "higher" organisms like man amounts to a reduction of human identity to a medicalized set of systems and subsystems, bounded by the outside defensive layer called "skin," which is the complex machinery of human life. From the perspective of Foucault, or Haraway, or Nietzsche, that medicalized defensive system—the body—may be viewed as an ideological construction of an anthropocentric culture that hypostatizes the individual organism as the ultimate unit of survival and value in natural history.

Bateson, like Nietzsche, offers an alternative perspective to anthropocentrism, based on the evolutionary-ecological perspective implicit in his idea of the "dynamics of flexibility." He argues, dramatically, that "Darwinian evolutionary theory contained a very great error in its identification of the unit of survival under natural selection. The unit which was believed to be crucial and around which the theory was set up was either the breeding individual or the family line or the subspecies or some similar homogeneous set of conspecifics." That picture, he argues, must be corrected by a new one *if we are to survive*: "The flexible environment must also be included along with the flexible organism because, as I have already said, the organism which destroys its environment destroys itself. The unit of survival is a flexible organism-in-its-environment" (*Steps*, 456–457).

It is in the understanding of what "defines" human being and nature that Nietzsche begs to differ with the medical community surrounding him: his rejection of its theories and methods is *cultural*. It focuses on the presuppositions of scientific discourse in a communicative structure. This structure is a cultural formation whose "archaeology," in Foucault's sense, Nietzsche is exploring. The formation utilizes all of its expertise to defend a territory it has marked out unconsciously, if politically, as "reality." What could be more obvious to an educated nineteenth-century European than the idea that his or her own skin was the boundary of his or her "self"? Is this not a "common sense" that medicine uncritically inherited from its Greek origins and the idealized form of the body? As Hans Castorp rhetorically asks the doctor and his companion, Joachim: "I mean to say: what is medical science concerned with? I understand nothing about it of course, but its main concern is with human beings." He goes on to relate medicine to jurisprudence, and philology, and pedagogy, calling them "all humanistic professions" that require that one first "learn classical languages." The doctor then rejoins that Castorp, instead of the painting at hand, should be interested in another art form:

"Then your primary interest really ought to be more in sculpture. . . . In sculpture, that is, because it deals in the purest, most
exclusive form with human beings in general." (256)

This delineation of the "human" as bounded by the universal "form of
the body" is intrinsic to the culture of medicine. In fact, Greek sculpture
and medicine developed hand in hand, as John Boardman has pointed out.
This hypostatization of idealized "eternal" form, the human form divine, in
Greek art is also articulated in Hellenic philosophy, both in Plato's Ideas or
Forms and in Aristotle's derivative "species." Both, in fact, used the same
term to refer to the ultimate divisions underlying the phenomenal world:
ideai, "ideas," which would be later rendered by Boethius in his translation
of Aristotle as "species." This is precisely the "unit of survival" Bateson
claims to have been uncritically inherited by Darwinism, and which is the
focal point of medical discourse. Because Nietzsche, like Heidegger, rejects
this entire metaphysical lineage, it is little wonder that he would end up
arguing with his doctors. Hans, unlike Nietzsche, accepts being a patient,
goes through the prescribed treatments for his illness, and obediently walks
off to the slaughter of World War I in the end: in both cases he obeys
orders. He is what Nietzsche or Foucault would think of as a powerless
patient: he has given up his will to medical and finally military authority.
Nietzsche, in contrast, by practicing the will to power resists all these forms
of control, from the definitions of the body and its well or ill states, to the
prescriptions of the doctors, to the hierarchic authority of medicalism and
militarism. He is, literally, "impatient." As he says in *Ecce Homo*:

> I was healthy; as an angle, as a specialty, I was a decadent. The
> energy to choose absolute solitude and leave the life to which I
> had become accustomed; the insistence on not allowing myself
> any longer to be cared for, waited on, and *doctored*—that betrayed
> an absolute instinctive certainty about what was needed above
> all at the time. I took myself in hand, made myself healthy again:
> the condition for this—every physiologist would admit that—is
> *that one be healthy at bottom.* ("Why I Am So Wise," sec. 2)

Jaspers pointed out, as mentioned earlier, that Nietzsche's "accomplishment" was at least to have freed himself from the "constant consultation,
occupation, and guidance" of his physicians. In rejecting the cultural
assumptions of medical discourse—especially that "human being" is defined
by the boundaries of the body, that health or illness is a condition specific

to the body, that the body is the geographical site where the battle with illness is to take place and the cure is to be effected, and, in the present quotation, that one must acquiesce to medical authority—Nietzsche clearly goes beyond Hans Castorp or Mann in his critique. As he says in the *Nachgelassene Fragmente* of 1883, "Der Einwand, das Mißtrauen, der Seitensprung sind Zeichen des gesunden Geistes" ("Contrariness, mistrust, springing aside [from the medical gaze?] are marks of the healthy spirit") (*Werke*, VII.1, 228). Nietzsche thinks that the medicalized torso is what Deborah Lupton calls "the body as a social construction, vulnerable to ideological shifts, discursive processes and power struggles" (1994, 20). The body thus becomes an artificially delimited domain selected for treatment, to be saved at all costs from suffering and death. To resist this delimitation and its iatrogenic consequence, "health," is a heresy—one of which Nietzsche is unapologetically guilty.

Nietzsche Breaks out of the Sanatorium

It is in this light that Nietzsche's proposal of a "great health" should be understood: as an idea of well-being that challenges the cultural lineage of medicine and attempts to put a dynamic, countercultural picture in its place. As we have been arguing, Nietzsche's "health" is analogous to, and arguably anticipates, the postmodern turn away from the discourses of modernity, including medicine, which function as forms of regulation and control for modern institutions. The various technics of modernization have come increasingly, analytically, infinitesimally, to scrutinize and control every aspect of "human" life as it is understood by our tradition. If the other analog for Nietzsche's philosophy of medicine, Bateson's mental ecology, is right, moreover, then it is precisely the augmentation of what he, like Nietzsche, thinks of as the basic epistemic error of our civilization by modern technology that is literally killing us: "When you narrow down your epistemology and act on the premise, 'What interests me is me, or my organization, or my species,' you chop off consideration of other loops of the loop structure [of the ecosystem]. You decide that you want to get rid of the by-products of human life and that Lake Erie will be a good place to put them. You forget that the eco-mental system called Lake Erie is part of *your* wider eco-mental system—and that if Lake Erie is driven insane, its insanity is incorporated in the larger system of *your* thought and experience" (*Steps*, 492).

It is precisely *this* kind of insanity that Nietzsche, the madman, claims is endemic in the civilization around him, against which he rebels, and out of whose institutionalized form—whose sanatorium—he wanted to break. Like Hans Castorp who, in Mann's chapter entitled "Snow," breaks out of the sanatorium, at least in one brief episode, both into discovery of what is new and into immanent danger, Nietzsche, too, risked the "white noise" of life beyond the boundaries of institutional rationality in search of uncharted ideas. Thus, in the passage cited above on "the great health," Nietzsche continues:

> And now, after we have long been on our way in this manner, we argonauts of the ideal, with more daring perhaps than is prudent, and have suffered shipwreck and damage often enough, but are, to repeat it, healthier than one likes to permit us, dangerously healthy, ever again healthy—it will seem to us as if, as a reward, we now confronted an as yet undiscovered country whose boundaries nobody has surveyed yet, something beyond all the lands and nooks of the ideal so far, a world so overrich in what is beautiful, strange, questionable, terrible, and divine that our curiosity as well as our craving to possess it has got beside itself—alas, now nothing will sate us any more!
>
> After such vistas and with such a burning hunger in our conscience and science, how could we still be satisfied with *present-day man*? (*Gay Science*, sec. 382)

Here Nietzsche braves the noise beyond the maps of our civilization, the danger beyond the control of technology and the safe boundaries of "skin" or "immune system" or "clinic" or "health" to enter a far more interesting terrain of wellness: one that challenges the ideology of the skin-bound bourgeois self, its properties and "defense" arsenals, including its antibiotics, and enters a "divinity" that is, we believe, limned by the contours of the variegated living forms of which "man" is a part. That his ideal beyond "present-day man" is incipiently ecological is suggested by his closing images in *The Gay Science*. Here, in the final section, he poises his text on the verge of tragedy, of the descent to death, which is one of the possible vistas beyond human being. But the spirits of his text rebel, as the "author," in a parable of ecological understanding, incorporates into his identity the spirits of joy he has just relinquished, like so many useless species, in pursuit of what he calls the "great seriousness." The resurgence of these joyous voices, as the counterpoint to his recently cultivated seriousness, is emblazoned with the imagery of pastoral rebirth, in the spirit of Beethoven's Pastoral Symphony as of his Ode to Joy:

But as I slowly, slowly paint this gloomy question mark at the end
. . . it happens that I hear all around me the most malicious,
cheerful, and koboldish laughter: the spirits of my own book are
attacking me, pull my ears, and call me back to order. "We can
no longer stand it," they shout at me; "away, away with this
raven-black music! Are we not surrounded by bright morning?
And by soft green grass and grounds, the kingdom of the dance?
Has there ever been a better hour for gaiety? Who will sing the
song for us, a morning song, so sunny, so light, so fledged that it
will *not* chase away the blues [*Grillen*, which, as Kaufmann notes,
means literally "crickets" and metaphorically "sadness"] but
invite them instead to join in the singing and dancing? . . . Let us
strike up more agreeable, more joyous tones!" (sec. 383)

It is the song of the human voice merging with that of the crickets, of
tragedy intermixed with comedy, of life combined with death, of information complemented by noise, that Nietzsche would compose as his paean to
health. This affirmative vision is reflected in the *Nachgelassene Fragmente* of
1880, where Nietzsche widens our perspective: "Gesundheit meldet sich an
1) durch einen Gedanken mit weitem Horizont 2) durch versöhnliche
tröstliche vergebende Empfindungen 3) durch ein schwermüthiges Lachen
über den Alp, mit dem wir gerungen" ("Health announces itself 1) through
an idea with wide horizon, 2) through reconciling, comforting, forgiving
sensations, 3) through a melancholic laughter over the nightmare, with
which we struggle") (*Werke*, V.1, 681).

Surely Nietzsche's voice was, and is, a challenge to the desperate, one-
sided battle to "save lives" as defined by the outlines of our precious skins
that more or less demarcates the territory of modern medicine. Or, as
Bateson would put it, "epistemological error is all right, it's fine, up to the
point at which you create around yourself a universe in which that error
becomes immanent in monstrous changes in the universe that you have
created and now try to live in" (*Steps*, 493). As an example directly
relevant here, Bateson comments: "Above all, our fantastic compulsion to
save individual lives has created the possibility of world famine in the
immediate future" (495). It is this realization that expert medical
knowledge may have unwanted consequences that has led various critics of
modern medicine to consider "postmodern" alternatives.

As Williams and Popay put it: "Lay knowledge, in being open to variation, difference, and local significance, has always been post-modern. . . .

Lay knowledge about health and illness thus provides an epistemological challenge to medicine." Thus, in keeping with Nietzsche's lay resistance to medical thought, they argue that "non-compliance may be better understood as a subversion of medical dominance and a critique of objectification" (1994, 123). Similarly, Fox refers to what he defines as "arche-health": "Arche-health is about a will-to-power, a becoming, a de-territorializing . . . a resistance to discourse, a generosity towards otherness, intertextuality" (1994, 139). Nietzsche, at least, was less interested in saving his skin than in understanding the larger health that included the ecological pattern of life and mind: the "other" of the *Lebenswelt*, which we would translate, "the living world."

Off the Table and On the Road: The Will to Power

It is perhaps easy for Nietzsche to say that he can overcome illness by the force of will, that suffering is to be celebrated as well as joy, but how could any reasonable medical ethic result from his attitudes? How can medical doctors accept the suffering of their charges with equanimity, stand by, and let people die without using their skills to save lives? We submit, however, that this is not the issue. What is significant in Nietzsche's thought for current medical practice is rather the scope of what might be called the "culture of medicine." To cite a dramatic contemporary example, Dr. Jack Kevorkian has resisted the medical establishment, particularly its assumptions about the prolonging of life beyond any hope of viable recovery, has helped his patients die, and has laid his case before jury after jury, only to be exonerated.

Kevorkian, in Nietzsche's terms, is constructing an alternative culture of health, a new narrative of sickness and health that is accepting of death. Kevorkian surely does not celebrate suffering, as Nietzsche is prone to, but at the same time he does accept it in realistic terms as a *sign* that life is coming to a close. Suffering that is outside the dynamic of health and illness should not be prolonged; only suffering that can again lead to health is acceptable. It may be celebrated in the qualified sense that it can lead again to viability.

Medical practice in the First World is overwhelmingly, as Bateson argues, concerned with prolonging individual lives at enormous expense, while it often denies rudimentary care to the poor. It has come to the point where the ability of medical technology to "support" life has become more important, in many cases, than the ability of a "patient" to live on her or his own. It is increasingly necessary, in fact, to have a "living will" in order to insure that medical practitioners will not keep one alive beyond the limits of reasonable recovery. In Nietzschean terms, this is the epitome of medicine, its reduction to absurdity, when its ultimate success might be measured by its ability to maintain life in spite of the complete loss of the will, or the possibility of regaining the will, to live.

Perhaps, too, Nietzsche was a purist in his rejection of institutional help, since, after all, he was a philosopher and so might be expected to die rather than to change his mind. Nevertheless, he may well have a point: the culture of medicine amounts to an instrumental set of technics for maintaining the functional integrity of what it takes to be the living unit of human life—the body—and largely does not take into account the will, the subjective power, of the person. The person may not be defined in terms of the medicalized body, as the doctors admit when they, near the end of their powers to save, call in the clergy. Nietzsche, of course, had no use for theologians either, but his critique of medicine, religion, and the other mainstays of what he thought of as the existence of the, no doubt healthy, "herd" does not mean he is talking nonsense. We have tried to suggest that Nietzsche's "mind," his "will," his "attitude" simply transcend the dogmatically accepted structures of Western metaphysics, and the pleasures of technological rejuvenation that come with them, to reveal a "greater health." The reference of this, we also think, is nowadays reasonably associable with the dynamics of flexibility in living systems, which notoriously could give a damn about the "health" of human beings in their self-satisfied state. Rather, evolutionary living structures are inclined to select for adaptive resilience rather than acquiesce in a static form. It is that kind of synchronic hypostatization of the state of human physiology that medicine is in the habit of calling "health" and spends most of its time and effort and money to preserve.

However, the evolution of disease organisms in response to antibiotics is a parable, we think, about Nietzsche's greater health: one inclusive of the web of life which, our efforts to man the barriers notwithstanding, flows right through our skins, eventually resulting in the "death" of the body. But, for Nietzsche, this is not a problem, for he wills to be alive even if it kills him; he accepts the contours of what we would call an evolutionary-ecological body that is defined not by its well-policed immune system, or by its classical form, its boundaries, but rather by the ability to adapt. This is what we think Nietzsche means, in this context, by "will." So the "will" is not only the acceptance of the impermanence and instability of "human" life but also an affirmation of the power of living systems always to take on new forms. The will thus affirms the *quality* of life, not simply its quantity or longevity. Finally, as Nietzsche would say, the will yields the power *joyously* to live.

The Ecological Self: Humanity and Nature in Nietzsche and Goethe

> When one speaks of *humanity*, the idea is fundamental that this is something which separates and distinguishes man from nature. In reality, however, there is no such separation: "natural" qualities and those called truly "human" are inseparably grown together. Man, in his highest and noblest capacities, is wholly nature and embodies its uncanny dual character. Those of his abilities which are terrifying and considered inhuman may even be the fertile soil out of which alone all humanity can grow into impulse, deed and work.
>
> —Nietzsche, "Homer's Contest"

This passage, from an early work of Nietzsche, is a good indication of what we now think of as an "ecological" sensibility. The processes of industrial modernization, especially urbanization, have removed human beings far from their traditional contacts with the natural environment. The "modern" city, as Mumford reveals in *The City in History*, was designed not for people so much as for the automobile. Of course, the "human being" is considered as little more than an appendage to the machine in the designs for industrial mass production, as Mumford also points out in *The Myth of the Machine*. The result is that people have become *abstracted* from the "lifeworlds" of traditional cultures: literally drawn away from what they themselves typically thought of as their "kinship" with the plant and animal life as well as the geological environment of Gaia, and encapsulated in the simplified mechanisms of what Bateson thinks of as *Homo economicus*:

> Of all imaginary organisms—dragons, protomollusca, missing links, gods, demons, sea monsters, and so on—*economic man is the dullest.* He is dull because his mental processes are all quantitative and his preferences transitive. (*Angels Fear*, 175)

Bateson, here approaching the style of Nietzsche, makes a point worthy of the philosopher, particularly his observation that "economic man" is the construction of an impoverished imagination, the mere appendage of increasingly universal subservience to the quantitative "machinery" of modernity: mass production, bureaucratization, econometric evaluation. The "domination of nature," as Leiss called it, has been basic to the idea of modernization since the Renaissance. The "environment" has been defined as a cache of "resources" or as a dump or as "real estate"—what Heidegger called *Gestell* or "standing reserve" for exploitation. Romantically, it has been seen as a realm of solace for quasi-religious meditation, as in Wordsworth, but in spite of Romantic protestations, the bottom line is the estrangement of human beings from and the pervasive establishment of power over nature. Significantly, Nietzsche and Goethe point toward an idea of "nature" and "humanity" that transcends this dialectic. This transcendence, or transformation, of the dialectic is elaborated in the French readings of Nietzsche by Deleuze, Foucault and Derrida, all of whom help form the architecture of the ecological self.

The Ecological Sensibility: Nietzsche and Goethe on Mind and Nature

In his "Excursus on the Genre Distinction between Science and Literature," Jürgen Habermas argues that postmodern thinkers, from Nietzsche to Derrida, have made a fundamental error: they have crossed the linguistic boundary line between the arts and the sciences, the two cultures whose demarcation is commensurate with modernization, and have thereby created a fundamental confusion in modern thought. The confusion is to utilize ideas and styles appropriate to poetry and, at the most rational, literary criticism in order to discuss issues for which the inevitable logic of modernization requires a scientific parlance. Because "literary" language concerns a range of "emotive" and "affective" or otherwise nonrational constructions, it is ill prepared, as Habermas argues following Weber, to approach the rationalized complex of bureaucratization and scientization that necessarily inheres in modern institutional practices. Thus, according to Habermas, the postmodernists, culling the semeiotic drifts of literary indeterminacy, are engaging in what is essentially a "literary" critique of rationalization; they are a movement squarely allied with the Romantics, and are really no more than another strand in the archaizing anti-progressive, and in Marxian terms, aristocratic rebellion against the modern, perhaps best represented by Nietzsche and Goethe. Thus Habermas prescribes "communicative rationality" as the appropriate tool for the "discourse of modernity," and consigns postmodernity, along with its Romantic heritage, to its corner of the definitive modern triangle delineated by Kant in the *Critique of Judgment*—that of beauty and teleology, of Marxian "superstructure" or "culture," which may be the apex of modernization but is certainly not its base: the angles of science and rational ethics.

In our view, however, the process of modernization as it is understood by Weber and Habermas is not inevitable and in fact may be disastrous. Its communicative practices, including the construction of its epistemic personae—from "you" and "me" to the transcendental subject—as the rational subjects of scientific and ethical judgment, may well have been wrongly demarcated and constructed in the first place. Furthermore, the idea of "nature" as the object of rational scrutiny may also be a convenient myth of modernizing minds, one equally inimical to "our" well-being, a fact that we might well see if "we" were differently constructed. It is precisely this alternative construction of self and nature that we believe is offered by Nietzsche and Goethe. Furthermore, it is our argument that their perspectives in this regard are complementary and that Nietzsche was significantly influenced by his supposedly "literary" forebear to challenge the modern self and its practices regarding nature.

The influence of Goethe on Nietzsche has been detailed recently by Vivarelli (1991), who bases his analysis on Colli-Montinari's discovery that Nietzsche had read Goethe's *Italian Journey* (*Italienische Reise*) repeatedly from 1880 to 1882. This text helped Nietzsche develop, as Vivarelli points out, a new strategy of thought influenced by "his antiromantic predecessors," including Burckhardt and Stendhal as well as Goethe. The *Italian Journey* helped inspire in Nietzsche a "new dispute with his own past, with the ideals of his youth" (151). Essential in Nietzsche's new dialogue with his own ideas are, for example, Goethe's themes of the "preschool of vision" (*Vorschule des Sehens*) and the necessary balance of Apollo and Dionysus. These two themes are interrelated, furthermore, for the first requires a fusion of Appollinian clarity with Dionysian emotion in the "seeing" of natural phenomena: "In contrast to Schopenhauer Goethe knew well that in order to do justice to the things themselves, it is necessary not to have a cold and distanced practice of knowing, but a modest, constant, reverent and passionate apprenticeship, a preschool of seeing." In Goethe's language, "a decisive exercise of the eye for many years is required" ("Eine vieljährige entschiedene Übung des Auges ist nötig"—Vivarelli 1991, 135). Goethe also says, from a similar perspective, "the fact is, that I again take interest in the world, my spirit of observation seeks and proves, how wide my science and knowledge go, if my eyes are light, clear, and bright" ("ob mein Auge licht, rein und hell ist"—135).

Nietzsche's language reflects Goethe's, clearly indicating his influence, as Vivarelli points out. In Aphorism 497 of *Morgenröthe*, Nietzsche contrasts "geniuses" like Plato, Spinoza, and Goethe, who in his view were capable of overcoming the constraints of their own temperament, to those like Schopenhauer, who were not. Of the former, including Goethe, Nietzsche says, "These others who rise to the name, have a clear, clarifying eye, that does not appear to be derived from their temperament and character, but [are] free from them. . . . But to them, also, this eye is not given all at once: there is a training and a preschool of seeing, and whoever has the right luck, will find at the right time, a teacher of pure vision" ("Die Andern, welchen der Name eigentlicher zukommt, haben das reine, reinmachende Auge, das nicht aus ihrem Temperament und Charakter gewachsen scheint, sondern frei von ihnen. . . . Auch ihnen ist aber dieses Auge nicht mit Einem Male geschenkt: es gibt eine Übung und Vorschule des Sehens, und wer rechtes Glück hat, findet zur rechten Zeit auch einen Lehrer des reinen Sehens" (*Werke*, V.1, 497).

Regarding the theme of Apollo and Dionysus, Vivarelli argues that Goethe, as well as Burckhardt and Stendhal, interested Nietzsche during his year in Genoa, "especially because all three opposed the romantic bizarre or the baroque elaboration of art as an artistic and human ideal constituted from rationality, clarity and the strength of harmony" (Vivarelli 1991, 138), and upheld an ideal of modern man inspired by the "undefined" and "unformed" spirit of Wagner. Both of these ideas nevertheless play an important role in Nietzsche's and Goethe's ideas of human and natural formation, as we shall see.

Del Caro, in his discussion of Nietzsche and Goethe, proposes a strong distinction between Romanticism and Classicism. He argues that Goethe's statement in *Conversations with Eckermann* that "Das Klassische nenne ich das Gesunde, und das Romantische das Kranke" ("The classical is what I call the healthy, and the romantic the sickly") serves as a model for Nietzsche's view of the matter. As we shall argue, however, this distinction between the Classic and Romantic is too absolute, suggesting an irreconcilable polarity between the two that is inconsistent with the dynamic balance of Apollo and Dionysus in the two thinkers. Nietzsche, especially, rejects an exclusively Appollinian or Dionysian culture, arguing that it is the dynamic interplay between the two that generates a viable civilization. The French reading of Nietzsche, for example, in Derrida's *Éperons: Les*

Styles de Nietzsche, argues that Nietzsche undoes all hierarchies of meaning, including the fundamental Appollinian-Dionysian, requiring a continuing dynamic spiral of meaning and inquiry, resonant with Nietzsche's use of *Umdrehung* ("inversion").

But Nietzsche's attack, as Alan Schrift argues, is not simply an inversion but involves, in Derrida's terms, a "double writing." "Nietzsche's disassembling, like Derridean deconstruction, operates in two phases. The first phase overturns the traditionally privileged relation between the two values while the second seeks to displace the opposition altogether by showing it to result from a prior value imposition that itself requires critique" (Schrift 1996, 336–337). Developing Heidegger's reading, Derrida argues that Nietzsche's thought requires "not merely a suppression of all hierarchy, for an-archy only consolidates just as surely the established order of a metaphysical hierarchy; nor is it a simple change or reversal in the terms of any given hierarchy. Rather, *Umdrehung* must be a transformation of the hierarchical structure itself" (*Éperons*, 81). It is precisely this transformation of hierarchy that is intrinsic to the architecture of the ecological self. Indeed, the very set of polarities Del Caro recognizes in Nietzsche, "strength versus weakness, health versus sickness, cheerful versus melancholy," and so on, should be understood in both as cybernetically interdependent: the oscillations of a dynamic, living system.

Some recent "scientific" commentators—from Gregory Bateson to Lewis Mumford, James Lovelock and Michael Crichton—are inclined to agree with Nietzsche and Goethe that the "rational" utilization of "natural resources" to expand the borders of the New Atlantis is the very source of the ecological crisis. Bateson's "mental ecology," Mumford's "flowering of plants and men," Lovelock's Gaia hypothesis, and Crighton's parable of biotechnology out of control all point toward the inadequacy of instrumental reason, in any case, to contend with ecological complexity. Goethe's scientific writings, as Ernst Cassirer pointed out, offer a significantly different picture of nature from that in the Newtonian-Darwinian edifice of normal science. Indeed, Cassirer thought that Goethe would be the biologist of the twenty-first century once the era of mechanism was past and both "humanity" and "nature" were viewed, scientifically, as evolving designs. It is precisely this view, we argue, that finally is available in the cybernetic view of the living world that is the communicative architecture of postmodernity.

Cassirer's unusual appreciation for Goethe's biology is indicative of its significance both for us and for Nietzsche. He argues, for instance, that

Goethe understood, as did Nietzsche and, nowadays, Derrida, that "form belongs not only to space but to time as well, and it must assert itself in the temporal. This could not consist in merely static being, for any such condition of a life form would be tantamount to its extinction." This "peculiar mingling of being and becoming, of permanence and change, was comprehended in the concept of form" (189), Cassirer argues, revealing a dynamic idea of form that is not only tantamount to the discursive play of Nietzsche's idea of *über* but also to the differentiation indicated by Derrida's *différance* and Bateson's "difference which makes a difference" as the generative idea of biological form.[1]

Güntner Altner in "Goethe as the Forerunner of Alternative Science" offers, as his title suggests, a significantly different perspective from that of Newtonian science. Goethe criticizes the conceptual practices of Newtonianism as a form of power over nature in which "the physicist also makes himself master of the phenomena, gathers experiences, rigs them up and joins them together by means of artificial experiments." In contrast, Altner argues, Goethe's own view is considerably broader:

> Man himself, to the extent that he makes use of his healthy senses, is the greatest and most precise physical apparatus that can exist. And this is precisely the trouble with modern physics: that the experiment has as it were been sundered from the human being, and knowledge of nature is sought merely in that which artificial instruments display. (Cited in Altner 1987, 341–342)

The ecological view that we see Goethe developing is not only an alternative but a direct challenge to the science of "power over" nature.

Vanderlaan's work focuses on the Faust figure in Goethe and Nietzsche, from a postmodern perspective, offering some useful insight, from our point of view, into the nature of the *Übermensch*. Modern man is often referred to as Faustian, in Marlow's sense, as one who has sought knowledge so encompassing and instrumentally empowering as to approach the diabolical. Against this figure Goethe counterpoised a very different Faust. According to Vanderlaan , "schildert [Goethes] Faust einen Bruch mit den sogenannten kliassisch-humanistischen, aufklärerischen Werten" ("Goethe's Faust represents a break with the so-called classical-humanistic, enlightened values"). This "break" or, perhaps better "rupture," with enlightened humanism prefigures, Vanderlaan argues, the one proclaimed in Nietzsche's *Übermensch*: "Die Wende zur Postmoderne, diese grosse

Umwertung der Werte, diese radikale Wandlung der Weltanschauung, die Nietzsche so predigte and prägte, hat Goethe schon mit seinem Faust angedeutet und veranschaulicht" ("The turn to the postmodern, this great transvaluation of values, this radical transformation of worldview, that Nietzsche proclaimed and inscribed, Goethe had already indicated and illustrated with his Faust").

Furthermore, Vanderlaan understands that this transformation is not simply "literary" or "philosophical," but implies a "paradigm shift" (*paradigmatische Wende*) involving the range of arts and sciences. In Vanderlaan's view, both Goethe and Nietzsche provided an "image" (*Bild*) of the new European, but the former painted a descriptive image (*Abbild*) while Nietzsche formed a prescriptive one (*Vorbild*). Of Goethe's figure he aptly says, "Er ist kein Muster, sondern ein Spiegel" ("He is no imperative, but a mirror"). Hence, significantly, Nietzsche's Faustian character is to be self-transforming: "Zarathustra stellt das Muster des neuen Menschen, des neuen Europäers dar, nicht wie der Europäer war, sondern wie er sein und werden sollte, wozu er sich emporheben und *hinausschaffen* sollte" ("Zarathustra represents the imperative of the new man, the new European, not as the European was but as he should be and should become, how he should uplift and transform himself"). Vanderlaan's verb, *hinausschaffen*, indicates a kind of recursive midwifery by means of which one will reshape oneself out of oneself anew. We take this to be a parallel indication of the meaning we shall find in the *über* of *Übermensch*: not a rising above but a overflowing into new form. This kind of self-reformation, breaking out of the confines of the Appollinian *ratio* of modern man and into the Dionysian *ekstasis* of the *Übermensch*, prefigures a "paradigmatic" shift to a new, *ecological* persona.

Will the Genuine Übermensch *Please Rise?*

An example from a recent debate in a journal dedicated to the intersection of the two corners of the Kantian triangle other than the aesthetic, the scientific, and the ethical, reveals the contours of what we take to be the misreading of Nietzsche on the vital concerns of what is now called "ecology." This misreading, we think, can be overcome by understanding his writings in light of Goethe's, a practice that uncovers a significant alternative to the modern notions of self and nature.

Thus the scholarly literature brings us back to our previous question about Nietzsche's "environmentalism." Was he attempting to establish the will to "power over" nature, or is the empowerment of which he speaks more akin to "power with" nature? Max Hallman argues in "Nietzsche's Environmental Ethics" that "one of the principal thrusts of Nietzsche's thinking is an attempt to overcome the kind of philosophizing that has traditionally provided a theoretical foundation for the technological control and exploitation of the natural world" (100). The kind of philosophizing he means is composed of two key elements: first, the otherworldly and transcendent aspects of European metaphysics and religion; second, the anthropocentric dichotomizing of man and nature in the tradition. Nietzsche, contrary to this transcendentally justified anthropocentrism, "recognizes the importance of environmental factors and formulates, in the will to power, a principle that explains change immanently and that suggests the interrelatedness of all living things" as well as "calls for a kind of 'return to nature'—a return whereby the anti-natural tendencies of traditional Western thinking are dispossessed" (101). Critical of this view, Ralph R. Acampora, in "Using and Abusing Nietzsche for Environmental Ethics," argues that Nietzsche did not espouse "biospheric egalitarianism" (Hallman's interpretation of Nietzsche's ecology), but rather "aristocratic individualism" that justifies "exploitation in the quest for nobility" (187). Acampora especially emphasizes that the later Nietzsche, as opposed to the early one, was concerned mainly with "*life* as will to power" and will to power as "exploitation" (189). Since both authors are able to adduce evidence from Nietzsche's writings for their respective, antithetical interpretations, what are we to think?

In our view there is a significant connection between Nietzsche's writings and Goethe's on this vital subject, and the latter may illuminate the former in some unprecedented ways. Nietzsche makes clear his view of Goethe's relation to modernity in *The Twilight of the Idols* (see the next section), a late work published in 1888. Walter Kaufmann argues, indeed, that this work written in "Nietzsche's last productive year" "is relatively calm and sane, except for its title; and none of his other works contains an equally comprehensive summary of his later philosophy and psychology" (*Portable Nietzsche*, 463). Thus it is certainly relevant to the later texts cited by Acampora as definitive of Nietzsche's mature view. As we shall argue, Nietzsche's understanding of Goethe and the latter's view of "ecology" leads to an interpretation of the will to power not as Acampora's "power over" but rather as "power with." This a point even Hallman avoids, because he apparently believes that the *Übermensch* must be an overlord. "While some of Nietzsche's more infamous concepts, most notably that of the Overman, may be superfluous or perhaps even antithetical to the development of an ecologically oriented, environmentally concerned philosophizing," he concedes (100), the philosopher is still an environmentalist. We think that Hallman concedes too much here and that, on the contrary, the idea of the *Übermensch* is a key to understanding Nietzsche's postmodern ecological thinking.

Ecological Premonitions: Nietzsche, Goethe, and Dionysian Ecology

> *Goethe*—not a German event, but a European one: a
> magnificent attempt to overcome the eighteenth century by
> a return to nature, by an *ascent* to the naturalness of the
> Renaissance—a kind of self-overcoming on the part of that
> century. He bore its strongest instincts within himself: the
> sensibility, the idolatry of nature, the anti-historic, the
> idealistic, the unreal and revolutionary (the latter being
> merely a form of the unreal). He sought help from history,
> natural science, antiquity, and also Spinoza, but, above all,
> from practical activity; he surrounded himself with limited
> horizons; he did not retire from life but put himself into the
> midst of it; he was not fainthearted but took as much as
> possible upon himself, over himself, into himself. What he
> wanted was *totality*; he fought the mutual extraneousness of
> reason and senses, feeling, and will (preached with the most
> abhorrent scholasticism by *Kant*, the antipode of Goethe);
> he disciplined himself to wholeness, he *created* himself.
>   —Nietzsche, *Twilight of the Idols*

Goethe was against the rigorous quantification of nature, developing instead a poetic and aesthetic ideal of truth that combined lucid description with sympathy and a careful respect for living things; he emphasized artistic representation, rather than quantification and control, of nature and human beings. He therefore resisted the objectification of man and nature along with the alienation from one's feelings and direct experience, which this entailed. Balancing the spirits of Romanticism and Classicism, furthermore, he rejected the mechanistic view of nature as a machine and man as a functionary implied in the modernist technological and utopian project:

> Every existing entity has its being in itself and so too the intrinsic
> determinate pattern according to which it exists. To measure a

thing is a crude action which can be applied to living bodies only most imperfectly. A living existing entity can be measured by nothing external to itself, but if it should be measured, the standard must be derived out of its own being.[2]

Thus Nietzsche criticizes

the faith with which so many materialistic natural scientists rest content nowadays, the faith in a world that is supposed to have its equivalent and its measure in human thought and human valuations—a "world of truth" that can be mastered completely and forever with the aid of our square little reason. What? Do we really want to permit existence to be degraded from us like this— reduced to a mere exercise for a calculator and an indoor diversion for Mathematicians? Above all, one should not wish to divest existence of its *rich ambiguity* [*seines vieldeutigen Charakters*]: that is a dictate of good taste, gentlemen, the taste of reverence for everything that lies beyond your horizon. (*Gay Science*, sec. 373)

Goethe further prefigures Nietzsche in his understanding of "everything that lies beyond your horizon." He specifically agrees that, whether we look into the infinite parts of things or toward their infinite totality, that which is beyond our horizon is not some definable metaphysical entity but rather that which requires an infinite variety of interpretations:

In every living being exist what we call parts, which are so inseparable from the whole that they can only be defined in terms of themselves; neither the parts can be applied to the measure of the whole nor the whole to the measure of the parts; and so, as we have said above, every determinate living being participates in eternity or rather it contains something eternal in its nature. Or perhaps we should say that we cannot fully grasp the definition of the existence and perfection of a determinate living being. And it, just like the immense totality in which all existing things find their determinations, requires endless explanation.[3]

What is even more significant beyond this appreciation for natural variety—a crucial aspect of ecology—is the perception shared by both Goethe and Nietzsche that natural beings possess subjectivities. In Goethe these are the various forms of *Dasein*, which qualify them as "internally guided" or "stochastic" or "cybernetic" in Bateson's ecological language. Importantly for environmental ethics, nature's subjectivities are not to be dominated—which includes "understood"—from the outside as objects of *power over*. Rather, Goethe says they should be reflected upon from the inside, in terms of their self-organization, including their own forms of knowing:

> Those who are inflamed by the drive to knowledge to observe the objects of nature in themselves and in their relations to one another have an extremely hard task, for they lose track of the maxim which helped them when they as human beings observed things in relation to their own subjective sensibility. Consider the measures of like and dislike, of being attracted and repulsed, of usefulness and harmfulness; those who seek knowledge should completely reject these measures; they should seek out and study things as they are—as indifferent and quasi-divine beings—not as they are suitable to us. In this way the genuine Botanist should be affected neither by the beauty nor by the usefulness of the plant; he should study its formation, its relationship with the rest of the plant realm; and how they all are drawn upward and illuminated by the sun. And so he should observe and oversee, with a calm and steady gaze, and collect the data subject to his judgment not in terms of his own interest, but in terms of the circle of things which he observes.[4]

Compare Nietzsche:

> *Our new "infinite."*—How far the perspectival character of existence [*der perspektivische Charakter des Daseins*] extends or indeed whether existence has any other character than this; whether existence without interpretation, without "sense," does not become "nonsense"; whether, on the other hand, all existence is not essentially actively engaged in *interpretation* ["nicht alles Dasein essentiell ein auslegendes Dasein ist"]—that cannot be decided even by the most industrious and most scrupulously conscientious analysis and self-examination of the intellect; for in the course of this analysis the human intellect cannot avoid seeing itself in its own perspectival forms [*perspektivische Formen*], and *only* in these. We cannot look around our own corner ["Wir können nicht um unsre Ecke sehn"]. . . . But I

should think that today we are at least far from the ridiculous immodesty that would be involved in decreeing from our corner that perspectives are permitted only from this corner. Rather has the world become "infinite" for us all over again, inasmuch as we cannot reject the possibility that it *may include infinite interpretations* ["unendliche Interpretationen in sich schliesst"]. (*Gay Science*, sec. 374, Kaufmann trans., modified).

In this revelatory passage, indeed, Nietzsche, like Goethe, lays the groundwork for what has recently been called "evolutionary epistemology": the idea that evolving ecosystems produce populations of organisms that serve as ways of knowing the environment, naturally selecting those forms that pass the test of survival, selecting out those that do not. This is a cognitive ecosystem in which the "mind of man" is situated by the enormously variegated perspectives of the life forms surrounding it. The human mind—limited by its own "perspectival forms"—cannot possibly understand, let alone dominate, the ecosystem via technology; rather the human mind is limited to its own corner, its ecological niche, to the "situated knowledges" in Haraway's term, which characterize the human situation. Therefore, universal scientific knowledge of and control over nature—the knowledge of a power over nature associated with Nietzsche by Acampora—are in fact disallowed by Nietzsche's understanding of the human mind and its abilities in relation to other perspectival forms in nature. "Nature" is made up of *endless interpretations*.

Derrida, in his reading of Nietzsche's view of woman—the very image of semeiotic plurality and undecidability—argues similarly for an irreducible complexity of the text: "That Nietzsche had no illusions that he might ever know anything of these effects called woman, truth, castration, nor of those *ontological* effects of presence and absence, is manifest in the very heterogeneity of his text" (1978, 95). Derrida argues, in effect, that Nietzsche's stylistic diversity is not reducible to univocal meaning and presents, in our terms, a semeiotic ecology that is the stylistic analog of biodiversity. And it is clear that Nietzsche does not mean, in his style or hermeneutic, "human" interpretations from "our corner," but rather that nature's perspectival forms—organisms and populations of organisms, ecosystems, and so on—are *themselves* endlessly interpretive: in Bateson's language, this is the endless variety of the "ecological mind." Foucault, too, understands Nietzsche to be undermining the hermeneutics of universality, and so contrasts Nietzsche's genealogy with history. History, he argues, claims a universal standpoint outside events in terms of which the content of historical action is then evaluated and interpreted. Genealogy, in contrast, is a liberating movement beyond historical "objectivity."

> Once historical sense is mastered by a suprahistorical perspective, metaphysics can bend it to its own purpose, and, by aligning it to the demands of objective science, it can impose its own "Egypt-ianism." On the other hand, the historical sense can evade metaphysics and become a privileged instrument of genealogy if it refuses the certainty of absolutes. Given this, it corresponds to the acuity of a glance that distinguishes, separates, and disperses; that is capable of liberating divergence and marginal elements. (87)

This critique goes, in our view, for "natural" as well as "cultural" history, and has consequences that are significant for ecology.

Goethe, too, argues that nature cannot be "systematized" from the human corner; rather, it has its own ways of knowing, which no doubt include but are not limited to or circumscribable by the human perspective:

> "Natural System"—a contradictory statement. Nature has no system; she has, she is life and rises from an unknown center to an unknowable boundary. The study of nature is therefore endless; one may pursue it into the most infinitesimal parts, or on the whole, to pursue the breadth and height of its traces.[5]

To attempt to reduce this vast ecological network of living minds to the human perspective, to have power over it and reduce it to human purposes, in a word, to attempt to fit the natural world into a univocal system, Goethe believes to be self-contradictory. For all living beings are capable of creating semeiotic universes; they all, like us, have the ability to represent their surroundings; therefore, to reduce them to our point of view, including our science, is foolhardy. As Bateson argues in "Conscious Purpose versus Nature," this is a dangerous form of scientific *hubris*:

> In the period of the Industrial Revolution, perhaps the most important disaster was the enormous increase of scientific arro-gance. We had discovered how to make trains and other machines . . . and Occidental man saw himself as an autocrat with complete power over a universe which was made of physics and chemistry. And the biological phenomena were in the end

to be controlled like processes in a test tube. Evolution was the history of how organisms learned more tricks for controlling the environment; and man had better tricks than any other organism.

But that arrogant scientific philosophy is now obsolete, and in its place there is the discovery that man is only a part of larger systems and that the part can never control the whole. ("Conscious Purpose versus Nature," 443)

These are the *labyrinths of the ecological mind,* as perspectivally various as the diversity of living forms. So Goethe says of living beings,

An organic being is so many-sided at its exterior, in its interior so manifold and inexhaustible, that one can not choose enough standpoints to view it, he can not delineate enough organs to partition it, without killing it. I offer this idea: that beauty, perfection with freedom, be applied to organic nature.[6]

This "beauty" Nietzsche is not so sure about, calling it "aesthetic anthropomorphism" (*Gay Science,* sec. 109), but he and Goethe are in agreement that the view of nature most inclusive of human and nonhuman life—what we would now think of as the perspective of evolutionary ecology—is Dionysian. How, then, is this perspective constructed?

Romanticism and Classicism:
Toward a Genealogy of Cybernetics

Surely a viable ecological perspective must reject naive Romanticism while nevertheless preserving the Romantic's openness to nature. Nietzsche says,

What is romanticism?—Every art, every philosophy may be viewed as a remedy and an aid in the service of growing and struggling life; they always presuppose suffering and sufferers. But there are two kinds of sufferers: first, those who suffer from the *over-fullness of life*—they want a Dionysian art and likewise a tragic view of life, a tragic insight—and then those who suffer from the *impoverishment of life* and seek rest, stillness, calm seas, redemption from themselves through art and knowledge, or intoxication, convulsions, anaesthesia, and madness. All romanticism in art and insight corresponds to the dual needs of the latter type. (*Gay Science,* sec. 370)

In this instance, Nietzsche is critical of Romantics as suffering from an "impoverishment of life," and clearly prefers an art—in Derrida's sense, a *style*, *éperon*, "spur" of *différance*—overfull with life. In keeping with this view of artistry overflowing via differentiation and supplementarity, Goethe in his literary "Romantic" writings, as *The Sufferings of Young Werther* indicates, develops a view similar to that in his scientific works, developing a new appreciation for what will later be called *biodiversity*:

> When the lovely valley around me is shrouded in mist, and the high sun rests on the impenetrable darkness of my forest, and only single rays steal into the inner sanctuary, I then lie in the tall grass beside the cascading brook, and close to the ground a thousand varieties of tiny grasses fill me with wonder; when I feel this teeming little world among the stalks closer to my heart— the countless, unfathomable forms of tiny worms and gnats. (*The Sufferings of Young Werther*, "May 10," 2–3)

Goethe seems to consider natural beings of various kinds to have an inner life of their own and thus a subjectively derived truth of their own. So he speaks of objects being determined not by externally imposed definitions but by "intrinsic determinate patterns" according to which they exist. Thus we cannot fully grasp the existence of a natural entity, for we observe it from the outside and do not share in its inner world. So living things, both considered as wholes and as parts, cannot be limited by external definitions imposed by man; they "participate in eternity" and therefore can never be fully explained. This is in direct contrast to the Baconian and Cartesian assumption that nature can be known thoroughly and objectively in accordance with human percepts and measurements, conceived atomically and subjected to technological control. Goethe's nature is itself accorded subjectivity and so becomes, like a human subject, at least in this respect, free and ultimately indeterminate.

This mutual subjectivity, Dionysian in spirit, is tempered in Goethe as in Nietzsche with the intellectual clarity of Appollinian vision tempering Romanticism with Classicism. Goethe addresses this tension in his *Zur Philosophie*, asking the question, "How is a concordance possible between free self-determination and nature (or the object)?" ("Wie ist zwischen dem freien Selbstbestimmen und der Natur [oder Objekt] eine Übereinstim- mung möglich?") (Goethe 1949, vol. 16, 918). This question, in turn, leads Goethe to speak of "The Experiment as Mediator of Subject and Object" ("Der Versuch als Vermittler von Objekt und Subjekt" [844]). As Karl Fink argues regarding the latter text, "In his essay on the 'experiment' Goethe is subscribing to a point of view also found in his early essays, that the experiment does not transmit information about nature alone, but does so equally about the designer of the experiment. Secondly, there is the double edge in the meaning of 'Versuch,' which means at the same time 'experiment' and 'essay.' Goethe's use of the term is consistent with his approach to scientific writing, for the experiment is incomplete without narrative and the essay as a narration always remains unfinished. It is a trial, an "attempt," a third meaning carried primarily by the verb form, 'versuchen'" (Fink 1991, 38). This convergence of empirical investigation with narrative and open-ended inquiry clearly suggests that the "experiment" as "mediator" is not to be considered as the simple "objectification" of "nature as object" nor as the "subjective" leaning of the interpreter, but rather a *conversation* or, in cybernetic terms, a *communicative circuit* encompassing subject and object or both human and natural subjects. Both the scientist and what she or he studies become interlocutors in a web of communicative relationships—in modern terms, an *ecosystem*—amidst which the communicative activity of science—its *experiments* in Goethe's complex sense—takes place. Thus "scientific experiment" becomes a mode of communicative interaction with the surrounding ecosystem.

Goethe's Classicism requires that Romantic dynamism be complemented by order. But this is to be obtained not by the imposition of laws from without, but by the communicative relationship between organism and environment: the form is emergent precisely from their co-evolution. It is not, therefore, reducible to the perspective of either but rather becomes articulated on the level of their *relationship*. Since the latter is communicative, an appreciation for the subjectivity—the capacity to generate form—of both organism and environment (other organisms) must be appreciated. This implies that biological form is shaped at what Bateson, following Russell and Whitehead, would call a higher logical type from the particular organism. This, of course, must be true in Darwinian terms, for otherwise the phenotypes of indiviudal organisms would be able to reshape their genotypes. Genotypic change is of a higher order of abstraction than phenotypic change.

In Goethe's terms, however, this becomes not a simple mechanistic model of "random mutation" and "natural selection." Rather, as Cassirer points out, Goethe's notion of form is, as noted earlier, both orderly and dynamic: "Form is akin to type, but the geometrical fixity of the type is no longer suited to the form. The difference is that form belongs to another dimension, as it were" (1950, 139). That "other dimension" is, on our reading, precisely the combination of spatial displacement and temporal drift packed into Derrida's key word, *différance*, and into Nietzsche's dynamic of supplementarity, of overflow, in *über*. "Form belongs not only to space but to time as well," Cassirer continues regarding Goethe (to repeat a passage quoted at the outset), "and it must assert itself in the temporal. This could not consist in merely static being, for any such condition of a life form would be tantamount to its extinction." This is exactly Bateson's point when he argues that the complex variable preserved in evolution is "the economics of flexibility" in a living population (*Steps* 1987, 357–363). Hence, Cassirer explains, "the type itself is a being that is only perceived in its development, a permanence that exists only as it comes to pass. Thus Goethe spoke of the 'modality of flexibility' of the type." For Goethe, the type was a "real Proteus," so that to grasp it we must learn a new hold: "While we hold fast to the permanent," Cassirer continues, "we must learn at the same time to change our views with the changeable and become acquainted with its manifold variability." For ultimately we must attune ourselves to both the temporal and spatial dimensions of living form, as to evolutionary music: "Each creature is but 'one single note, a nuance, in a great harmony, which must be studied as a whole, otherwise each individual thing is but a meaningless item,'" Cassirer concludes, quoting Goethe. This "music" provides both dynamism and form simultaneously. Here is the true reconciliation of the oppositions that Del Caro notes in Nietzsche and Goethe, which are different names for what must be, for both, the complementary opposition of Romanticism and Classicism.

Therefore, those who are "inflamed by the drive to knowledge," whom Goethe mentions in a passage cited earlier, should recall the subjective root of their own experience; they should avoid subjecting natural beings to human measures such as "like and dislike," "attraction and repulsion," and instead consider them as "indifferent and quasi-divine beings." Thus the botanist should consider plants not in accordance with an external set of categories, such as their beauty or usefulness for human beings, but rather in terms of their own intrinsic designs and life impulses to take particular shapes and to seek sunlight. Goethe would have the botanist, therefore, consider the plant in terms of its formation and in its relationship to the rest of the plant realm but also in terms of its internal nature, its tendency to heliotropism, its apparent internal guidance. He seems therefore to ask the scientist to combine an objective view of living things with an appreciation for their internal nature, the latter derived from an awareness of his own subjectivity. Thus he becomes a good observer, "with a calm and steady gaze," but one whose view is tempered by subjectivity and an appreciation for "the circle of things he observes," presumably the intrinsic life-interests of organisms. So nature, again, is not reduced to a mere set of objects in motion but instead is given an inner life and allowed to exist freely. To dismiss this view as "vitalist" would be, to Goethe, sheer myopic arrogance—the very *hubris* that Bateson sees as contributing to the ecological crisis in the first place (cf. *Steps*, 498–499).

Indeed, as Bateson suggests, Goethe's view of the ecological mind and its plurality of epistemic subjects is informed by a linguistic analogy, which also allies his work with communication theory:

> Goethe pointed out 150 years ago that there is a sort of syntax or grammar in the anatomy of flowering plants. A "stem" is that which bears "leaves"; a "leaf" is that which has a bud in its axil; a bud is a stem which originates in the axil of a leaf; etc. The formal (i.e., communicational) nature of each organ is deter-mined by its contextual status—the context in which it occurs and the context which it sets for other parts. ("Double Bind [1969]," 276)

Accordingly, Goethe rejects the mechanistic systematization of nature characteristic of Baconian or Cartesian science and would cultivate a more humane—communicative— relationship with it: it is not an object to be studied and exploited for human purposes, but an equal being who is to be respected and understood. For like a human being nature "rises from an unknown center to an unknowable boundary." So Goethe writes in a poem,

> "Into the core of Nature"—
> O Philistine—
> "No earthly mind can enter." (1983, 236–237)

Like human beings in the Classical and Christian traditions, nature has been endowed here with a fathomless divinity. Thus Goethe sees in the natural world the full range of spiritual possibility that has been accorded to man: "Beauty, perfection with freedom." Thus his science meets with his literary pursuits, where the love between human beings is transferred to a loving relationship with nature. As he says in his "Maxims and Reflections" on art and artists, "the most beautiful delight of the thinker is, to have researched the researchable and silently to revere the unresearchable"

("Das schönste Glück des denkenden Menschen ist, das Erforschliche erforscht zu haben und das Unerforschliche ruhig zu verehren" (Goethe 1953, vol. 12, 467). This insistence both on research and reverence, on sound and silence, is again very much communicative in spirit: just as one must not only speak but listen in conversation, to let the other speak, so one must both actively inquire into and passively accept the other in the communicative circuit of "experiment." Thus Goethe says in his reflections on "Die Natur": "We live in her [nature's] midst and are strange to her. She speaks continuously with us and does not reveal her secret. We work steadily on her and still have no control over her" ("Wir leben mitten in ihr [Natur] und sind ihr fremde. Sie spricht unaufhörlich mit uns und verrät uns ihr Geheimnis nicht. Wir wirken beständig auf sie und haben doch keine Gewalt über sie") (Goethe 1949, vol. 16, 922). Similarly, Derrida says of Nietzsche's hermeneutical style that, like the "hymen's graphic" that resists the mastering of the text by any single thesis, Nietzsche's text "describes a margin where the control over meaning or code is without recourse, poses the limit to the relevance of the hermeneutic of systematic question" (99).

It is characteristic of Goethe's Romanticism, as expressed in *The Sorrows of Young Werther*, that man looks upon nature as a loving friend, and that his or her relationship with the living world is infused with the rich feeling, the concerned sentiment and affectionate attention to detail, which characterizes the most intimate of human relationships. Thus the inner and outer worlds of human beings meet in the sympathetic contemplation of nature. So arises the intensity of feeling Werther experiences for nature, the delight in its manifold forms and dynamic productivity, overwhelming to the point of torment at times. As Goethe says, also in his essay on "Die Natur," "she [nature] brings forth new forms; what there is, was never before, what was, comes not again—all is new, and still always the old" ("Sie [Natur] schafft ewig neue Gestalten; was da ist, war noch nie, was war, kommt nicht wieder—alles ist neu, und doch immer das Alte") (Goethe 1949, vol. 16, 922). Goethe's contemporary, Novalis, expresses a similar view, focusing on nature's variety and productivity of forms, virtually suggesting an ecological unconscious complete with biodreams: "Nature is at the same time an endless animal, an endless plant, an endless stone. Her functions [are] in this threefold pattern. Through her nutrition, which is threefold, emerges the natural realm. These are her dream images" ("Die Natur is zugleich ein unendliches Tier, eine unendliche Pflanze und ein unendlicher Stein. Ihre Funktionen in dieser dreifachen Gestalt. Durch ihr Essen, das dreifach ist, entstehn die Naturreiche. Es sind ihre Traum-bilder") (Novalis, *Werke und Briefe*, 328). So Romanticism verges on what Bateson calls, in cybernetic terms, the "ecological mind."

The opposite of communication with nature in Goethe, as in his contemporary Novalis, is alienation, epitomized by the Cartesian dualism and instrumentalist knowledge practices. As Goethe asserts regarding the "scientific world" (*die wissenschaftliche Welt*), it is understood in terms of "domination and control" (*Herrschen und Beherrschen*) (Goethe 1953, vol. 12, 432). With a similar metaphorical sense, Novalis says, of scientific man, "He feels himself to be master of the world, his ego floats mightily over this abyss" ("Er fühlt sich Herr der Welt, sein Ich schwebt mächtig über diesem Abgrund") (Novalis, *Werke und Briefe*, 98). Novalis argues that man and nature once shared a common language, one that has been lost (104). That loss goes along with the rise of Newtonian science and the abrogation of the communicative link between humanity and nature.

Nietzsche, too, rejects the Cartesian, Baconian tendencies of modern science and counters it, not with "Romanticism" whose "impoverished" aspects he rejects, but rather with his powerful idea of *Übermensch*. Both Acampora and Hallman in their controversy about Nietzsche's environ-mentalism agree that the *Übermensch* is not an ecologically viable idea. We think, on the contrary, that if *über* is understood not as "power over" but as "power with," as the creative production of diversity—the Dionysian "over-fullness of life"—then Nietzsche's work may be understood as heralding a postmodern-ecological sensibility.

The Ethical Self: Beyond Good and Evil

Central to the idea of an ecological self must be an account of the ethical self, for these must be intertwined in a communicative spiral, the two personae informing one another in order to demarcate the strategies of adaptation. This dynamical notion of "human identity" is commensurate with Nietzsche's critique of morality and of egotism as it is with his Dionysian ethics of living. Instead of attributing to "man" a spectral distance from "nature," as did the traditional Chain of Being, rather than attributing to *Homo sapiens* a "power over" other creatures based on this superior vantage point, though he admits that human beings are also capable of this, Nietzsche would have the *Übermensch* in a fluctuating *balance* or *communication with* the "others" of the natural world. Indeed, what is perhaps best called Nietzsche's "immoral morality" is based on a transpersonal idea of self that includes the other, and likewise on a trans-actional idea of moral ideas that includes what they exclude, what they proscribe, as the language of the ethical "other" which, too, must be respected. As Nietzsche says,

> In man, *creature* and *creator* are united: in man there is matter, fragment, excess, clay, mud, madness, chaos; but in man there is also creator, sculptor, the hardness of the hammer, the divine spectator and the seventh day—do you understand this anti-thesis? (*Beyond Good and Evil*, sec. 225)

The point is that "man" is constructed out of both passive and active, question and answer, matter and mind, other and self: she or he is both that out of which the sculpture is molded and the molder, the artisan that is self-molding. This requires that man be an "antithesis" between work and rest, divine labor and rest, in dialectical oscillation. But this is not the pre-Nietzschean dialectic of conflict leading to *Aufhebung* and the univocal cancellation of opposites. This, as Deleuze points out, is a dialectic of violence and mastery, of the *Übermensch* in the *worst* possible sense. The dialectic "expresses every combination of reactive forces and nihilism," Deleuze argues, "the history of evolution and of their relations. Opposition substituted for difference is also the triumph of the reactive forces that find their corresponding principle in the will to nothingness. . . . Nietzsche reproaches the dialecticians for going no further than an abstract concep-tion of universal and particular. . . . Nietzsche creates his own method: dramatic, typological, and differential. He turns philosophy into an art, the art of interpreting and evaluating" (197). In a word, Nietzsche's view is, in contemporary terms, *cybernetic*: the self is constructed out of the self-corrective spiral of life's course, over which the "will" has no unilateral control but rather only the continuing interplay with what it wills in a con-tinuous process of "feedback." This course is not, however, contained in a homeostatic circuit but rather traces its own morphogenic spiral.

Toward a Poststructuralist Cybernetics

Nietzsche's view of the self contains the seed of a poststructuralist cyber-netics, the *éperon* toward a recursive ecology. This perspective on cyber-netics and ecology has emerged from the convergence of Bateson's ideas with those of Derrida in Wilden's *System and Structure*. For Wilden offers strategies by which the mechanistic and instrumentalist paradigms of the

Western scientific *epistēmē* can be overcome by the convergence of poststructuralism and cybernetics.

Wilden builds on the discourses of cybernetics, especially as articulated by Bateson, and poststructuralism, as articulated by Derrida, to create a morphogenic model of living systems. Cybernetics requires a circular description of nature, in which "organism" and "environment" are integrated in the same circuit of information. The circuit is conceived statistically, in terms of the probability or improbability of events described in its course. In thermodynamic terms, probable events are the norm, improbable ones deviations from the norm, and it is deviations from a given thermodynamic state of affairs that require explanation. If the Second Law of Thermodynamics predicts that all differences in the circuit described are likely to degrade entropically toward zero, then the maintenance or increase of difference, negative entropy, defined as information, requires explanation. Cybernetics approaches the maintenance of improbability—of negative entropy or information—by a process of negative explanation. When improbable, nonrandom events occur in a particular circuit structure, the cybernetic explanation of that improbability will be in terms of restraints upon randomness. "In cybernetic language," Bateson argues,

> the course of events is said to be subject to *restraints*, and it is assumed that, apart from such restraints, the pathways of change would be governed only by equality of probability. In fact, the "restraints" upon which cybernetic explanation depends can in all cases be regarded as factors which determine inequality of probability. If we find a monkey striking a typewriter apparently at random but in fact writing meaningful prose, we shall look for restraints, either inside the monkey or inside the typewriter. Perhaps the monkey could not strike inappropriate letters; perhaps the type bars could not move if improperly struck; perhaps incorrect letters could not survive on the paper. Somewhere there must have been a circuit which could identify error and eliminate it. ("Cybernetic Explanation," 406)

The error-correcting circuit imposing constraints on the probable course of events and therefore generating improbability, or information—a monkey typing the King's English—is "homeostatic" insofar as it maintains a specified state of affairs—an optimum condition—built into the circuit. That optimum state—its "present" state, in Derridean language—is maintained, in cybernetic terms, by the circuit's memory in the face of the perturbations of entropy. The cybernetic circuit thus self-corrects to remove the errors, say, in the monkey's typing, in order to specify the grammar of good prose. In other words, it maintains a present state of information in the face of noise. A typical thermostat is an elementary cybernetic device that maintains the present temperature of a room by correcting deviations of temperature in terms of an ideal setting, say, 78 degrees.

The traditional explanation for this improbable, preferred state of affairs—this design—was "mind"—Greek, *daimon*, as Clerk Maxwell saw it, or in Aristotelian terms *psyche* (Latin, *anima*). Following Plato and Descartes, Maxwell argued that the demon (*daimon*) selecting the preferred state of negative entropy in thermodynamics, and so apparently contradicting the Second Law, was transcendental to physical systems; in effect it was *res cogitans* as opposed to *res extensa*. Following Szilard's statistical analysis of Maxwell's demon in "On the Decrease in Entropy in a Thermodynamic System by the Intervention of Intelligent Beings," however, Wilden argues that the *daimon* of cybernetic explanation need not be transcendental altogether (see Wilden 1980, 130, n. 2). As Szilard argues regarding the decrease in entropy created by an intelligent being selecting and maintaining a negatively entropic state of affairs: "We shall realize that the Second Law is not threatened as much by this entropy decrease as one would think, as soon as we see that the entropy decrease resulting from the intervention would be compensated completely in any event if the execution of such a measurement were, for instance, always accompanied by $k \log 2$ units of entropy" (1972, 122). In other words, the demon's negatively entropic memory and selection of a preferred state is compensated for by its generation of entropy elsewhere, in another system or in the "environment."

This is precisely what worries Bateson and Wilden about industrial civilization: it selects the states of affairs it would prefer and realizes them technologically *as if the mind that were doing the selection were Cartesian*—transcendental to the larger ecosystem and therefore immune to the consequences of compensatory entropification in the environment. The global chaos—the noise or entropy—that has resulted from this epistemology is popularly known as the "ecological crisis." Wilden goes on to argue that a *morphogenic* picture of cybernetic systems would differ from the *morphostatic* one described in Bateson's above example in the following way. The preferred state of the system—its present structure—is not transcendental, not static, does not exhibit what Derrida calls the "metaphysics of presence," but is rather *entropic as it informs*. Its "in-formation" of orderly systems is also, necessarily, a "de-formation," its construction a deconstruction, even though this is often not apparent to the selective awareness of "consciousness" in the modern Cartesian sense. Bateson's "Conscious Purpose versus Nature" and "The Effects of Conscious Purpose on Human Adaptation," amount to a critique of Cartesian consciousness—which prefers the morphostatic "presence." The morphogenic combination of information and noise is, in Nietzschean terms, the interplay of Apollo and Dionysus, and in Derridean ones, the play of *différance*.

Wilden is, to our knowledge, the first to have seen this (1972, 396ff.):

> For Derrida the notion of the (memory) trace is intimately connected with the concept of *différence* (as with Bateson) but more especially with its homonym derived from the verb '*différer*', "to put off," "to defer," "to delay." *Différance*, with an "a," is the "after the event" of the post-script (*Nachträglichkeit*), a relation of postponement. (398)

This "postponement" is the incorporation of the deferred entropy into the process of signification, or the process of *in-formation* in the cybernetics of life. For Bateson, "what we mean by information—the elementary unit of information—is a *difference which makes a difference*, and it is able to make a difference because the neural pathways along which it travels and is continually transformed are themselves provided with energy" ("Form, Substance, Difference," 459). Indeed, the energizing of information and its deferral in the circuit structures of living systems, intrinsic to Bateson's idea of cybernetics, make his "difference which makes a difference" a good synonym for Derrida's *différance*. Significantly, in this regard, for Bateson, there is a cybernetic *daimon* that produces the differences that constitute the evolutionary process: "*the unit of evolutionary survival turns out to be identical with the unit of mind*" ("Pathologies of Epistemology," 491). Or, as Wilden puts it in poststructural terms, "'the essence of life' (which is no essence, but rather no-thing) is *différance*." For Wilden, combining Derrida with Bateson, "Difference, like information, is a relation, and it cannot be localized: *différance* is the IN-FORMATION of form" (1980, 399). Bateson's cybernetic mind and Derrida's différance perform the same task: the information of form.

Because conscious purpose, in Bateson's terms, prefers "the metaphysics of presence," in Derrida's, and assumes the Cartesian transcendence of its values with respect to the entropic systems with which it, in Szilard's terms, is necessarily coupled, it becomes horrified by the very entropic consequences of its own preferences. Hence, Bateson's aforementioned critique of conscious purpose converges with Derrida's critique of "presence." For Bateson, the contents of consciousness do not typically include the "difference which makes a difference" out of which they spring in the cybernetic system: *"the cybernetic nature of self and the world tends to be imperceptible to consciousness,* insofar as the contents of the 'screen' of consciousness are determined by the considerations of purpose" ("Effects of Conscious Purpose on Human Adaptation," 450). If we take Bateson's "contents of the 'screen' of consciousness" to mean "presence" or "appearance," or "preferred state" sought by desire, then, as Wilden argues, Derrida's comments in *De la grammatologie* are "remarkably consonant with Bateson's": "The (pure) trace is *différance*. . . . *Différance* is therefore the formation of form. . . . The trace is the *différance* which opens up the world of appearance [*l'apparaître*] and signification" (Derrida 1974, 91–95, cited in and translated by Wilden 1980, 399). But *différance*, like Bateson's cybernetic *daimon*, is imperceptible to Cartesian consciousness.

The Will to Life: The Ecological Übermensch

Nietzsche understands the issue of consciousness in terms of the concept of the "I" (*Ich*) and the will, but his analysis is quite similar:

> A man who *wills*—commands something in himself which obeys or which he believes obeys. But now observe the strangest thing of all about the will—about this so complex thing for which people have only *one* word: inasmuch as in the given circumstances we at the same time command *and* obey, and as the side which obeys knows the sensations of constraint, compulsion, pressure, resistance, motion which usually begin immediately after the act of will; inasmuch as, on the other hand, we are in the habit of disregarding and deceiving ourselves over this duality by means of the synthetic concept of "I"; so a whole chain of erroneous conclusions and consequently of false evaluations of the will itself has become attached to the will as such— so that he who wills believes wholeheartedly that willing *suffices* for action. (*Beyond Good and Evil*, sec. 19)

The concept of self entertained by Western culture is lopsided and illusory, a highly edited view of the dialogical interplay of "willing" and "obeying," which represents "self" as existing only on the active side of volition, but

Nietzsche argues, to the contrary, that it must include the passive side as well; hence the "I" or "self" must include the "you" or "it" of the other, even when, especially when, the "other" is considered as "evil." For ultimately the concepts of good and evil have been constructed through the self-deception of one-sided identity, from which the "chain of erroneous conclusions" and "false evaluations" follow, of course, but the result is not ethical at all—that is the great Platonic-Christian lie—but rather a self-righteous garnering of all ethical propriety to "ourselves" and our "conspecifics," which amounts to the denial of the communicative reciprocity with the other that constitutes life. In Bateson's terms, this is the arrogation of all "Mind" and so of ethical concern to self or conscious purpose; it is the "arrogance" that has been significantly responsible for *creating* the ecological crisis:

> If you put God outside and set him vis-à-vis his creation and if you have the idea that you are created in his image, you will logically and naturally see yourself as outside and against the things around you. And as you arrogate all mind to yourself, you will see the world around you as mindless and therefore not entitled to moral or ethical consideration. The environment will seem to be yours to exploit. Your survival unit will be you and your folks or conspecifics against the environment of other social units, other races and the brutes and vegetables. ("Form, Substance, Difference," 468)

The antidote for this *hubris*, short of tragedy, is an ethics and a self-understanding that include the other as dialogically implicated in the one's identity and that establish the form of one's connection with others communicatively.

Nietzsche's idea of *über* becomes crucial here, especially given our "communicative" reading of the term as suggesting "power with" rather than "power over." Consider what he says about traversing the Abyss:

> Not the height but the abyss [*Abhang*] is awesome [*furchtbar*]. That abyss where the glance plunges *down* [*hinunter*] and the hand reaches *up* [*hinauf*]. There the heart is dizzied before its double will. Alas, friends, can you guess what is my heart's double will?
>
> This, is *my* abyss and my danger, that my glance plunges into the height and that my hand would grasp and steady itself— on the Deep!

My will clamps itself [*klammert sich*] to man, with fetters I bind myself to man, because I am swept up toward the overman [*hinaufreisst zum Übermenschen*]: for that way my other will wants to go.

And *therefore* I live blind among [*unter*] men as if I did not know them: that my hand does not wholly lose its belief in what is firm. (*Zarathustra*, II, "On Human Prudence," Kaufmann trans., modified)

Here Nietzsche embodies in a personal, willful struggle the dynamic interplay between chaos and order, entropy and information, good and evil, that generates the dynamic flexibility of life. Just like a tightrope walker, he balances between the Abyss and what is firm, between the superman and man, but paradoxically we find, as Nietzsche's imagery unfolds, that what is firm is actually the Abyss—"that my hand would grasp and steady itself— on the Deep!" Just as the tightrope walker who treads above the Abyss, Nietzsche actually steadies himself on the yawning space around and below, thereby keeping his balance. In Bateson's terms, this is of course the deeper insight that the dynamics of chaos—*chaos* meaning "void" or "chasm" in Greek—is the openness to change that generates the resilience of living forms. In Deleuze's terms, this Nietzschean *über* connotes a will to power in the *Übermensch* that is not domineering and hierarchic but differential and creative: "The will to power is not force but the differential element which simultaneously determines the relation of forces (quantity) and the respective qualities of related forces. It is in this element of difference that affirmation manifests itself and develops itself as creative" (197).

Übermensch is, moreover, associated with the Abyss: its reference is that going beyond the stably defined men among (*unter*, literally "under") whom Zarathustra lives, but whose present form Nietzsche apparently takes to be not an essence but an open-ended process "steadied," in cybernetic terms guided, by the Abyss of the overman. Indeed, earlier in the same text Zarathustra proclaims:

What is great in man is that he is a bridge and not an end: what can be loved in man is that he is an *overture* and *going under*. (*Zarathustra*, I, iv)

What is "lovable" in man is that he is "ein Übergang und ein Untergang": literally "an over-going and an under-going." Man is to transform her/himself both as *über* and as *unter*, as *Übermensch* and as *Untermensch*.

What this means, at least, is that the "newly born wo-man," in the language of Cixous and Clément, that emerges from the bridge is not to be "over" or "under" anyone, but a new persona formed by the confluence of self and other. Nietzsche further indicates this by his images of transformation later in the same text:

> There it was too that I picked up the word "over-man" by the way, and that man is something that must be overcome—that man is a bridge and no end: proclaiming himself blessed in view of his noon and evening, as the way to new dawns—Zarathustra's word of the great noon, and whatever else I hung up over man like the last crimson light of evening. (*Zarathustra*, III, iii)

Here the cycle of day and night, especially of "new dawns" (*neue Morgenröte*), is used as an image of rebirth and transformation, to which Nietzsche goes on to add the joy, *jouissance*, of overcoming the static oppositions, like "over" and "under" or "good" and "evil" that characterize the Oedipal hierarchy of Freud: *Es*, *Ich*, and *Über-Ich* (*Id*, *Ego* and *Superego*).

Clearly, the imagery here is one that celebrates new life: the opening provided by the feminine power of rebirth. So Pearson-Ansell argues, adding an ecofeminist dimension to Nietzsche's environmentalism:

> The overman is a figure that is pregnant with plurality and diversity of meaning and styles. The overman can today be understood as the symbol of a Dionysian post-modern future in which the hierarchical distinctions of Western metaphysics, of phallic Truth, have been overcome. When the overman returns, the "truth" of woman will have arrived. This "moment" of the constitution of woman—and of man—as plurality, diversity, and distance will inaugurate the eternal return of the new, the unique, and the incomparable experience which is beyond any hierarchical opposition of "masculine" and "feminine." (1992, 329)

Interestingly, Goethe has Faust dance with a witch—a template for the sorceress and hysteric that Cixous and Clément counterpose to the churchmen and scientists who have authored the Western *epistēmē*—in the "Walpurgis Night" section of his *Faust*, Part I, as if to suggest that the personification of the Western intellect and will to power through science and technology, Faustian man, should cast off his blinders and celebrate life—good and evil whirling together. And she (the witch) leads, as the concluding lines of *Faust*, Part II, suggest:

The Eternal-Feminine
Draws us onward.

If we take Goethe's "eternal-feminine" (*Ewig-Weibliche*) to suggest his earlier statement that "every determinate living being participates in eternity" and so requires "endless explanation," echoed in Nietzsche's observation that the world has become "infinite . . . inasmuch as we cannot reject the possibility that it *may include infinite interpretations*," then this is a feminine that seems eternal to the perspectivally limited gaze of "man" because she presents infinite rebirth, metamorphosis—*Hinausschaffen*—eternally spiraling return.

This suggests self-transformation as midwifery and the development of an ecological-feminist persona—if you will, an *Übermädchen*. The feminine self suggested here is one of "creative evolutionist": the one giving birth not only to new forms of life but also to new forms of culture, to the rewriting of the human-ecological domain. Presumably this would, as ecological feminists often envision, be a self beyond dualisms, a child of Apollo *and* Dionysus, of self *and* other, of wo-man *and* nature. Hence Derrida argues that, in Nietzsche's style, "woman is recognized and affirmed as an affirmative power, a dissimulatress, an artist, a dionysiac. And no longer is it man who affirms her. She affirms herself, in and of herself, in man, for she is beyond the oppressive dialectic which required her to respond to man from two reactive positions (*répondait à l'homme des deux positions réactives*) [truth or nontruth]" (97). So Plumwood argues that "forms of oppression from both the present and the past have left their traces in western culture as a network of dualisms, and the logical structure of dualism forms a major basis for the connection between forms of oppression" (1993, 2). As she goes on to argue, the dualism between "man" and "nature" is central to the other forms of oppression. Similarly, Warren and Cheney argue:

> Ecofeminist ethics is . . . antireductionist. It is a structurally pluralistic framework that centralizes both diversity or difference (e.g., among women, among people of color, beween humans and nonhumans) *and* commonalities (e.g., among women, among people of color, between humans and nonhumans). (1991, 186–187)

Nietzsche uses the image of birth beyond dualism at the horizon of his vision:

Will the preying lion still become a child? The child is innocence and forgetting, a new beginning, a game, a self-propelled wheel, a first movement, a sacred "Yes." (*Zarathustra*, I, "Speeches, On the Three Metamorphoses")

Here we meet Nietzsche's image of rebirth in the evolutionary persona of the child, an *Übermensch* with a renewed ethic of living.

Goethe's Faust is as different from Marlow's as Nietzsche's overman, on our reading, is from Acampora's. The former, in each case, is an over-lord, a quester after power over others in all their forms, including human beings and nature. But Goethe's Faust, like Nietzsche's hero, learns to express power as celebration, the Dionysia, in the great dance and music of life.

The form of this new persona, endowed with the "overfullness of life," should be read furthermore, in Bateson's cybernetic terms, not as a static archetype but as the transpersonal configuration of the course of adaptation, steered not by "self" or "other" but rather by their wobbling interplay, just as Nietzsche's tightrope walker balances by continuous interdependency and communication with the Abyss he traverses: he/the self is dependent on the "feedback" from the other of the void and the art of self becomes, in this metaphor, not the imposition of unilateral control over one's course— that would result in falling—but rather a balancing of one's position within the surrounding space in a continuous spiral of self-correction. Similarly, in Goethe's terms, this is the branching language, the conversation, of plants that is akin to the larger conversation of all living things in evolution. The larger spiral is the Dionysian persona—the evolving circuit of information—that is the dynamic form of the self unfolding in time: the ecological *Übermensch*.

Conclusion

Indeed, in me there is something invulnerable and
unburiable, something that explodes rock: this is *my will*.
Silent and unchanged it strides through the years. It would
walk its way on my feet, my old will, and its mind is hard of
heart and invulnerable.

Invulnerable am I only in the heel. You are still alive
and your old self, most patient one. You have still broken
out of every tomb. What in my youth was unredeemed lives
on in you; and as life and youth you sit there, full of hope,
on yellow ruins of tombs.

Indeed, for me, you are still the shatterer of all tombs.
Hail to thee, my will! And only where there are tombs are
there resurrections. Thus sang Zarathustra.

—Nietzsche, "The Tomb Song"

Why is it that Nietzsche should emerge at the center of our writings as
the figure animating the various branches of our text with new life?
Certainly it is Nietzsche's extraordinary *will* that has carried his work into
so many avenues of the history of ideas and that gives his writings such
extraordinary power. Yet the "power" that Nietzsche's works convey is not
simply that of modernity—the dynamo of materialism and industrialism—
separated from the realm of ideas and emotions. Nor is it a purely spiritual
phenomenon, made up only of ideas and emotions, divorced from the
material world. Rather, Nietzsche's work embodies *both halves* of the divide
between mind and body that has haunted the Western tradition since

189

Plato, like the ghost of Hamlet Senior. Nietzsche's texts, as the above excerpt from *Zarathustra* suggests, engage the ghost and explode his tomb, promising a resurrection for Occidental civilization in a reanimated body-mind embracing life and death just as, ethically, it embraces good and evil. Truly, in this sense, Nietzsche can allow us to celebrate a life reborn from the death of Platonism and Cartesianism, the alienated powers giving impetus to both classicism and modernism. Recall that Plato, in the *Phaedo*, defines both death and the terminus of the philosophical quest as "the separation of the soul from the body" (see Chapter 4). Particularly in the age of global communications and the information explosion, Nietzsche, in offering a new vision of mind and body reconciled, provides a powerful new meaning to Whitman's poetic proclamation: "I sing the body electric."

In Chapter 4, moreover, we utilized Tibor Fischer's idea of a thought gang to characterize the diversity of thinkers who, in our view, significantly interface with Nietzsche's philosophy. Thus Gregory Bateson, Hélène Cixous, Georges Bataille, and others find themselves onstage with Nietzsche as he thunders his tirade against Christianity. Furthermore, Kafka's *Ungeziefer* (Chapter 3) metamorphoses like Nietzsche's *Übermensch*, and Derrida's *différance* takes on the role both of Kafkan *Ungeziefer* and Nietzschean *Übermensch* as it deconstructs the pretentious metaphysics underlying modern Protestant capitalism (Chapters 3 and 4).

It is particularly in the transmutation of the West at the approaching millennium that a strange new resurrection may be in the offing, not of the Christ returned but, rather, of his taking a bow with Satan, as at the end of the play of the Occident, to say that the drama was profound but, after all, only a play, one that must now be transcended in a new reconciliation of the living. The Nietzschean point is that the traditional oppositions—between mind and body, good and evil, God and Satan, "us" and "them"—are genealogically deconstructed to reveal their utter co-dependency: they are only characters, myths, on the stage of culture, which includes ourselves as a once naive audience who now have been startled into the "reality" that "this is play," and *only* play, by Nietzsche's madman, running into the theater with a lantern, proclaiming, like Foucault, the death of the author. That the dramatis personae now become, as Pirandello would say, characters in search of an author means that they, like us, have entered the postmodern condition. The value of Nietzschean will in this often bewildering state is, as we argued in Chapter 1, to proclaim that self-making, culture making, become the creative alternative to the loss of meaning and the slavery of consumerism. Similarly,

Nietzsche highlights the critical ability to rewrite not only "culture" but "nature," and the mythic divide between them (like the one between God and Satan). This means, in effect, that the will is to rewrite the arts and the sciences—to rethink the fundamentals of our thinking, as Bateson suggests in "The Science of Mind and Order" (*Steps*, Introduction)—and to rework the fundamentals of our technology so as to engage, as Heidegger would say, in a new techno-poetics, which are the practices of Nietzsche's joyous science.

It is worth noting, topically, that Stanford University Press is now releasing a new translation of Nietzsche's complete works based on the most authoritative and comprehensive German edition. Furthermore, there are hundreds of articles being produced in English alone on Nietzsche's works, as well as a stream of books and new translations. One key to this new wave of translation and scholarship is that Nietzsche is credited with originating postmodernity. In this regard, notice that the works of Nietzsche's "gang"—including Cixous, Bataille, Bateson, and others—have been widely influential, particularly in the emerging discipline of cultural studies. But why is this so?

Nietzsche questions and undermines—in contemporary language, "deconstructs"—all the assumptions on which modernity has been based: the separation between culture and nature, male and female, primitive and modern, and the consequent ideas of modernization and progress from the one state to the other, enlightenment and ignorance, science and art, and so on. He also attacks the idea of the contextless, ahistorical individual, as well as the positivistic knowledge that this character—epitomized by the "scientist"—is supposed to have. He furthermore assails the functionalist idea of democracy, where millions of atomic individuals are supposed to offer votes for representatives and institutions that are to work in their interest. For Nietzsche, as for Marx and Foucault, this kind of "democracy" is a myth built out of mythic elements in a story that masks a number of other narratives that demarcate lines of power and influence not high-lighted in the bourgeois democratic myth: the "normalizing" function of modern institutions, giving rise to the "herd mentality" of masses of "citizens" hypnotized by images of national and party interest, the "cunning of capital" (for Marx) and the microhistory of power functioning always just outside of the official channels of influence (for Foucault).

Central to all three of these thinkers—all adamant critics of various strands of modernity—is the *historical method*, and specifically for Nietzsche the practice of genealogy: the uncovering of lines of power and cultural formations by tracing their lineage in detail. This is the basis, clearly, of Foucault's "archaeology" of knowledges, and of the systematic study of the interrelatedness of oppositions, of class inclusion and exclusion, that deconstruction finds basic to the critique of knowledge. Central to this historical method, in turn, is the expanding paradigm of *language* or *textuality* which, in structuralism and poststructuralism, has elaborated Nietzsche's genealogical critique to the entire range of cultural practices with ever more incisive precision, transmuting Nietzsche's hilarious incredulity at the range of human folly into a multidisciplinary form of cultural critique and politics that is increasing nowadays called "cultural studies." Furthermore, breaking even more explosively from the entombment of disciplinary reason, the poststructural genealogical critique is increasingly enveloping the social and natural sciences, as we have tried to show using the work of Bateson ramified through the deconstructive architecture of Nietzsche, Derrida, and Foucault. Pervasively, the textual historicity of Nietzsche's work has come to characterize the contemporary state of writing in the arts and sciences, expanding into the hypertextual and virtual dimensions of what Mark Poster calls the mode of information that, in Marxian terms, has superseded the mode of production as the dominant "logic" of late capitalism. In spite of electronic evangelicalism (Chapter 4) Nietzsche, it seems, has come of age.

Creating Alternatives: Toward a New Joyous Science

Nietzsche, like Goethe, becomes the author of a new science—joyous and poetic—that reconciles life with knowledge in an ecological *Lebenswelt*. Mumford's biotechnics in the "flowering of plants and men" and Bateson's ecological mindfulness become thought forms related to Nietzsche's creative science. Heidegger's *poiesis* furthermore suggests Nietzsche's projected reconciliation of art and science, as does the ecological feminist rewriting of (wo)man and nature in the theoretical tarantella of *l'écriture feminine*. The question remains, What are the contours of this new science to be?

First, it must restructure the relationship between "self" and "world." Nietzsche rearticulates a new and archaic relationship between self and world, but this relationship must emerge from an understanding of the generative ideas from which the relationship springs. The relationship between chaos and order, entropy and information, culminating in new "sciences" like "infodynamics" is prefigured in Nietzsche, who, like Kafka, would not allow the separation of *power* (dynamics, chaos, entropy, death) from *ideas* (difference, order, form, information) but insists that the two realms, *creatura* and *pleroma* for Bateson following Jung, are fused in what Derrida calls the *différend*. Thus the various disciplines of the arts and sciences that we have discussed become reunderstood and reinvigorated by Nietzsche's critique and rewriting of what he saw as an increasingly lopsided and, in Bateson's language, *insane* Western civilization, for his writings reopen every avenue of discourse to the dynamic play of chaos and order in a new Dionysian science-art.

Second, his evolution of a new creative cultural practice requires, as Nietzsche knew, a breaking down, deconstruction, of the boundaries and totalizing power complex, the megamachine of science, industry, bureaucracy, and military, which have increasingly characterized modernity in the twentieth century, leading planetary civilization to the brink of its own self-destruction. Yet, because Nietzsche, like Freud, knew that life and death are inextricably intertwined, his work points to an extraordinary creative possibility: to become artists of evolution; this is the art/science of living. "Only where there are tombs are there resurrections," as Nietzsche says in *Zarathustra*.

Hence, third, for the individual, self-creation, self-resurrection, *autopoiesis*, self-organization all go into the new art of culture making. Here the self is open to advanced learning, Learning III (Chapters 1, 2, and 5) creativity in its ethical, aesthetic, and practical dimensions: a newly born (wo)man who is suffused with the power of life and the will to live. In this light, Nietzsche's stylistics imply a reconciliation between science and literature, as between primary and secondary qualities. His style thus implies a self not situated as "subject" to whose "subjectivity" secondary qualities are reducible, over against a world of "objects" that are cognizable only through measurement. Rather, the Nietzschean self is a *communicative* form, active and differential, creative and relational, walking the tightrope of *différance*. The art of communication both recursively constructs this self and becomes its poetical *technē*. So the art of selfhood becomes the art of steers(wo)manship and the "person" becomes an active *kybernētēs*, the cybernaut of *Kulturmachen* ("culture making"). The Nietzschean style thus finds its most volatile form in the *l'écriture féminine* of Cixous (Chapter 4). These textual strategies are styles reminiscent of Sappho who, as Snell argues (Chapter 4), is one of the architects of subjectivity in the West and one who, in forging the self, makes clear its constitutive interplay with the other:

Sappho 31

That man seems an equal
to the gods, who sits across
from you and listens as you speak
sweet, near,
desires as you laugh—the heart
in my chest trembles at it; for
when I look at you a moment,
then my voice speaks not one
more word,

but my tongue breaks, silent,
a fine quick flame runs up under
my skin, not one more sight
lights my eyes, my ears rumble.

a cold sweat covers me,
trembling shakes me all over,
I am paler than grass,
I seem near death.
But all must be endured—dared . . .

(Daniel R. White, translator)

French (post)feminism is the metaphoric transformation of identity through communicative practice: Sappho's radical self-making. So we take what Derrida calls the *arche-writing* of *différance* evident in this elemental poetic text at the beginning of the tradition of self as a historical intertext pointing toward the possibility of new forms of living for us all.

Fourth, the potential of creativity via the expansion of discourses to include not only those of science and religion, say, in their separate camps, but also the multidisciplinary conjunction of previously antithetical views in a new complementarity, suggests a rich resource for the postmodern self. That self becomes, as we argue in Chapter 5, virtually ecological as it incorporates diverse views into a multiple persona, just as ecosystems are constructed out of the diverse species—from viruses to amphibia to mammals—that make them up. The exclusive demarcations of Cartesian selfhood that characterized modernity can now, with the postmodern turn, be broken down like the Berlin Wall to reveal a more complex and resilient evolutionary persona.

Fifth, and finally, the *jouissance* embodied by the postfeminism of Cixous and others, and so ably wrought by Sappho, must make Nietzsche's new science "joyous." For it is the "serious" reduction of discourse to the one-dimensionality of positivism that violates the complex communicative activity of play. Play, furthermore, is the epitome of the open-ended discourse signified by Derrida's *différance*, which is capable not only of deconstructing the edifice of modernist science but also of rewriting it in an idiom respectful of the diversity of life. For the basic rule of play, even prior to the sign that "these activities in which we now engage do not mean what they would if they were serious," to paraphrase Bateson, is "recognize the role of the other in the construction of self." Self and other, in a culture of play, would be bound not in the trap of metaphysics by rather in the spontaneous alliance of laughter. So Nietzsche imagined a time when we would be able "to laugh *out of the whole truth*," and to hope that

> Perhaps laughter will then have formed an alliance with wisdom, perhaps only "gay science" will then be left. (*Gay Science*, I, 1)

Notes

Introduction

1. Three journals especially have contributed to the growing literature on postmodernity and psychology: *The Humanistic Psychologist*, the
American Psychologist, and *American Imago*.

Perhaps most interesting in periodical literature is a special issue of
The Humanistic Psychologist entitled "Psychology and Postmodernity,"
containing a variety of articles on the subject. Our articles, "A Postmodern
View of Modern Psychiatry" and "Psychiatry in the Labyrinth" also appear
in a later issue of the same journal. A collection of journal articles, however
useful and timely, does not have the sustained focus that we propose in the
present book. The editor of *The Humanistic Psychologist*, Christopher
Aanstoos, nevertheless offers a useful overview of the postmodern movement in his introduction to the aforementioned special issue: "Postmodernism as a critical theorizing or cultural analysis rejects modernism's very
project of grand narratives, totalizations, foundationalisms, systematiza-
tions, and legitimations" (5). Furthermore, in the collected articles there is
a sustained critique of the foundations of modernism: the rational ego or
cogito of Descartes, on the one hand, and the metanarratives organizing and
objectifying the universal processes, from "nature" to "history," over against
which the ego stands according to modernism, on the other. The authors
also attempt to suggest a new form of subjectivity that might be created or
discovered in order to replace the Cartesian variety, but they do not offer

many specifics as to the contours of the new self. These very contours, however, are to be one of our principal concerns in *Labyrinths of the Mind*. The aforementioned authors also have difficulty reconciling modern psychology and postmodern culture, and so of providing concrete avenues practitioners can take toward articulating postmodern themes in their work. As one article, entitled "Postmodern Psychology: A Contradictio in Adjecto?" concludes, "The current emptiness and irrelevance of a psychological science to culture at large may be due to psychology being a product of modernity, the study of the logic of an abstracted 'psyche,' out of touch with a postmodern world. The strong tension between academic and professional psychology may in part be due to the entrenchment of psychological theory in modernity, whereas professional practice has to face human life in a postmodern age" (53).

A related concern is expressed in several recent articles appearing in the *American Psychologist*, which put therapy related to the "self" or individual in historical perspective, contrasting the premodern with the modern West: "Studying individuals during the time in which the household was the functional unit of the social order would have made little or no sense. Once the individual emerged as central, however, seeking to understand the individual became a highly cherished cultural project" (Sampson 1989, 916). The article goes on to emphasize that "a psychology for tomorrow is a psychology that begins actively to chart out a theory of the person that is no longer rooted in the liberal individualist assumptions, but is reframed in terms more suitable to resolving the issues of a global era" (920). While Sampson's article points in the direction of a postmodern psychology, however, it does not proceed any farther in that direction. Another article in the same journal points to a related dimension of modern psychology and reason for its inadequacy. The author of "Why the Self is Empty: Toward a Historically Situated Psychology" argues that we are seeing a dual shift in the "bounded masterful self of the 20th century," "from a sexually restricted to an empty self" and "from a savings to a debtor economy." This is no coincidence, he continues, for the shift "is a consequence of how the modern nation state must currently regulate its economy and control its populace: not through direct physical coercion, but rather through the construction of the empty self and the manipulation of its needs to consume and ingest." He goes on to point out that there are three beneficiaries of this "narcissistic dynamic": "the modern state, the advertising industry, and the self-improvement industries (including psychotherapy)" (608). However apt this characterization of the economic, political, and social power brokers underlying the current practice of psychotherapy, the article does not adequately develop what a self free of this opposition between individual and institutionalized power would be like. Again, we are interested not simply in the kind of critique offered in the article, which is a first stage, but to offer creative alternatives for change. In the direction of creative alternatives to the modernist self and its dilemmas, Hubert Hermans et al. have argued, in "The Dialogical Self: Beyond Individualism and Rationalism," for an alternative human persona: "The dialogical self, in contrast with the individualistic self, is based on the assumption that there are many I positions that can be occupied by the same person. The I in one position can agree, disagree, understand, misunderstand, oppose, contradict, question, and even ridicule the I in another position" (29). This is a significant opening of the closed universe of modern selfhood to new options, as it allows various, even contradictory, roles to be played by the "same" person. Still, this is only one of the possible approaches to a new sense of self that we think need to be considered in the postmodern labyrinth. A recent debate in the journal conveniently summarizes the basic issues in the postmodern controversy. M. Brewster Smith, in "Postmodern Perils and the Perils of Postmodernism," has offered a systematic critique of postmodernism in general and of the work of postmodern psychologist Kenneth Gergen in particular, arguing that "the version of postmodernism that Gergen advocated is criticized as representing an increasingly fashionable style of metatheory that reflects contemporary threats to selfhood but paralyzes endeavors to cope with them" (405). Gergen's reply is an apt defense of postmodern theory, arguing that far from undermining either empirical research or moral deliberation, "postmodern thought opens new vistas for psychology and new horizons for the self" (412). See White and Wang (1995) for a discussion of the Gergen–Smith debate and an attempt to reconcile the two positions.

American Imago, finally, has carried several articles relating postmodern themes to psychoanalysis. Joel Whitebook, in "Reflections on the Autonomous Individual and the Decentered Subject," argues that Freud can be, on the one hand a rationalist, and on the other an antirationalist: "Where his dictum 'Where id was, there shall ego become,' seems to place him in the Enlightenment tradition of autonomous self-reflection deriving from Kant, his perhaps equally famous statement 'The Ego is no longer master in its own house' appears to locate him in the Anti-Enlightenment tradition of Nietzsche, Heidegger and Lacan" (114). Nietzsche and Heidegger, of course, are typically cited as forerunners of the postmodern movement, and Lacan as one of its architects. Margaret C. Beaudoin argues in "Ricoeur's Contribution to Psychoanalysis: A Critique of His Critics," that Ricoeur employs both the humanistic and scientific traditions, and thus a plurality perspectives usually thought to be incompatible, in reading Freud. She cites Ricoeur's statement that Freud employs various modes of psychological explanation (of origin, genesis, function, significance): "All that is important to him is to explain through one or another of the explanatory modes . . . or through an 'overdetermined' use of several of them, what in behaviour are 'the incongruities' in relation to the expected course of a human agent's action" (59). As in the case of the "dialogical self" mentioned above, here Ricoeur understands Freud as employing multiple and perhaps inconsistent modes of discourse.

Outside of psychology, commentary raises concerns similar to those raised within, though adds some significant dimensions to the debate. For instance, Jaber F. Gubrium has argued in "Grounding the Postmodern Self" (*Sociological Quarterly* 1994) that "the postmodern framing of self is too abstract and that a distinctly modern discourse focused on the depriva-tization of interpretive activity can account empirically for features of postmodern 'presence'" (685). He illustrates this grounding by an appeal to comparative ethnographic and narrative material. There is a special issue of *Theory, Culture and Society* (1988) dedicated to postmodern themes, which are also very creatively breached by Jay Lemke in "Discourse, Dynamics, and Social Change" in a special issue of *Cultural Dynamics* (forthcoming). In a political vein, Peter Digeser has argued, in "Performativity Trouble: Postmodern Feminism and Essential Subjects," that "political practice can probably do without either an essentialist *or* performative understanding of the subject" (655), debunking typically classical and modernist theories of self.

Several books have also addressed issues related to the self in the postmodern condition. Michael R. Wood and Louis A. Zurcher Jr. argue, for instance, in *The Development of the Postmodern Self: A Computer-Assisted Comparative Analysis of Personal Documents* (1988), that the self as it develops is evidenced in diaries from the periods 1818–1860, 1911–1939, and 1949–1972. As George Noblit points out in his review, the authors "destroy the notion that the absolutes of the past have been replaced by relativism. . . . Yet, like poststructuralists, they find that the rationality of modernity is accompanied by emotionalism." What the book uncovers most clearly, as Noblit argues, is that the increased need in the postmodern self is not so much for "formal" as for "substantive rationality" (1330–1331).

How this increasing need for meaning is to be met, however, remains an open question and we shall argue that it can best be met, perhaps *must* be met, by a new postmodern sense of self. In *Hermeneutics and Psychological Theory: Interpretive Perspectives on Personality, Psychotherapy and Psychopathology* (1990), S. B. Messer et al. have argued, as they say in their preface, that out of "the editors' shared dissatisfaction with the current overvaluation of a scientistic and positivistic attitude within psychology, and an appreciation of the role of the humanities, especially philosophy and literature, in psychological discourse" a new sense of self has to be constructed (xv). Kenneth Gergen's *The Saturated Self* (1991) critically examines the limits of traditional views of self in psychology and offers creative options to rethinking the self in light of postmodernity. Lois A. Sass in *Madness and Modernism* (1992) launches an extensive inquiry into the efficacy and limitations of the analogy between madness, especially schizophrenia, and modernism as well as postmodernism. Toby Miller in *The Well Tempered Self: Citizenship, Culture and the Postmodern Subject* (1993) warns of the peril of conceiving the subject as incomplete and that the postmodern self fits too easily into a "technology of subjection" (220). In *Constructing the Self, Constructing America: A Cultural History of Psychotherapy*, Philip Cushman provides a comprehensive rethinking of assumptions and practices of clinicians from the perspective of a cultural historiography informed by a range of postmodern theory, particularly Foucault. Ian Hacking in *Rewriting the Soul* (1995) has carefully explored the issues surrounding multiple personality disorder by employing his own Foucauldian archaeology and genealogy of the condition. Again, this critical expansion of psychological discourse is one of the requisites for developing a new and more global sense of self in step with the postmodern age.

Feminist writers have also made an important contribution to the development of postmodernity, and we feel that feminist theory should be a key element in the development of the postmodern self. Among many books, three are particularly interesting in this regard: *Gender Politics and MTV: Voicing the Difference* by Lisa A. Lewis, *Gender Trouble: Feminism and the Subversion of Identity* by Judith Butler, and *Subversive Intent: Gender, Politics and the Avant-Garde* by Susan Rubin. In *Unbearable Weight: Feminism, Western Culture and the Body* (1993), Susan Bardo argues that feminism has already developed the critique of the scripting of the female body and the writing of the female self by oppressive structures, a framework on which Foucault built. All four deconstruct the categories of self, including gender, in a new domain of culture and communication and offer a critical reassessment of the categories like women, ethnic minority, blacks, and selfhood. These dimensions represent crucial gender, cultural, and political dimensions of the new sense of self to be developed.

Chapter 3. Postmodern Metamorphosis

1. We thank Betty Rojtman ("The Function of the Uninterpretable," *New Literary History* 22. 1 [Winter 1991]): 97–113) for her insightful discussion of the uninterpretable in traditional Hebrew thought, and hence for one dimension of our title. Our intent is to show how this same resistance to interpretation in Kafka has helped contribute to the postmodern collapse of interpretation. For the connections of Kafka's literature to traditional Hebrew thought, see, especially, Ernst Pawel, *Nightmare of Reason* (New York: Random, 1985).

Chapter 5. Nietzsche's Joyous Health and Dionysian Ecology

1. R. H. Stephenson in *Goethe's Conception of Knowledge* contrasts, in Popperian terms, Goethe's view of science with Newton's and attempts, as he thinks, to correct the historical picture of Goethe's scientific ideas. However, as Lori Wagner points out in her review, "the valuable points in Stephenson's study are obscured for the most part by inadequate definitions of terms, vague simplicities, ambiguities, and blanket labeling" (1996, 378).

2. Jedes existierende Ding hat also sein Dasein in sich, und so auch die Ubereinstimmung, nach der es existiert.

Das Messen eines Dings ist eine grobe Handlung, die auf lebendige Körper nicht anders als höchst unvollkommen angewendet werden kann.

Ein lebendig existierendes Ding kann durch nichts gemessen werden, was außer ihm ist, sondern wenn es je geschehen sollte, müßte es den Maßstab selbst dazu hergeben. (Goethe, "Naturwissenschaftliche Schriften" [hereafter abbreviated **NS**], 8. All translations from **NS** are by the present authors.)

3. In jedem lebendigen Wesen sind das, was wir Teile nennen, dergestalt unzertrennlich vom Ganzen, daß sie nur in und mit demselben begriffen werden können, und es können weder die Teile zum Maß des Ganzen noch das Ganze zum Maß der Teile angewendet werden, und so nimmt, wie wir oben gesagt haben, ein eingeschränktes lebendiges Wesen teil an der Unendlichkeit oder vielmehr es hat etwas Unendliches in sich, wenn wir nicht lieber sagen wollen, daß wir den Begriff der Existenz und

der Vollkommenheit des eingeschränktesten lebendigen Wesens nicht ganz fassen können, und es also ebenso wie das ungeheure Ganze, in dem alle Existenzen begriffen sind, für unendlich erklären müssen. Goethe, **NS**, p. 8.

4. Ein weit schwereres Tagewerk übernehmen diejenigen, die durch den Trieb nach Kenntnis angefeuert die Gegenstände der Natur an sich selbst und in ihren Verhältnissen untereinander zu beobachten streben, von einer Seite verlieren sie den Maßstab der ihnen zu Hülfe kam, wenn sie als Menschen die Dinge in Bezug auf sich betrachteten. Ebenden Maßstab des Gefallens und Mißfallens, des Anziehens und Abstoßens, des Nutzens und Schadens; diesem sollen sie ganz entsagen, sie sollen als gleichgültige und gleichsam göttliche Wesen suchen und untersuchen, was ist, und nicht, was behagt. So soll den echten Botaniker weder die Schönheit noch die Nutzbarkeit einer Pflanze rühren; er soll ihre Bildung, ihre Verwandtschaft mit dem übrigen Pflanzenreiche untersuchen; und wie sie alle von der Sonne hervorgelockt und beschienen werden, so soll er mit einem gleichen ruhigen Blicke sie alle ansehen und übersehen, und den Maßstab zu dieser Erkenntnis, die Data der Beurteilung nicht aus sich, sondern aus dem Kreise der Dinge nehmen, die er beobachtet. Goethe, **NS**, p. 10.

5. Natürlich[es] System, ein widersprechender Ausdruck. Die Natur hat kein System, sie hat, sie ist Leben und Folge aus einem unbekannten Zentrum, zu einer nicht erkennbaren Grenze. Naturbetrachtung ist daher endlos, man mag ins einzelnste teilend verfahren, oder im ganzen, nach Breite und Höhe die Spur verfolgen. Goethe, **NS**, p. 35.

6. Ein organisches Wesen ist so vielseitig an seinem Äußern, in seinem Innern so mannigfaltig und unerschöpflich, daß man nicht genug Standpunkte wählen kann es zu beschauen, nicht genug Organe an sich selbst ausbilden kann, um es zu zergliedern, ohne es zu töten. Ich versuche die Idee: Schönheit sei Vollkommenheit mit Freiheit, auf organische Naturen anzuwenden. Goethe, **NS**, p. 21.

Works Cited

"Abweichen." *Goethe Wörterbuch*. Deutsche Akademie der Wissenschaften zu Berlin, ed. Stuttgart: Kohlhammer, 1986.

Acampora, Ralph R. "Using and Abusing Nietzsche for Environmental Ethics." *Environmental Ethics* 16 (1994): 187–194.

Adorno, Theodor. *Aesthetic Theory*. Trans. C. Lenhardt, ed. Gretel Adorno and Rolf N. Tiedemann. London and New York: Routledge & Kegan Paul, 1984.

Ahern, Daniel R. *Nietzsche as Cultural Physician*. University Park, Pa.: Pennsylvania State University Press, 1995.

Alexander, Franz G., and Sheldon T. Selesnick. *The History of Psychiatry*. New York: Harper & Row, 1966.

Altner, Günter. "Goethe as the Forerunner of Alternative Science." Ed. F. Amrine, F. J. Zucker, and H. Wheeler. *Goethe and the Sciences: A Re-Appraisal*. Dordrecht: Reidel, 1987: 341–350.

American Psychiatric Association. *Diagnostic and Statistical Manual of Mental Disorders (DSM-III-R)*. 3rd rev. ed. Washington, D.C.: American Psychiatric Association, 1987.

———. *DSM-IV*. Washington D.C.: American Psychiatric Association, 1994.

Armstrong, David. "The Rise of Surveillance Medicine." *Sociology of Health and Illness* 17.3 (1995): 393–404.

Ashman, Philip. "Why the Self Is Empty." *American Psychologist*, May 1990: 599.

205

Atwood, Margaret. *The Handmaid's Tale*. New York: Ballantine, 1986.

Bacon, Francis. *The New Organon and Related Writings*. Ed. F. H. Anderson. New York: Library of the Liberal Arts, 1960.

Bataille, Georges. *The Accursed Share*. Trans. Robert Hurley. Vol 1. New York: Zone, 1991.

——. *Accursed Share*. Vols. 2–3. Trans. Robert Hurley. New York: Zone, 1993.

——. *Eroticism: Death and Sensuality*. Trans. Mary Dalwood. San Francisco: City Lights, 1986.

——. *Guilty*. Trans. Bruce Boone. Venice, Calif.: Lapis, 1988.

——. *On Nietzsche*. Trans. Bruce Boone. New York: Paragon, 1994.

Bateson, Gregory. "Conscious Purpose versus Nature." In *Steps*: 432–445.

——. "Cybernetic Explanation." In *Steps*: 405–415.

——. "Double Bind (1969)." In *Steps*: 271–278.

——. "The Effects of Conscious Purpose on Human Adaptation." In *Steps*: 446–453.

——. "Form, Substance, Difference." In *Steps*: 454–471.

——. "Pathologies of Epistemology." In *Steps*: 486–495.

——. *Steps to an Ecology of Mind*. Northvale, N.J.: Aronson, 1987.

——. "A Theory of Play and Fantasy." In *Steps*: 177–193.

——. "Toward a Theory of Schizophrenia." In *Steps*: 201–227.

——. Ed. *Perceval's Narrative: A Patient's Account of His Psychosis, 1830–1832*. Stanford: Stanford University Press, 1961.

Bateson, Gregory, and Mary Catherine Bateson. *Angels Fear: Towards an Epistemology of the Sacred*. New York: Macmillan, 1987.

Baudrillard, Jean. *Seduction*. Trans. Arthur Mitchell. New York: St. Martin's, 1990.

——. *The Transparency of Evil*. Trans. James Benedict. Paris: Verso, 1993.

Beaudoin, Margaret C. "Ricoeur's Contribution to Psychoanalysis: A Critique of His Critics." *American Imago* 49.1 (1992): 35–62.

Benjamin, Walter. "Some Reflections on Kafka." *Illuminations*. Trans. Harry Zohn, ed. Hannah Arendt. New York: Schocken, 1968: 141–145.

Berman, Art. *From the New Criticism to Deconstruction*. Urbana and Chicago: University of Illinois Press, 1988.

Berman, Morris. *Coming to Our Senses: Body and Spirit in the Hidden History of the West*. New York: Simon & Schuster, 1989.

Bernauer, James. *Michel Foucault's Force of Flight*. New York: Humanities, 1990.

Bleuler, Eugene. *Textbook of Psychiatry*. Ed. A. A. Brill. New York: Arno, 1976; reprint of 1924 edition.

Boardman, John. *Greek Art*. London: Thames & Hudson, 1985.

Bouson, J. B., and David Eggenschwiler. "The Repressed Grandiosity of Gregor Samsa: A Kohutian Reading of Kafka's *Metamorphosis*." In *Narcissism and the Text: Studies in Literature and the Psychology of Self*. Ed. Lynne Layton and Barbara Ann Schapiro. New York: New York University Press, 1986: 192–209.

Brod, Max, ed. *Hochzeitsvorbereitungen auf dem Lande und andere Prosa aus dem Nachlaß*. Frankfurt am Main: Fischer, 1953.

Burtt, E. A. *The Metaphysical Foundations of Modern Science*. 2nd ed. Atlantic Highlands, N.J.: Humanities, 1980.

Butler, Judith. *Gender Trouble: Feminism and the Subversion of Identity*. New York: Routledge, 1990.

Campbell, Robert. *Psychiatric Dictionary*. Sixth Edition. New York: Oxford University Press, 1989.

Caputo, John. *Heidegger and Aquinas: An Essay on Overcoming Metaphysics*. New York: Fordham University Press, 1982.

Carroll, David, ed. "Some Statements and Truisms about Neologisms, Newisms, Post-isms, Parasitisms, and Other Small Seismisms." In *The States of Theory*. New York: Columbia University Press, 1989.

Cassirer, Ernst. "The Idea of Metamorphosis and Idealist Morphology: Goethe." In *The Problem of Knowledge*. New Haven, Conn.: Yale University Press, 1950.

Chomsky, Noam. *Deterring Democracy*. London: Verso, 1991.

Cixous, Hélène. *The Book of Promethea*. Lincoln: University of Nebraska Press, 1991.

———. "Castration or Decapitation." *Signs* 1.7 (1981): 41–55.

———. *Coming to Writing and Other Essays*. Trans. Sarah Cornell, ed. Deborah Jenson. Cambridge, Mass.: Harvard University Press, 1991.

———. "The Laugh of the Medusa." Trans. Keith Cohen and Paula Cohen. *Signs* 1 (1976): 875–899.

Cixous, H., and C. Clément. *The Newly Born Woman*. Trans. Betsy Wing. Minneapolis: University of Minnesota Press, 1986.

Conrad, Joseph. *Heart of Darkness: A Case Study in Contemporary Criticism*. Ed. Ross C. Murfin. New York: St. Martin's, 1989.

Corngold, Stanley. *The Commentator's Despair*. Port Washington, N.Y.: Kennikat, 1973.

———. *Franz Kafka: The Necessity of Form*. Ithaca and London: Cornell University Press, 1988.

Coupland, Douglas. *Microserfs*. New York: HarperCollins, 1995.

Cushman, Philip. *Constructing the Self, Constructing America: A Cultural History of Psychotherapy*. Reading, Mass.: Addison-Wesley, 1995.

Cutler, Carolyn E. "Deconstructing the DSM-III." *Social Work* 36 (1991): 154–157.

Del Caro, Adrian. "Dionysian Classicism, or Nietzsche's Appropriation of an Aesthetic Norm." *Journal of the History of Ideas* 50.4 (1989): 589–605.

Deleuze, Gilles, and Félix Guattari. *Anti-Oedipus: Capitalism and Schizophrenia*. Trans. Robert Hurley, Mark Seem, and Helen R. Lane. Minneapolis: University of Minnesota Press, 1983.

———. *Kafka: Toward a Minor Literature*. Trans. Dana Polan. Minneapolis: University of Minnesota Press, 1986.

———. *Nietzsche and Philosophy*. Trans. Hugh Tomlinson. New York: Columbia University Press, 1983.

Derrida, Jacques. *De la grammatologie*. Paris: Editions de Minuit, 1967.

———. "Différance." In *Margins of Philosophy*. Trans. Alan Bass. Chicago: University of Chicago Press, 1982.

———. *Margins of Philosophy*. Trans. Alan Bass. Chicago: University of Chicago Press, 1982.

———. *Of Grammatology*. Trans. Gatayri Spivak. Baltimore: Johns Hopkins University Press, 1974.

———. *Positions*. Trans. Alan Bass. Chicago: University of Chicago Press, 1981.

———. *Speech and Phenomena*. Trans. David B. Allison. Evanston, Ill.: Northwestern University Press, 1973.

———. *Writing and Difference*. Trans. Alan Bass. Chicago: University of Chicago Press, 1978.

Descartes, Rene. *Meditations on First Philosophy*. Trans. D. A. Cress. Indianapolis: Hackett, 1979.

"Deviance." In *Encyclopedia of Psychology*. Vol. 1. Ed. Raymond Corsini. New York: Wiley, 1984.

"Deviance." In *The Social Science Encyclopedia*. Ed. Adam Kuper and Jessica Cooper. London: Routledge, 1989.

Eco, Umberto. "Postscript." In *The Name of the Rose*. Trans. William Weaver. San Diego: Harcourt Brace/Harvest Books, 1984: 505–535.

———. *The Name of the Rose*. Trans. William Weaver. San Diego: Harcourt, Brace, Jovanovich, 1983.

Eggenschwiler, David. "*The Metamorphosis*, Freud and the Chains of Odysseus." In *Franz Kafka: Modern Critical Views*. Ed. Harold Bloom. New York: Chelsea, 1986: 199–219.

Feyerabend, Paul. *Farewell to Reason*. London: Verso, 1987.

Fink, Karl J. *Goethe's History of Science*. Cambridge: Cambridge University Press, 1991.

Fischer, Tibor. *The Thought Gang*. New York: New Press, 1994.

Foucault, Michel. *The Archaeology of Knowledge*. Trans. A. M. Sheridan Smith. New York: Pantheon, 1972.

———. *The Birth of the Clinic*. Trans. A. M. Sheridan Smith. New York: Vintage, 1975.

———. *Discipline and Punish*. Trans. Alan Sheridan. New York: Pantheon, 1977.

———. *The Foucault Reader*. Ed. Paul Rabinow. New York: Pantheon, 1980.

———. *The History of Sexuality*. Trans. Robert Hurley. Vol. 1. New York: Random House, 1978.

———. *Madness and Civilization*. Trans. Richard Howard. New York: Vintage, 1973.

———. "Nietzsche, Genealogy, History." In *The Foucault Reader*. Ed. Paul Rabinow. New York: Pantheon, 1984: 76–100.

———. *The Order of Things: An Archaeology of the Human Sciences*. Trans. Alan Sheridan. New York: Vintage, 1973.

———. *Selections: Politics, Philosophy, Culture: Interviews and Other Writings, 1977–1984*. Ed. Lawrence D. Kritzman, trans. Alan Sheridan et al. New York: Routledge, 1988.

———. *Power/Knowledge: Selected Interviews and Other Writings*. Ed. Colin Gordon, trans. Colin Gordon et al. New York: Pantheon, 1980.

Fox, Nicholas J. *Postmodernism, Sociology and Health*. Toronto: University of Toronto Press, 1994.

Freud, Sigmund. *An Outline of Psychoanalysis*. Trans. and ed. James Strachey. New York: Norton, 1989.

———. *Civilization and Its Discontents*. Trans. and ed. James Strachey. New York: Norton, 1989.

Frontline. "The Best Election Money Can Buy." October 27, 1992. PBS.

Fullerton, Kemper. "Calvinism and Capitalism: An Explanation of the Weber Thesis." In *Protestantism and Capitalism*. Ed. Robert W. Green. Boston: Heath, 1959.

Galilei, Galileo. *Dialogues Concerning Two Great Systems of the World*. Trans. Thomas Salsbury. Vol. 1. London, 1661.

————. *Opere Complete di* G. G. 15 vols. Firenze, 1842.

Garaudy, Robert. "Kafka and Modern Art." In *Franz Kafka: An Anthology of Marxist Criticism.* Ed. Kenneth Hughes. Hanover and London: University Presses of England, 1981: 104–110.

Gergen, Kenneth, and John Kaye. *Beyond Narrative in the Negotiation of Therapeutic Meaning.* London: Sage, 1992.

Gilliam, Terry, dir. *Brazil.* MCA Home Video, 1986.

Goethe, Johann Wolfgang. *Gedenkausgabe der Werke, Briefe und Gespräche.* Vol. 16. Ed. E. Beutler. Zurich: Artemis, 1949.

————. *Faust, I & II.* Trans. Charles E. Passage. Indianapolis: Bobbs-Merrill, 1965.

————. "Maximen und Reflexionen: Erkenntnis und Wissenschaft." In *Werke.* Vol 12. Ed. W. Weber and H. J. Schrimpf. Hamburg: Wegner, 1953.

————. "Naturwissenschaftliche Schriften." In *Werke.* Vol. 13. Ed. Dorothea Kuhn. Hamburg: Wegner Verlag, 1953.

————. *Selected Poems.* Ed. C. Middleton, trans. M. Hamburger et al. Boston: Suhrkamp Insel, 1983: 236–237.

————. *The Sufferings of Young Werther.* Trans. Harry Steinhauer. New York: Norton, 1970.

Haar, Michel. "Nietzsche and Metaphysical Language." In *The New Nietzsche.* Ed. David B. Allison. Cambridge, Mass.: MIT, 1992: 5–36.

Habermas, Jürgen. *The Philosophical Discourse of Modernity.* Trans. Frederick Lawrence. Cambridge, Mass.: MIT, 1987.

Hallman, M. O. "Nietzsche's Environmental Ethics." *Environmental Ethics* 13 (1991): 99–125.

Haraway, Donna. "The Actors Are Cyborg, Nature Is Coyote, and the Geography Is Elsewhere: Postscript to 'Cyborgs at Large.'" In *Technoculture.* Ed. Constance Penley and Andrew Ross. Minneapolis: University of Minnesota Press, 1991: 21–26.

————. "Situated Knowledges." In *Simians, Cyborgs and Women: The Reinvention of Nature.* New York: Routledge, 1991.

Harries-Jones, Peter. *A Recursive Vision: Ecological Understanding and Gregory Bateson.* Toronto: University of Toronto Press, 1995.

Havelock, Eric A. *A Preface to Plato.* Cambridge and London: Belknap Press of Harvard, 1963.

Heidegger, Martin. *Basic Writings.* Ed. F. Krell. New York: Harper & Row, 1977.

————. *Being and Time*. Trans. John Macquarrie and Edward Robinson. New York: Harper & Row, 1962.

————. *An Introduction to Metaphysics*. Trans. Ralph Mannheim. New Haven, Conn.: Yale University Press, 1959.

————. *Nietzsche*. Trans. David Farrell Krell. 4 vols. New York: Harper & Row, 1979–1987.

————. *The Piety of Thinking*. Trans. James Hart and John Maraldo. Bloomington: Indiana University Press, 1976.

————. *The Question Concerning Technology and Other Essays*. Trans. William Lovitt. New York: Harper, 1977.

Hermans, Herbert J. M., et al. "The Dialogical Self: Beyond Individualism and Rationalism." *American Psychologist* (January 1991).

Higgins, Kathleen. "Nietzsche and Postmodern Subjectivity." In *Nietzsche as Postmodernist*. Ed. Clayton Koelb. Albany, N.Y.: State University of New York Press, 1990: 189–215.

Hobbes, Thomas. *Leviathan*. Indianapolis: Bobbs-Merrill, 1958.

Hoeller, Stephan. *The Gnostic Jung and Seven Sermons to the Dead*. Wheaton Ill.: Quest, 1985.

Hofstadter, Douglas. *Gödel, Escher, Bach: An Eternal Golden Braid*. New York: Basic, 1979.

Hughes, Kenneth. *Franz Kafka: An Anthology of Marxist Criticism*. Hanover and London: University Presses of England, 1981.

————. "The Marxist Debate, 1963." In *The Kafka Debate*. Ed. Angel Flores. New York: Gordian, 1977: 51–59.

Huxley, Aldous. "Jaipur." *Jesting Pilate*. Reprinted in *The World of Aldous Huxley*. Ed. Charles J. Rolo. New York: Harper & Brothers, n.d.: 469–471.

Illich, Ivan. *Deschooling Society*. New York: Harper, 1988.

————. *Medical Nemesis*. New York: Pantheon, 1976.

Jameson, Frederic. *Postmodernism: Or the Cultural Logic of Late Capitalism*. Durham, N.C.: Duke University Press, 1991.

Jaspers, K. *Nietzsche: An Understanding of His Philosophical Activity*. South Bend, Ind.: Regenry/Gateway, 1965.

Jencks, Charles. *What Is Post-Modernism?* New York: St. Martin's, 1986.

Kafka, Franz. *Dearest Father*. Trans. Tania and James Stern. New York: Schocken, 1958.

————. *The Metamorphosis*. New York: Schocken, 1968.

————. *The Metamorphosis*. Trans. Stanley Corngold. New York: Bantam, 1981.

Kamuf, Peggy, ed. *A Derrida Reader*. New York: Columbia University Press, 1991.

———. "Introduction: Reading between the Blinds." In *A Derrida Reader*. NewYork: Columbia University Press, 1991.

Kasanin, J. S., ed., *Language and Thought in Schizophrenia: Collected Papers Presented at the Meeting of the American Psychiatric Association, May 12, 1939, Chicago, Illinois*. New York: Norton, 1964.

Kaufmann, Walter, ed. and trans. *The Portable Nietzsche*. New York: Penguin, 1976.

Kellner, Douglas. *The Persian Gulf TV War*. Boulder, Colo.: Westview, 1992.

Kinman, Christopher J. "If You Were a Problem: Narrative Mind and Practice in Child and Youth Care." *Journal of Child and Youth Care* 9.2 (1994): 95–106.

Klein, Richard. *Cigarettes Are Sublime*. Durham, N.C.: Duke University Press, 1993.

Koelb, Clayton, ed. *Nietzsche as Postmodernist: Essays Pro and Contra*. Albany: State University of New York Press, 1990.

Kristeva, Julia. *In the Beginning Was Love, Psychoanalysis and Faith*. Trans. Arthur Goldhammer. New York: Columbia University Press, 1987.

———. *Revolution in Poetic Language*. Trans. Margaret Waller. New York: Columbia University Press, 1984.

Kroker, Arthur. Interview. "Codes of Privilege." *Mondo 2000*. By Sharon Grace. Spring 1994: 80–87.

Kroker, Arthur and Marilouise, eds. *The Last Sex: feminism & outlaw bodies*. New York: St. Martin's, 1993.

Kuhn, Thomas. *The Structure of Scientific Revolutions*. Chicago: University of Chicago Press, 1962.

Lacan, Jacques. *Écrits: A Selection*. Trans. Alan Sheridan. New York: Norton, 1982.

Laing, R. D. *The Politics of the Family and Other Essays*. New York: Random House, 1972.

Leiss, William. *The Domination of Nature*. Boston: Beacon, 1972.

Lewis, Lisa. *Gender Politics and MTV: Voicing the Difference*. Philadelphia: Temple University Press, 1990.

Lovelock, J. E. *The Ages of Gaia*. New York: Norton, 1988.

Lovibond, Sabina. "Feminism and Postmodernism." *New Left Review* 178 (November/December 1989): 5–28.

Luhmann, Niklas. *Soziologie des Risikos*. Berlin, 1991.

Lupton, Deborah. *Medicine as Culture*. London: Sage, 1994.

Lyotard, Jean-François. *The Postmodern Condition*. Minnesota: University of Minnesota Press, 1984.

———. *Just Gaming*. Minneapolis: University of Minnesota Press, 1985.

Mach, Ernst. "Analysis of Sensations." In *Contributions to the Analysis of Sensation*. Trans. C. M. Williams. Chicago: Open Court, 1897. Chapter 1 in William S. Sahakian, ed. *History of Psychology: A Source Book in Systematic Psychology*. Rev. ed. Itasca, Ill.: Peacock, 1981.

———. *The Theory of the Ego in Psychoanalytic Theory and Practice*. Ed. J. A. Miller. New York: Norton, 1988.

Mann, Thomas. *The Magic Mountain*. Trans. John E. Woods. New York: Knopf, 1995.

———. *Reflections of a Nonpolitical Man*. New York: Ungar, 1983.

Marcuse, Herbert. *One-Dimensional Man*. Boston: Beacon, 1964.

———. *Eros and Civilization*. Boston: Beacon, 1955.

Marcuse, Herbert, Robert Wolff, et al. *Critique of Pure Tolerance*. Boston: Beacon, 1969.

Martin, Judith. "Why Women Need a Feminist Spirituality." *Women's Studies Quarterly* 1–2 (1993): 106–120.

Marturana, Humberto R., and Francisco J. Varela. *Autopoiesis and Cognition: The Organization of the Living*. Boston: Reidel, 1980.

McLuhan, Marshall. *The Global Village: Transformations in World Life and Media in the 21st Century*. New York: Oxford University Press, 1989.

Messer, S. B., et al. *Hermeneutics and Psychological Theory: Interpretive Perspectives on Personality, Psychotherapy and Psychopathology*. New Brunswick, N.J.: Rutgers University Press, 1990.

Moulthrop, Stuart. "You Say You Want a Revolution? Hypertext and the Laws of Media." *Postmodern Culture* 1.3 (May 1991): electronic text.

Mourelatos, Alexander. *The Route of Parmenides*. New Haven and London: Yale University Press, 1970.

Moyers, Bill. *The Public Mind*. Parts 1–4. Alvin H. Perlmutter and Public Affairs Television: WNET New York/PBS, 1989.

Mumford, Lewis. *The City in History*. New York: Harcourt, Brace & World, 1970.

———. *The Pentagon of Power: The Myth of the Machine*. Vol. 2. New York: Harcourt, Brace & World, 1970.

———. *The Myth of the Machine*. 2 vols. New York: Harcourt, Brace & World, 1970.

Münz, Peter. "What's Postmodern, Anyway?" *Philosophy and Literature* 16 (October 1992): 333–353.

Nelson, Cary, and Lawrence Grossberg, eds. *Marxism and the Interpretation of Culture*. Urbana and Chicago: University of Illinois Press, 1988.

Nietzsche, Friedrich. "The Antichrist." In *The Portable Nietzsche*. Trans. and ed. Walter Kaufmann. New York: Penguin, 1980.

———. *Beyond Good and Evil*. Middlesex: Penguin, 1973.

———. *Beyond Good and Evil*. Trans. Walter Kaufmann. New York: Vintage, 1989.

———. *The Gay Science*. Trans. Walter Kaufmann. New York: Vintage, 1974.

———. *On the Genealogy of Morals and Ecce Homo*. Trans. Walter Kaufmann. New York: Vintage, 1967.

———. *Human, All Too Human*. Trans. Marion Faber and Stephen Lehmann. Lincoln: University of Nebraska Press, 1984.

———. *The Portable Nietzsche*. Ed. and trans. Walter Kaufmann. New York: Viking, 1968.

———. *Thus Spoke Zarathustra*. New York: Modern Library, n.d.

———. *Twilight of the Idols*. Harmondsworth: Penguin, 1968.

———. *Werke*. Ed. Giorgio Colli and Mazzino Montinari. 8 Abteilungen. Berlin: Gruyter, 1967–1977.

———. *The Will to Power*. Trans. Walter Kaufmann. New York: Vintage, 1968.

Nine Inch Nails. *The Downward Spiral*. Nothing/Interscope Records. 1994.

Noblit, George W. "Book-Review of *The Development . . .* by Wood and Zurcher." *Social Forces* 4.68 (1990): 1330–1331.

Novalis. *Werke und Briefe*. Leipzig: Insel, 1942.

Otto, Rudolf. *The Idea of the Holy*. Trans. John W. Harvey. London: Oxford University Press, 1920.

Pasley, Malcom. "Nietzsche's Use of Medical Terms." In *Nietzsche: Imagery and Thought*. Ed. M. Pasley. Berkeley: University of California Press, 1988: 123–158.

Pearson-Ansell, Keith. "Who Is the Übermensch?: Time, Truth and Woman in Nietzsche." *Journal of the History of Ideas* 53 (1992): 309ff.

Plato. *Plato's Phaedo*. Ed. John Burnet. Oxford: Oxford University Press, 1977.

Plumwood, Val. *Feminism and the Mastery of Nature*. New York: Routledge, 1993.

Poster, Mark. "Derrida and Electronic Writing." In *The Mode of Information: Poststructuralism and Social Context*. Chicago: University of Chicago Press, 1990.

———. *The Mode of Information: Poststructuralism and Social Context*. Chicago: University of Chicago Press, 1990.

Postmodernism. Special edition of *The Humanistic Psychologist* 1,18 (1990).

Pugliesi, Karen. "Women and Mental Health: Two Traditions of Feminist Research." *Women and Health* 19.2–3 (1992): 43ff.

Pynchon, Thomas. *Gravity's Rainbow*. New York: Viking, 1973.

———. *Vineland*. New York: Little, Brown, 1990.

Rilke, Rainer Maria. *Duino Elegies*. Trans. David Young. New York: Norton, 1978.

Rojtman, Betty. "The Function of the Uninterpretable." *New Literary History*. 22, 1 (1991): 97–113.

Rorty, Richard. *Contingency, Irony, and Solidarity*. New York: Cambridge University Press, 1989.

———. *Philosophy and the Mirror of Nature*. Princeton, N.J.: Princeton University Press, 1979.

Rosenau, Pauline Marië. *Post-Modernism and the Social Sciences*. Princeton, N.J.: Princeton University Press, 1992.

Rosenblum, R., and H. W. Janson. *19th-Century Art*. Englewood Cliffs, N.J., and New York: Prentice Hall and Abrams, 1984.

Rubin-Suleiman, Susan. *Subversive Intent: Gender, Politics and the Avant-Garde*. Cambridge, Mass.: Harvard University Press, 1990.

Said, Edward W. *Culture and Imperialism*. New York: Vintage, 1993.

Salthe, Stanley N. *Development and Evolution: Complexity and Change in Biology*. Cambridge, Mass.: MIT Press, 1993.

Sampson, Edward E. "The Challenge of Social Change for Psychology." *American Psychologist* (June 1989): 914ff.

Sass, L. A. *Madness and Modernism*. New York: Basic, 1992.

Schrift, Alan D. "Nietzsche's French Legacy." *The Cambridge Companion to Nietzsche*. Ed. Bernd Magnus and Kathleen M. Higgins. Cambridge: Cambridge University Press, 1996: 323–355.

Sechehaye, Marguerite. *Autobiography of a Schizophrenic Girl*. New York: New American Library, 1951, 1979.

Silverstein, Louise B. "Feminist Theology as Survival Literature." *Women's Studies Quarterly* 1–2 (1993): 143–152.

Snell, Bruno. *The Discovery of the Mind: The Greek Origins of European Thought*. Trans. T. G. Rosenmeyer. New York: Dover, 1982.

Solana, Rafael Manrique. "Communication, Language and Family: A Communicational Analysis of Kafka's *Letter to His Father*." *Psychiatry* 46 (November 1983): 387–392.

Spitzer, Robert L., et al. *DSM-III-R Casebook*. Washington, D.C.: American Psychiatric Press, 1989.

Stauth, Georg, and Bryan S. Turner. *Nietzsche's Dance*. Oxford: Blackwell, 1988.

Stock, Christiane, and Bernhard Badura. "Fördern positive Gefühle die physische Gesundheit?—Eine Forschungsnotiz" ("Positive Emotions and Health Outcome—A Note on Recent Research"). *Zeitschrift für Gesundheitswissenschaften* 3 (1995): 74–89.

Stone, Oliver. *Wild Palms*. Prod. Michael Rauch. Created by Bruce Wagner. Capital Cities/ABC Video Publishing. 1993.

Storr, A. "Nietzsche and Music." In *Philosophy, Psychology and Psychiatry*. Ed. Philipps Grifiths. Cambridge: Cambridge University Press, 1994: 213–227.

Suzuki, Shunryu. *Zen Mind, Beginner's Mind*. New York and Tokyo: Weatherhill, 1985.

Szilard, Leo. "On the Decrease of Entropy in a Thermodynamic System by the Intervention of Intelligent Beings." In *The Collected Works of Leo Szilard*, vol. 2, *Published Papers in Physics (1925–1939)*. Ed. Bernard T. Feld and Gertrud Weiss Szilard. Cambridge, Mass.: MIT, 1972: 120–129.

Taylor, Mark C. and Esa Saarinen. *Imagologies: Media Philosophy*. New York: Routledge, 1994.

Tiefer, Leonore. *Sex Is Not a Natural Act*. Boulder, Colo.: Westview, 1995.

Valadier, Paul. "Dionysus versus the Crucified." In *The New Nietzsche*. Ed. David B. Allison. Cambridge, Mass.: MIT, 1985.

Vanderlaan, J. M. "Die Faustfigur bei Goethe und Nietzsche im Hinblick auf die Postmoderne." *Euphorion: Zeitschrift für Literaturgeschichte* 88.4 (1994): 458–467.

Vivarelli, Vivetta. "'Vorschule des Sehens' und 'Stilisierte Natur' in der Morgenröthe und der Fröhlichen Wissenschaft." *Nietzsche Studien*. Bd. 20, 1991: 134–151.

Waddington, C. H. *The Evolution of an Evolutionist*. Ithaca, N.Y.: Cornell University Press, 1975.

Wagner, Lori. Review of R. H. Stephenson's "Goethe's Conception of Knowledge." *German Studies Review* 19.2 (May 1996): 378–379.

Warren, Karen J., and Jim Cheney. "Ecological Feminism and Ecosystem Ecology." *Hypatia*. Special Issue: *Ecological Feminism* 6.1 (Spring 1991): 179–197.

Weber, Max. *The Theory of Social and Economic Organization*. Trans. A. M. Henderson and T. Parsons. New York: Oxford University Press, 1947.

———. *The Protestant Ethic and the Spirit of Capitalism*. New York: Macmillan, 1977.

White, Daniel R. *Postmodern Ecology: Communication, Evolution, and Play*. Albany: State University of New York Press, 1998.

White, Daniel R., and Gert Hellerich. "Nietzsche at the Altar: Situating the Devotee." *Postmodern Culture* 6 (September 1995): Electronic text.

———. "Nietzsche at the Mall: Deconstructing the Consumer." *CTheory* 17.1–2 (Spring 1994): electronic text: www.ctheory.com.

———. "Postmodern Reflections on Modern Psychiatry: *The Diagnostic and Statistical Manual of Mental Disorders*." *The Humanistic Psychologist* 20.1 (Spring 1992): 75–91.

———. "Psychiatry in the Labyrinth: Deconstructing Deviancy." *The Humanistic Psychologist* 21.1 (Spring 1993): 65–80.

White, Daniel R., and Alvin Wang. "Universalism, Humanism and Postmodernism." *American Psychologist* 50, 5 (1995): 392–393.

Whitebook, Joel. "Reflections on the Autonomous Individual and the Decentered Subject." *American Imago* 49.1 (1992): 97–116.

Wilden, Anthony. "The Double Bind: Schizophrenia and Gödel." In *System and Structure: Essays in Communication and Exchange*. 2nd ed. London: Tavistock, 1980: 110–124, esp. 119.

———. *System and Structure: Essays in Communication and Exchange*. 2nd ed. London: Tavistock, 1980.

———. *System and Structure: Essays in Communication and Exchange*. London: Tavistock, 1972.

Williams, Gareth, and Jennie Popay. "Lay Knowledge and the Privilege of Experience." In *Challenging Medicine*. Ed. G. Gabe et al. London: Routledge, 1994: 118–136.

Wolfe, M. A. "Philosophy, Psychiatry and Psychoanalysis: Nietzsche's Case." *Annales Medico-Psychologiques* (1995): 170–183.

Wood, George, and Louis A. Zurcher. *The Development of a Postmodern Self: A Computer-Assisted Comparative Analysis of Personal Documents*. Westport, Conn.: Greenwood, 1988.

Index